Work-based Learning

SRHE and Open University Press Imprint
General Editor: Heather Eggins

Current titles include:

Catherine Bargh *et al.*: *University Leadership*
Ronald Barnett: *The Idea of Higher Education*
Ronald Barnett: *The Limits of Competence*
Ronald Barnett: *Higher Education*
Ronald Barnett: *Realizing the University in an age of supercomplexity*
Neville Bennett *et al.*: *Skills Development in Higher Education and Employment*
John Biggs: *Teaching for Quality Learning at University*
David Boud *et al.* (eds): *Using Experience for Learning*
David Boud and Nicky Solomon (eds): *Work-based Learning*
Etienne Bourgeois *et al.*: *The Adult University*
Tom Bourner *et al.* (eds): *New Directions in Professional Higher Education*
John Brennan *et al.* (eds): *What Kind of University?*
Anne Brockbank and Ian McGill: *Facilitating Reflective Learning in Higher Education*
Stephen Brookfield and Stephen Preskill: *Discussion as a Way of Teaching*
Ann Brooks: *Academic Women*
Sally Brown and Angela Glasner (eds): *Assessment Matters in Higher Education*
John Cowan: *On Becoming an Innovative University Teacher*
Heather Eggins (ed.): *Women as Leaders and Managers in Higher Education*
Gillian Evans: *Calling Academia to Account*
David Farnham (ed.): *Managing Academic Staff in Changing University Systems*
Sinclair Goodlad: *The Quest for Quality*
Harry Gray (ed.): *Universities and the Creation of Wealth*
Andrew Hannan and Harold Silver: *Innovating in Higher Education*
Norman Jackson and Helen Lund (eds): *Benchmarking for Higher Education*
Merle Jacob and Tomas Hellström (eds): *The Future of Knowledge Production in the Academy*
Mary Lea and Barry Stierer (eds): *Student Writing in Higher Education*
Elaine Martin: *Changing Academic Work*
Ian McNay (ed.): *Higher Education and its Communities*
David Palfreyman and David Warner (eds): *Higher Education and the Law*
Craig Prichard: *Making Managers in Universities and Colleges*
Michael Prosser and Keith Trigwell: *Understanding Learning and Teaching*
John Richardson: *Researching Student Learning*
Stephen Rowland: *The Enquiring University Teacher*
Yoni Ryan and Ortrun Zuber-Skerritt (eds): *Supervising Postgraduates from Non-English Speaking Backgrounds*
Maggi Savin-Baden: *Problem-based Learning in Higher Education*
Peter Scott (ed.): *The Globalization of Higher Education*
Peter Scott: *The Meanings of Mass Higher Education*
Anthony Smith and Frank Webster (eds): *The Postmodern University?*
Colin Symes and John McIntyre (eds): *Working Knowledge*
Peter G. Taylor: *Making Sense of Academic Life*
Susan Toohey: *Designing Courses for Higher Education*
Paul R. Trowler: *Academics Responding to Change*
David Warner and David Palfreyman (eds): *Higher Education Management*
Diana Woodward and Karen Ross: *Managing Equal Opportunities in Higher Education*

Work-based Learning

A New Higher Education?

Edited by
David Boud and
Nicky Solomon

The Society for Research into Higher Education
& Open University Press

Published by SRHE and
Open University Press
Celtic Court
22 Ballmoor
Buckingham
MK18 1XW

STOCKTON - BILLINGHAM

LEARNING CENTRE

COLLEGE OF F.E.

374.941

email: enquiries@openup.co.uk
world wide web: www.openup.co.uk

and 325 Chestnut Street
Philadelphia, PA 19106, USA

First published 2001

Copyright © The editors and contributors, 2001

All rights reserved. Except for the quotation of short passages for the purposes of
criticism and review, no part of this publication may be reproduced, stored in a
retrieval system, or transmitted, in any form or by any means, electronic, mechanical,
photocopying, recording or otherwise, without prior permission of the publisher
or a licence from the Copyright Licensing Agency Limited. Details of such
licences (for reprographic reproduction) may be obtained from the Copyright
Licensing Agency Ltd of 90 Tottenham Court Road, London, W1P 9HE.

A catalogue record of this book is available from the British Library

ISBN 0 335 20580 1 (pb)   0 335 20581 X (hb)

Library of Congress Cataloging-in-Publication Data

Work-based learning: a new higher education? / edited by David Boud and
Nicky Solomon.
       p. cm.
   Includes bibliographical references and index.
   ISBN 0–335–20581–X – ISBN 0–335–20580–1 (pbk.)
   1. Education, Cooperative–Great Britain–Case studies.   2. Education,
Cooperative–Australia–Case studies.   3. Apprenticeship programs–Great
Britain–Case studies.   4. Apprenticeship programs–Australia–Case studies.
5. Career education–Great Britain–Case studies.   6. Career education–Aus-
tralia–Case studies.   7. School-to-work transition–Great Britain–Case
studies.   8. School-to-work transition–Australia–Case studies. I. Boud, David.
II. Solomon, Nicky, 1951–

   LC1049.W67 2001
   378.1'627–dc21   00–044122

Typeset by Graphicraft Limited, Hong Kong
Printed in Great Britain by St Edmundsbury Press, Bury St Edmunds, Suffolk

Contents

List of Contributors   vii
Acknowledgements   ix
Abbreviations   x

Part 1: Framing Work-based Learning   1
1   New Practices for New Times   3
    David Boud, Nicky Solomon and Colin Symes
2   Repositioning Universities and Work   18
    David Boud and Nicky Solomon
3   Knowledge at Work: Issues of Learning   34
    David Boud
4   Creating a Work-based Curriculum   44
    David Boud

Part 2: Case Studies   59
5   From Once Upon a Time to Happily Ever After: The Story of
    Work-based Learning in the UK Higher Education Sector   61
    Norman Evans
6   Making It Work Institutionally   74
    Derek Portwood
7   Ensuring a Holistic Approach to Work-based Learning:
    The Capability Envelope   86
    John Stephenson
8   Working with Partners to Promote Intellectual Capital   103
    Jonathan Garnett, Alison Comerford and Neville Webb
9   The Possibilities in a Traditional University   113
    Lynne Caley
10 Implementing Work-based Learning for the First Time   126
    Jenny Onyx
11 Smart Work: What Industry Needs from Partnerships   141
    Nicholas Shipley

12   A Challenge to Assessment and Quality Assurance
     in Higher Education   155
     Richard Winter
13   Setting the Standards: Judging Levels of Achievement   167
     Frank Lyons and Mike Bement
14   Earning Academic Credit for Part-time Work   184
     Iain S. Marshall and Lynn S. M. Cooper

Part 3: Past, Present and Future   201
15   Capital Degrees: Another Episode in the History of
     Work and Learning   203
     Colin Symes
16   Future Directions for Work-based Learning:
     Reconfiguring Higher Education   215
     David Boud and Nicky Solomon

Index   228

List of Contributors

Mike Bement is Director of Postgraduate Studies for the Partnership Programme, University of Portsmouth.

David Boud is Professor of Adult Education at the University of Technology, Sydney.

Lynne Caley is Senior Programmes Manager in the Cambridge Programme for Industry at the University of Cambridge.

Alison Comerford works for Bovis Construction (UK).

Lynn S. M. Cooper is a visiting lecturer at Napier University, Edinburgh.

Norman Evans is Visiting Professor at Goldsmiths' College, University of London, and was formerly Founding Director and now Trustee of the Learning from Experience Trust.

Jonathan Garnett is Director of the National Centre for Work Based Learning Partnerships (NCWBLP) at Middlesex University.

Frank Lyons is Director of the Partnership Programme at the University of Portsmouth.

Iain S. Marshall is a senior lecturer at Napier University, Edinburgh.

Jenny Onyx is an associate professor and former Head of the School of Management in the Faculty of Business at University of Technology, Sydney.

Derek Portwood is Emeritus Professor of Work-based Learning at Middlesex University, where he founded, and was the inaugural Director of, the National Centre for Work Based Learning Partnerships (NCWBLP).

Nicholas Shipley is Manager, Work-based Learning Programs for the Faculty of Business and Insearch at the University of Technology, Sydney.

Nicky Solomon is a senior lecturer at the University of Technology, Sydney.

John Stephenson is Professor of Learner-Managed Learning at Middlesex University, London.

Colin Symes is a research fellow with the Research into Adult and Vocational Learning group at the University of Technology, Sydney, and a lecturer in the School of Cultural and Language Studies at the Queensland University of Technology.

Neville Webb is a principal consultant with Webb Associates (UK).

Richard Winter is Professor of Education at Anglia Polytechnic University.

Acknowledgements

We would like to acknowledge the contributions of the many people and institutions that have been instrumental in both the conceptualization and execution of this book.

We would like particularly to thank two groups of colleagues at the University of Technology, Sydney for the many ways they have directly and indirectly contributed to the development of this book. The first are those in a number of faculties involved in developing work-based learning. We have learned from their engagement with work-based learning and in finding ways to implement it effectively in a new context. The second are our colleagues in the Faculty of Education, particularly members of the Research in Adult and Vocational Learning group. They have enabled us to locate better the practice of work-based learning in a wider set of emerging ideas about working knowledge. The idea for the book developed during a period of sabbatical leave in the UK during 1998. Of particular help during that time was the support provided to David Boud at two institutions active in work-based learning. The first was from the Centre for Policy Studies in Education and the School of Continuing Education at the University of Leeds, the second the International Centre for Learner-managed Learning at Middlesex University.

A very important acknowledgement must go to Colin Symes – one of our colleagues in the Research in Adult and Vocational Learning group. Colin's editing expertise has been critical in the final preparation of this manuscript. Colin's fine textual skills, generosity in time and intellectual insights have been invaluable.

Abbreviations

APEL	accreditation of prior and experiential learning
APL	accreditation of prior learning
CAT Registry	Credit Accumulation and Transfer Registry
CNAA	Council for National Academic Awards
CBI	Confederation for British Industry
CPD	continuing professional development
CPI	Cambridge Programme for Industry
FEU	Further Education Unit
HE	higher education
HEQC	Higher Education Quality Council
MSC	Manpower Services Commission
NCWBLP	National Centre for Work-based Learning Partnerships
NCVQ	National Council for Vocational Qualifications
OECD	Organisation for Economic Cooperation and Development
PSI	Policy Studies Institute
QAA	Quality Assurance Agency
RPL	recognition of prior learning
SMEs	small and medium-sized enterprises
TEC	Training and Enterprise Council
TQM	total quality management
UfI	University for Industry Ltd
UTS	University of Technology, Sydney
WBL	work-based learning

Part 1

Framing Work-based Learning

Part 1

1

New Practices for New Times

David Boud, Nicky Solomon and Colin Symes

Higher education is in the midst of an unprecedented era of change. Governments are keen to reduce public expenditure. There are demands to increase the numbers and diversity of students. Alongside these continuing imperatives looms a crisis in the nature of the knowledge for which universities previously stood. Innovative responses are required, but the forms and magnitude of the innovations needed go far beyond what has been contemplated to date.

This book is located as part of these major challenges to higher education. It deals with one of the responses that these challenges have provoked – the move to new forms of work-based learning (WBL). None of us know whether this will turn out to be a major or a minor part of the response of higher education institutions to the challenges they are facing. We do know, though, that it is one of the very few innovations related to the teaching and learning aspects of post-secondary education that is attempting to engage seriously with the economic, social and educational demands of our era. In doing so, it provides a fundamental challenge to existing practices and provides new possibilities for post-secondary pedagogy and education.

What is this work-based learning and what is it trying to do? What examples exist of the practices it is promoting? What are the issues involved? What problems and difficulties need to be addressed if it is to be effective? These are some of the themes that this book addresses. Its contributors are drawn from among the pioneers of work-based learning in the UK and Australia. They examine what has been achieved in the way of work-based learning and what is the nature of the new learning practices that are emerging. It has been written alongside *Working Knowledge: The New Vocationalism and Higher Education* (Symes and McIntyre 2000). This book also considers work-based learning, but in a somewhat broader context, addressing the socio-economic forces which have given rise to this innovation and have helped to make it part of the landscape of higher education. Both books are the outcomes of the same research group, Research on Adult and Vocational Learning (RAVL), a key university research strength at the University of Technology, Sydney (UTS).

The present book has a single focus on the new practice of work-based learning. It explains how it developed and why it is significant, and describes its key features and how it is being used. As the first book to be published that examines the range of different approaches that are being adopted under the name of work-based learning, it aims to provide a foundation for further explorations and research. While it is not a 'how-to-do-it book', it does provide a framework for the development of work-based learning programmes. This framework is outlined in Part 1, which deals with the curriculum and learning aspects of work-based learning. It also provides guidance on implementation matters. The framework draws on the best of present practice to outline the challenges posed by work-based learning and how they have been addressed. Some of the practice is discussed in Part 2, which provides a series of case studies of work-based learning.

The book focuses throughout on the form of work-based learning that takes place within partnerships between educational institutions and other enterprises. This is not to suggest that equally valid forms of work-based learning cannot take place under other arrangements. However, without the explicit and tangible support of the organizations in which learners work and an acceptance by the educational institutions that learning is an activity to be engaged widely, not just by an elite, there are severe limits to what can be achieved.

What is work-based learning?

Work-based learning is the term being used to describe a class of university programmes that bring together universities and work organizations to create new learning opportunities in workplaces. Such programmes meet the needs of learners, contribute to the longer-term development of the organization and are formally accredited as university courses. There is a wide variation in the mix of elements they include, ranging from little more than a lightly tailored version of an existing course delivered in the workplace with some work-related assessment activities to programmes which focus more closely on the needs of learning in work. At the more interesting end of the spectrum are those programmes which depart substantially from the disciplinary framework of university study and which develop new pedagogies for learning. It is on these that this book focuses. This is not to suggest that hybrids of work-based learning and conventional study are not possible or appropriate in some circumstances, but before developing them it is necessary to understand the varieties which can be crossed to form the new hybrids.

Work-based learning programmes typically share the following six characteristics. First, a partnership between an external organization and an educational institution is specifically established to foster learning. This organization may be in the private, public or community sector of the economy.

Partnerships are required to enable infrastructure to support learning to be established. If learning is to occur in the workplace, then it is necessary to ensure that the conditions which prevail there are suitable and that learning projects are undertaken in cooperation with the given needs of a workplace. It would be a very demanding process to establish afresh for any given learner if a relationship did not already exist between the educational institution and the employer. While independent study courses in which students design their own courses have been available for many years, they are oriented to students who already possess relatively sophisticated learning skills and who are self-starters. Work-based learning requires more formal arrangements, which are overseen by the establishment of partnerships. These partnerships are of benefit to both parties. For the employer they create an ongoing relationship with an educational institution that comes to understand the needs of the organization and provide a flexible approach to the learning needs of employees and the organization itself. For the educational institution they create links with new areas of educational need and diversify their sources of income.

Work-based learning partnerships consist of formal arrangements between educational institutions and other organizations. These take a variety of forms, but often they consist of a contractual arrangement or memorandum of agreement in which the responsibilities of each partner are identified. Typically, they will cover matters such as how many students might be catered for, over how many years, what support for learners will be provided within the organization, how work-based learning links to corporate capabilities and so on.

Second, learners involved are employees of, or are in some contractual relationship with, the external organization. They self-select into the programme, but groups may be targeted according to priorities established by the organization. Learners negotiate learning plans approved by representatives of both the educational institution and the organization. Different learners will follow quite different pathways.

Learners have different needs and these change over time. Their requirements typically do not fit into any standard pattern of courses. Therefore a learning plan has to be created for each learner. In order to ensure that this plan can be supported and resources to pursue it made available, it has to be agreed to by all the parties concerned. The negotiation of the learning plan provides an opportunity for each party to communicate its needs clearly to the others and a greater understanding and commitment achieved than in circumstances where a plan is proposed and either agreed or rejected.

Third, the programme followed derives from the needs of the workplace and of the learner rather than being controlled or framed by the disciplinary or professional curriculum: work is the curriculum.

Work is the curriculum because the learning exigencies of work do not commonly map on to the disciplinary and professional structures of educational institutions. Workplaces are not structured in ways that coincide with the disciplinary boundaries of university faculties. Knowledge is represented in different forms in business and industry that use and generate knowledge for different purposes and ends. If the learning that is undertaken is to be used to influence and shape an organization, it must be represented in forms that it can utilize.

Fourth, the starting point and educational level of the programme is established after learners have engaged in a process of recognition of current competencies and identification of the learning they wish to engage in rather than on the basis of their existing educational qualifications.

Each individual will commence study at a different point according to their previous educational experience, training opportunities and aspirations. The level of qualification in which individuals enrol and their exit points need to be established by taking all these factors into account. A somewhat stricter definition of recognition of prior learning is often used in work-based learning programmes than in other courses involving the assessment of prior experiential learning. Current competencies refer to what students can do now, not what they can demonstrate they have achieved in the past. This focus on current knowledge is needed if realistic learning plans are to be effectively implemented. This means that a graduate might pursue an undergraduate level course rather than a postgraduate one through work-based learning. Likewise, an undergraduate could be enrolled in a postgraduate course.

Fifth, a significant element of work-based learning is that learning projects are undertaken in the workplace. These are oriented to the challenges of work and the future needs of the learner and the organization. Routine training for current work responsibilities is generally excluded. Learners draw on advice and support from within their organization and from the educational institution in which they are enrolled. They are encouraged to locate resources to contribute to their learning wherever they might be found. Modules from educational providers or training courses offered elsewhere may be used as part of an overall learning plan.

While work-based learning programmes can be constructed from any coherent mixes of activities it is the pursuit of learning projects in the workplace that tends to characterize such programmes. These projects could form a major or a minor part of the overall activities. Learning is designed not just to extend the knowledge and skills of the individual, but to make a difference to the organization. Projects are undertaken not just to equip students to contribute to the organization, but to make a tangible step towards doing so. Organizational and individual capabilities are thus linked. This grounds learning and gives a focus to it. It enables managers and supervisors to see that learning is not a self-indulgent activity, but actually contributes to the enterprise and needs to be supported by it.

Sixth, the educational institution assesses the learning outcomes of the negotiated programmes with respect to a framework of standards and levels. Such a framework is necessarily transdisciplinary.

The framework of standards and levels is a key element in the educational quality assurance process. While the learning should be of benefit to the organization, it must be accepted by the educational institution if a formal qualification is to be awarded. During times when continuity of employment is no longer guaranteed, the learner wants a qualification that facilitates access to employment pathways. A framework of standards and levels which crosses the subject boundaries of education is needed because it will be rare for any given learning plan to fall exclusively within any given subject area and it is necessary to maintain standards across plans at a given level. While there has been considerable discussion in the UK of having a framework that operates across universities, responsibility for this presently resides with the institution that accredits the programme.

Unlike in most conventional courses, there is not a fixed syllabus, core content or essential disciplinary material in a work-based learning programme. The only units not negotiable in most work-based learning programmes are those that act as a framework to hold the programme together. So, for example, there might be an introductory unit called 'Portfolio and Proposal', which acts as a vehicle for students to prepare documentation of their prior learning and the learning plan for the rest of the course. Similarly, there might be units or modules that introduce strategies and techniques for learning-how-to-learn within work situations. The case studies in Part 2 provide examples of these facets of work-based learning.

There may also be 'capstone' units at the end of programmes in which students draw together, analyse and reflect on their studies and demonstrate how they meet the desired learning outcomes. This is especially relevant in programmes that involve complex mixes of existing course units, in-house training and a variety of workplace studies. All these non-negotiable features are process-oriented units which seek to provide means whereby students can operate effectively in a work-based learning environment in which significant parts of the learning outcomes are in terms of planning, organizing and monitoring one's own learning.

This is not to say that academic disciplines have no place in work-based learning. Anything that helps students to meet their desired learning outcomes and the requirements of the university can be included.

Work-based learning: a short history of a practice

While there are many antecedents for these linkages between learning and work, their configuration into the programmes outlined above is quite new. Without the experience gained in the use of past educational innovations, it would probably not have been possible for educational institutions to meet the challenges of work-based learning. The practices which have influenced the development of work-based learning include the following:

1. *Work placements and sandwich courses.* The idea of students spending an extended period of time in authentic work contexts is a common feature not just of particular professional courses – teaching, nursing, social work – but also more generally (see Fowler 1988). The sandwich course,

or cooperative education programme as it is called in some countries, involves one or more placements of up to a year in a relevant job as part of an undergraduate degree and is an established part of the academic profile of many universities and colleges. Although it originated in techno-logical faculties it has been adopted more widely. Many of the institutions (e.g. the former polytechnics in the UK) adopting work-based learning have extensive prior experience of work placements and sandwich courses. In recent years, practice-based education of these kinds has been undergoing a period of development to ensure that the experiences gained by students are integrated with the desired learning outcomes of the course, rather than a gratuitous experience of work.

2. *Independent studies and negotiated learning.* In the 1970s a few institutions in the UK, other European countries and the USA, started to offer university education which did not fit the traditional pattern of students following a series of subjects defined by the institution. Students could create their own degree programmes, individually (independent studies or self-directed learning), with a group (negotiated curriculum) or with respect to a major problem (project-orientation) (Boud 1988). A key feature of all these approaches was that the course undertaken was not defined in advance but was negotiated between teachers and students. Institutional changes were made to provide an infrastructure to support such approaches and to provide ways of recognizing the academic achieve-ments gained from them. As with sandwich courses, a few institutions became well known proponents of such approaches.

3. *Access and the accreditation of prior experiential learning.* As higher education has expanded in the past two decades, many initiatives have been intro-duced to ensure that the benefits of university study are not restricted to the educationally privileged. Access programmes have been established to provide a bridging experience for students so they could operate successfully in university courses and ways were found of recognizing achievements that did not conform to standard entry qualifications. Uni-versities found that they had to create course units which did not fit their existing course structures, liaise with other institutions to negotiate transitional arrangements and develop ways to assess the learning achieve-ments of students no matter how they had been obtained.

4. *Generic competencies and capabilities.* Another antecedent element of work-based learning arose in the 1990s. As a smaller proportion of the intake of students wanted to complete single-subject degrees and the range of choice, even within conventional courses, increased dramatically, it became no longer possible for university standards to be overseen by dis-ciplinary groups. What counted for a degree owed more to the cultural practices of a discipline than to any well articulated account of what students would take from their experience. Prompted also by continuing and long-standing complaints by employers that graduates were defici-ent in skills such as communication, teamwork and self-planning and development, universities began to engage in their own consideration of

a competency agenda. A number of issues were involved. What is to be expected of all graduates? How can learning outcomes be represented? How do we know if we are being effective in our wider range of educational responsibilities? Statements of graduateness or educational capabilities or generic competencies were developed to capture these imperatives. They were then used to review courses, provide frameworks for student choices through a programme and assess outcomes.

5. *Labour and learning.* The idea that learning should be linked to work has a noble educational ancestry. Its philosophical roots can be traced to John Dewey, and still earlier to John Locke and Jean-Jacques Rousseau. In Dewey's educational philosophy work was always a pivotal element. He argued that the theme of work could be an organizing principle of the curriculum, and that the conventional disciplines of study could be taught through it. Dewey's ideas, though not informing work-based learning in any direct sense, are part of the discourse heritage upon which it draws.

Experience with these five sets of antecedents has provided institutions with the educational expertise and language needed to meet the challenges of work-based learning. They loosened the rigidities of administrative and teaching practice and created an awareness that teaching and learning in higher education need not be campus-based, follow a standard set of courses, require identical entry qualifications, start at the same point for everyone or be framed by the disciplines. New learning technologies were invented to cope with the challenges of flexibility. These included the negotiated learning contract, the portfolio of records of learning achievements and the recognition of prior learning.

What kinds of organizations are involved in work-based learning?

At the time of writing, the majority of work-based learning partnerships appear to have been established between major regional, national or multinational enterprises. There were smaller numbers with government departments or local authorities and fewer again with community and arts organizations and the voluntary sector (see Saunders 1995). There are some examples of partnerships with small business. It is not surprising that it has taken off in those areas with the greatest resources to devote to learning and those organizations that have staff appointed to promote and oversee training and development.

The organization has to be committed to making an investment in the learning of its employees and willing to take a longer view than the completion of immediate performance or productivity requirements. Within an organization workplaces with sufficient flexibility to enable work-based learning projects to be undertaken are needed. In particular, workplace supervisors and managers in the operational parts of an organization need to share the commitment to learning and staff development of those senior managers involved in establishing a work-based learning partnership. Of course, it is not possible to assume that work is stable. A commitment across an organization is required to accommodate the deployment and changing nature of work assignments. Work-based learning plans must be able to change with the change in work activities. This may restrict those who might become involved.

As far as higher education institutions are concerned, those forming partnerships have been relatively large and diverse universities. While on balance there are more from the former polytechnic sector in the UK and the former college of advanced education sector in Australia, there are many examples of traditional universities, and indeed at least one ancient university. Institutions must have sufficient flexibility to be able to respond to learning demands which cross their internal structures and staff who are able to orient themselves around the needs of learners rather than see their teaching role as inducting students into their own subjects.

Who are the learners and the employers, and what do they want?

The full range of the diversity of learners and organizations benefiting from work-based learning is yet to be mapped. However, the following vignettes represent some typical examples. They illustrate the need to consider learner and setting together, unlike other forms of access and educational provision which try to disengage learners from the settings in which they operate. Some focus more on the needs of the employee, some on those of the organization of which they are a part.

Case A: Learning through work

Alex is a supervisor on a production line for consumer products. She left school with few qualifications and married young. After raising a family she joined her present company as an 'unskilled' worker and has worked in various jobs on the factory floor. She has been active in lobbying for and setting up an after-school care centre now used by the children of many of her co-workers. Her involvement in this made her realize that she needed to learn and she has taken classes in a local community centre to improve her writing skills. She is keen to extend her learning and believes she is 'as good as' the graduates she has encountered. She has been instrumental in making changes to the organization of work on the production line, which have resulted in improved quality of working environment for the workers and increased workflow. Alex doesn't like classrooms as they remind her of school. She wants to learn in order to equip herself to take on roles in production management because she thinks she can make a difference in the company. Work-based learning enabled Alex to construct a programme for herself. She will need to construct a portfolio to demonstrate her capacity to enrol in a course at undergraduate level. She will draw on a combination of units from several courses being offered in flexible learning mode, participate in an in-house training programme and undertake a series of workplace learning projects.

Case B: Dealing with dislocation

Brian is a professional engineer employed by a multinational construction company. His work takes him to construction sites in different parts of the world, sometimes for up to six months. He has completed some postgraduate study in engineering, but it is impossible for him to continue this study as he moves too frequently. He has considered distance learning, but there are few courses offered anywhere and they all involve elements that Brian doesn't see as relevant to his interests. He enrols in a work-based learning master's programme. This gives him recognition for some of his existing engineering units. For the rest he plans a major learning project which contains elements that can be conducted at different work sites and is not campus dependent.

Case C: Meeting the needs of performance and recognition

Chris is a graduate who works in a large company in the financial services sector. The company has introduced an improved performance management policy for all staff in Chris's division. Part of the performance management agreement involves employees developing learning plans to complement their performance targets. Her company believes that this will encourage its employees to focus attention on the learning needs of their changing forms of work. Chris has learned about a new programme being offered jointly by her employer and a university in the same city. This has been designed to fit the performance enhancement processes, but will also give her the opportunity for her to work towards a graduate diploma. Chris is aware that the financial services sector is always undergoing restructuring and she wants to ensure that her learning is recognized outside the company. She enrols in the work-based learning course and includes in her learning plan a course offered by a management consultancy that does a lot of work with her company which has also been accredited by the university. She also includes a unit from the university's graduate certificate in e-commerce offered online. The remainder of the plan involves a sequence of projects that link directly with the implementation of financial software in her section.

Case D: Addressing organizational priorities

Drew is a middle manager in a medium-sized utility company. His company is facing an overwhelming challenge from the deregulation of prices through the industry. The strategic objective of the firm is to reduce costs at all levels in order to survive. The managing director had been impressed with a work-based learning programme he saw in another industry, but considered it too individualistic. He therefore negotiated with the university to introduce it for all middle-level staff around the learning theme of cost reduction. He was able to reassure his managers that it wasn't his intention to downsize the firm and that he wanted to achieve his goals without losing staff if at all possible. The staff involved in work-based learning went through a search group conference exercise and formed themselves into cross-departmental teams. Within the teams each person developed work-based learning plans that related directly to the overall goal and to the particular objectives of the team. The managing director sees work-based learning as a way of bringing together the non-negotiable imperative of the company with the development of staff in such a way that they can feel ownership of the resulting changes.

Case E: Flexible professional development

Elaine holds a senior position in the staff development division of a government department. The department has in the past sponsored professional staff to undertake postgraduate qualifications broadly connected to their work. While these were regarded by the staff who took part as relevant, the senior executive of the department had formed the view that there were insufficient benefits to the department in the light of the relatively generous financial support provided. Discussions had been held with one university, but the faculty involved had asserted that all the units offered were designed to be relevant and that students had the opportunity to include consideration of issues related to their work as part of their assignments. The response of another university was different. They were able to offer a master's programme that allowed for a mix of accredited in-service courses offered within the faculty, a few of the existing master's subjects and extended work-based learning projects in which learners examined some of the major challenges facing them in the changing working environment. Through work-based learning the department has been able to shift the emphasis on professional development from an essentially individualistic benefit to one which brings together the needs of the staff and the organization.

What will the learner do?

The scenarios outlined above show that different students will have quite different experiences according to their background, their aspirations and the expectations of the organization that employs them. However, what might a student enrolled in a work-based learning course expect to find? Let us take Chris as an example.

Information about opportunities for study through work-based learning is spread through Chris's organization by the human resources department. It explains how a degree or diploma can be obtained through a combination of recognition of existing learning, the taking of various units from the university in a flexible mode and the undertaking of learning activities associated with work. It suggests that the programme can be tailored for each individual staff member. It explains that work-based learning is of benefit to both the individual and the organization. For staff members, it enables them to undertake further study and gain recognized qualifications in ways linked to their work interests. For the organization, it extends the expertise of staff without them having to take time off work and it addresses the challenges to the organization in such a way as to contribute to its future effectiveness. The information illustrates some of the activities that might be included in a work-based learning programme.

Chris expresses interest and enrols in a series of workshops over a few weeks. These involve her in reflecting on her present achievements, identifying what she wants to learn and documenting this in a form which will enable her starting point and level of qualification to be assessed. In Chris's case she does not receive any learning credits as assessment of her learning portfolio indicates that other than her undergraduate degree she does not have learning outcomes directly related to her proposed course. Her friend Robin was the leader of a project involving the implementation of a new product and gained 25 per cent of the credits towards a master's degree based on an assessment of the academic equivalent outcomes she was able to demonstrate.

As part of the workshops Chris formulates a learning plan. This outlines the goals she will pursue through the work-based learning course, the activities she will engage in, including the course modules both from the university and as part of the organization's staff development programme, and the learning projects Chris will undertake in the workplace. The plan also identifies the learning outcomes being pursued and the ways in which they will be assessed. As part of the negotiation of the final plan Chris discusses her proposals with both her immediate manager and her university learning adviser. These discussions focus on whether the programme is realistic, can be resourced and will meet the outcomes desired. The plan is signed when all three parties are in agreement.

Over the next two years, Chris completes course modules from the university, participates in a training programme run by a consultant and engages in three interlinked work-based learning projects that are submitted for assessment. She forms a peer learning group with three of her colleagues who work in the same building. They meet at lunchtime once a week and discuss their experiences of work-based learning. She is also part of a larger e-mail list consisting of all those students who participated in the workshops and she sometimes joins in the discussions of issues that are raised. She says that she needs these other forms of contact so that she doesn't lose touch with being a student as well as an employee.

As she works through the tasks she has set herself, she uses the strategies she learned in the university workshops to reflect on and document her achievements in the context of the statement of university standards and levels she was provided with. She finds this demanding and seeks meetings with her academic adviser to understand what critical reflection means in the context of the knowledge she has gained.

Chris has managed to fit part of the work into her normal working day and was pleased to discover that part of the learning she needed to do was more or less identical to that required by her normal job. What she did take home was some of the reading required for her study, as she couldn't fit that into the interruptions of the office. Much of the documentation she completed at work, but she was not able to disengage from the demands of her workflow and undertake the reflection required.

On successful completion of all the elements of her original plan, she graduates with a graduate diploma.

Structure and organization of the book

The book has three parts. The first, consisting of four chapters, including this one, places work-based learning in the context of changes to work and the demands on higher education institutions. It provides some background to the emergence of work-based learning. Chapter 2 explores in more detail the nature of the challenges that have been outlined in this chapter and locates them in the context of the changing nature of work and organizational culture. It also explores the changing nature of knowledge production in contemporary culture, and suggests that the move on the part of corporations to develop their own research and development capacities has caused an identity crisis for the university. This theme is further explored in Chapter 3, where the nature of contemporary knowledge production is more specifically examined along with the implications that the changes to this production have for learning, particularly within the academy. It is suggested that in the context of these changes work-based learning has much that is seductive about it, for universities, for employers and for students. It considers questions of how to avoid the problems of learning becoming too specific to particular work contexts. Chapter 4 looks at the pedagogical ramifications of work-based learning, particularly in terms of the reformation of the university curriculum. It provides guidelines in terms of how work-based learning should be framed and located, and the kinds of best practice that it should uphold.

Issues of work-based learning practice are more thoroughly explored in Part 2, which consists of a series of case studies of such learning in the UK and Australia.

Norman Evans in Chapter 4 describes work-based learning in a historical context in the UK in the 1980s. He discusses the social and economic challenges of the time and the emerging need for higher education and employers to work together to address them. He focuses on the pivotal issue of access to higher education, the role of the recognition of prior learning and the codification of academic credit in opening new opportunities in higher education. Evans writes from the perspective of one of the key players of the time who was involved in many of the influential discussions and who helped to shape the direction which work-based learning subsequently took.

Derek Portwood in Chapter 6 examines the initiatives of Middlesex University in work-based learning. He has been instrumental in supporting networks of institutions involved in work-based learning in the UK and overseas. In his chapter he stands back from his involvement to consider how work-based learning can be made to work within a university. This is one of the most difficult and sensitive challenges faced within institutions that are structured to support quite different kinds of course provision. Portwood addresses issues of establishing credibility, developing tools for work-based learning programmes and ensuring that it pays its way.

John Stephenson is known from his long involvement in the development of independent studies courses and more recently in the Education for Capability movement and the University for Industry (UfI). His extensive experience with the educational practices of negotiated learning have led him to reflect in his chapter on the educational frameworks which are necessary for work-based learning programmes to be meaningful and co-herent for learners. In Chapter 7 he draws attention to the importance of viewing such programmes as a whole, not as aggregations of discrete and disparate parts. His important contribution to the debate is the idea of what he terms the 'capability envelope'. This enables learners and those who advise them to see all elements of a work-based learning programme holistically. This envelope prompts us to consider what practices and activities are needed to equip students to operate in the challenging context of work-based learning and to reflect on the contributions work makes to their learning activities.

Unless the needs of industry are explicitly addressed, work-based learning cannot be effective. Chapter 8 discusses the partnership – which is central to work-based learning – that developed between a company and a university and how the needs of the various parties involved were met. It focuses on how the university can accommodate the needs of industry and how these are reflected in a programme. This accommodation is manifested in the authorship of the chapter. Jonathan Garnett is from Middlesex University, one of the pioneers of work-based learning, and currently probably its largest provider; Alison Comerford is a training manager from Bovis Construction, a large multinational engineering management company; and Neville Webb is a private training consultant who works with Bovis.

Lest it be thought that work-based learning can only find a place in ex-polytechnics, Lynne Caley in Chapter 9 describes such learning in the

University of Cambridge. The challenges of finding a way of working collaboratively with external organizations confront all universities, but each has to find its own way of addressing them. Through the Cambridge Programme for Industry, the University of Cambridge has developed ways of contributing to continuing professional education that engages with organizations as well as individuals.

The next two chapters discuss work-based learning in Australia. Getting started in work-based learning confronts academic departments with many issues that they are normally able to avoid. Jenny Onyx was a head of school in a faculty of business at a time when work-based learning was introduced. Even though the faculty prided itself on its relationships with industry, the kinds of issues that the introduction of a new partnership raised were difficult and complex. In Chapter 10 Onyx gives her own perspective on the initial stages of implementation and the many difficulties she faced and overcame.

Nicholas Shipley in Chapter 11 provides a perspective on the needs of employers. He has been involved in the difficult process of liaising between companies and a university in helping each to appreciate the perspective of the other. He sets the discussion of work-based learning in an organizational context and notes the competing demands now evident in business. He identifies the organizational drivers of work-based learning from the perspective of business and industry and examines how these have influenced the character of the partnerships that have developed within the university. He raises the important question of what it is that organizational partners hope to derive from a university that they cannot themselves deliver.

Anglia Polytechnic University has adopted a different approach to work-based learning partnerships from Middlesex and Portsmouth. Unlike these institutions, which established a centralized operation for programmes throughout the university, Anglia started with partnerships between particular faculties and particular employers. Richard Winter was involved at an early stage in the developments at Anglia and has written extensively about the issues that he and his colleagues confronted (Winter and Maisch 1996). In Chapter 12 Winter looks at the issues involved in the quality assurance of work-based learning programmes. He argues that the assurance issues associated with work-based learning not only challenge conceptions of what is required for conventional programmes, but that the quality assurance frameworks that have proved necessary for the new programmes provide a basis for all higher education. He suggests that the public specification of educational outcomes conforms more to quality assurance requirements than do traditional courses that are taken to be a yardstick for the higher education sector as a whole.

One of the main contributions universities can make to work-based learning partnerships is in validating standards of achievement. Both learners and the organizations in which they operate can be assured that the outcomes that have been achieved are equivalent to those from recognized qualifications. Setting the standards and monitoring the quality of learning is a central concern to all programmes. Frank Lyons and Mike Bement are

from the University of Portsmouth, another of the pioneering UK universities in the field of work-based learning, one with particular experience
in programmes in the high technology area. In Chapter 13 they discuss the
various quality issues that arise and how they have been addressed. They
pay particular attention to judgements about the amount of academic credit
given for different purposes and how this is assessed. They report on debates
about levels of achievement and the development of frameworks of standards
and levels of achievement associated with different academic qualifications.

The last chapter in Part 2 focuses on the application of work-based learning in a somewhat different framework. Most of the examples of work-based
learning represented in this book involve entire programmes of study. However, it is possible to use aspects of the thinking behind work-based learning
within existing courses. Iain Marshall and Lynn Cooper in Chapter 14 illustrate how this might be done by utilizing the kinds of typical part-time work
experience with which a full-time undergraduate student in a conventional
course might be involved. Part-time employment is used to allow students
to undertake projects in their workplaces as a contribution to their undergraduate studies.

In Part 3 a review is conducted of the current state of work-based learning
and the immediate issues it needs to confront if it is to find a secure place
in the university. Colin Symes provides an account of work-based learning
from a more 'contextual' perspective and argues that the case studies in
Part 2 demonstrate the degree to which work-based learning has exploited
the policy envelope of flexibility and access. He suggests that its emergence
is another aspect of the ongoing 'tailorization' of higher education – the term
that he has coined to describe the diversification of provision that is a marked
feature of the contemporary university. In the final chapter Boud and Solomon adopt a more speculative frame of reference. They move on from the
pressing problems of the present, and consider how work-based learning
might advance education and learning in the university of the future. They
identify a number of research and teaching issues that need further examination if work-based learning is to have a secure place in the university.

References

Boud, D. (1988) Moving towards autonomy, in D. Boud (ed.) *Developing Student Autonomy*. London: Kogan Page.

Fowler, G. (1988) An overview of vocational aspects of higher education in selected countries, in H. Silver (ed.) *Vocational Training in Higher Education*. London: Higher Education Institute.

Saunders, M. (1995) The integrative principle: higher education and work-based learning in the UK. *European Journal of Education*, 30(2): 203–16.

Symes, C. and McIntyre, J. (2000) *Working Knowledge: The New Vocationalism and Higher Education*. Buckingham: SRHE/Open University Press.

Winter, R. and Maisch, M. (1996) *Professional Competence and Higher Education: The ASSET Programme*. London: Falmer Press.

2

Repositioning Universities and Work

David Boud and Nicky Solomon

The vignettes in Chapter 1 are typical snapshots of work-based learning programmes. Collectively these snapshots indicate the seductive appeal of work-based learning partnerships to various kinds of organizations and a diverse range of employees. For organizations, work-based learning offers a vehicle for linking individual learning to the development of corporate capabilities. It is a strategy for facilitating change and for retaining good employees. For employees, work-based learning provides an opportunity for gaining qualifications that incorporates their existing knowledge and experiences and that links learning to current workplace performance needs as well as to career development goals. Furthermore, although not visible in the vignettes, work-based learning has a seductive quality to the third participant, the university. Work-based learning enables universities to be collaborators with organizations rather than competitors in the competitive qualification market. This is important for the university's positioning of itself at a time when the market place rewards close cooperative relationships between higher education learning and the 'real' world. Work-based learning provides the university with the opportunity to establish long-term relationships with corporations and this potentially has an impact on many kinds of education and research, ranging from new forms of course provision to collaborative research projects. Indeed, this kind of reading of work-based learning reveals the unambiguously attractive reciprocal gains for all its participants.

Nevertheless, this is not the only story to tell about work-based learning. Academics participating in work-based learning, as well as those observing it at a sceptical distance, share an understanding of the variety of challenges that work-based learning presents to academic work. In this chapter the focus is on a different kind of story – a story that exposes and explicates these challenges and the conditions within which they have emerged. This particular story draws on our experiences and efforts in theorizing as well as in designing and delivering work-based learning programmes within a higher education setting. Through these experiences we have confronted head-on the multiple conceptual and practical challenges to our identity, institutional structures and work practices. All of these challenges have contributed to a disturbance of our understanding of the role and function of higher education, our understanding of what is legitimate academic knowledge and what are academic standards, our belief in the resilience of our discipline and in our teaching and learning practices.

Is work-based learning such a radical challenge?

In the spirit of an examination of the challenges, an initial question that requires some consideration is: 'Are the challenges faced by academics and learners overstated?' In other words, could it not be argued that work-based learning partnerships are a 'natural' step in the educational developments of universities? In support of this line of argument we can turn to the widespread increased emphasis on professional and vocational practice in higher education undergraduate and postgraduate courses over the past decade. This emphasis is not just part of the rhetoric but is visible in many academic programmes where students' learning experiences no longer sit neatly inside the boundary of the academy. Many courses already use workplace problems as a learning resource, offer professional placements and include workplace action learning projects and individual negotiated learning contracts. Furthermore, recently the boundary between learning gained in educational institutions and learning outside these institutions has been blurred through the recognition and accreditation of prior learning (RPL and APL). This has enabled non-traditional entry into university courses as well as credit for advanced standing. Advocates of work-based learning, as several case studies in Part 2 demonstrate, have been able to exploit this to further their interests.

While initially these kinds of initiatives may have troubled conventional pedagogical and disciplinary practices, increasingly they are becoming accepted as part of the repertoire of higher educational offerings, in which case it seems likely that work-based learning in this respect will become a 'normal' component of the university.

Or does work-based learning represent a much more significant shift? We suggest that work-based learning is different enough to warrant a careful examination of its practices and what they signify. At the same time, we do not mean to suggest that work-based learning, in itself, signifies the end of higher education as we know it. Such a suggestion ignores the complexities around existing academic practices and the numerous other challenges faced by higher education institutions and academics. But we do suggest that work-based learning draws attention to a radical shift in our assumptions about 'legitimate' knowledge and learning.

While the focus of this book is on a particular set of work-based learning practices (those exemplified in Part 2), we would argue that work-based learning epitomizes many of the tensions in contemporary academic work. These are a consequence of the changing relationship between knowledge and the academy in the university in these 'new times'. Of significance is that these changes have meant that the university is becoming more open within its internal structures, as evident in the increased number of cross-faculty courses and cross-disciplinary research institutes, centres and concentrations. But it is also more open in its relationship with the outside world, as seen in the increasing number of entrepreneurial and research relationships with industry and government bodies (Turpin *et al.* 1996). These openings are both cause and effect of the reduction in status of universities as primary producers of a particular kind of knowledge, as well as the loss of their monopoly over knowledge production and legitimation (Solomon and Usher 1999). These losses not only have a symbolic significance, but also have a considerable number of practical consequences. One such is the legitimation of work-based learning as a normal trajectory of academic study.

In work-based learning, the practices associated with the 'openness' of its structures (both within the university and in its external relationships) present many challenges to administrators, to academics and to students. Indeed, as signalled in the way it is spoken and written about, 'openness' is a key feature of work-based learning. It is frequently marketed in terms of its 'openness'. For example, it is implicit in its promise to be 'flexible' enough to enable the customization of each partnership and each learning programme, to allow for non-conventional access to higher education learning and to cater for 'different learners' following 'different pathways'. The practices and processes attached to all of these promises draw attention to the emerging struggles within the academy over the customization of its provision and curriculum structures.

Discretionary change

An important feature and outcome of the partnership and of its curriculum processes is a lack of *discretion* around work-based learning practices. The concept of discretion is a useful one in drawing attention to what is so radical in work-based learning. The more typical workplace learning episodes, such as professional placements and learning contracts, usually sit discretely within conventional course structures and understandings about academic knowledge and learning, and are accompanied by equally familiar teaching and learning practices. Furthermore, arguably, in these cases, the power or right of deciding the scope of such embedded learning still resides with academics and within the academy. Accountability lies in the hands of the academy and the disciplinary community.

None of this applies to work-based learning. Academics involved in work-based learning no longer have the sole right to decide what is to be learnt or how it is to be learnt. The accountability is no longer self-referential but extends into the boundaries of the workplace. Moreover, at the macro-level, the primary point of departure is not a conventional area of knowledge or learning but rather work, the workplace and the learner. In work-based learning the structural arrangements, as well as the sequence of learning episodes, begin with the learners and their workplaces, and end with the university. Subject units are subordinate to the programme of work. This is in contrast to more conventional university courses, which begin with the university and its conceptions of what is legitimate knowledge, before moving to the workplace and the learner.

Some of these changes have been foreshadowed by the influences of professional bodies on the curriculum or on, for example, the amount of practice teaching in teacher education. But significantly these have been mediated through quasi-educational bodies representing the interests of the profession, while in work-based learning the influence of organizational and professional practices is felt in a more direct way, at the interface with the workplace.

A key concept, related to the changes in the discretionary practices of the academy and the loss of singular control of work-based learning awards, is the co-production of knowledge and of the learning experience. As indicated in our first chapter, work-based learning involves partnerships involving many different kinds of relationships. The award is initiated by and organized around a contractual partnership between the university and an organization. This is then complemented by a contractual agreement with each learner as the learners write themselves into the partnership with an individualized learning programme that has been negotiated in partnership with an academic and a workplace manager. Furthermore, representatives from the workplace and the university supervise work-based programmes. All of these relationships, processes and 'products' have to take into account the different social structures, histories and understandings about knowledge and learning of each of the various partners.

The process of developing a work-based learning partnership and a work-based learning programme involves working with rather than ignoring these differences. This is not to argue that in conventional learning experiences the learning process is a non-interactive or uncontested one. Such an argument ignores the way the processing of new knowledge always connects with the learners' existing experiences and knowledge. However, in work-based learning, these processes are visible and indeed part of the learning experience. In other words, the negotiations and discussions, necessarily, are 'on the table'.

Moreover, the 'partnership' model actually foregrounds the different relationships through which the curriculum unfolds. The use of the word 'partnership' with students is not part of the conventional discourses of higher education learning. Those discourses reflect and contribute to a kind of unilateral control (Heron 1988) by the academy which is symptomatic of a model of learning that is hierarchical and authoritarian. By contrast, the 'partnership' discourse suggests a more equitable decision-making process.

However, the more democratic drift in work-based learning is not necessarily an unproblematic one. Indeed, we would argue that the collaborative processes in the co-production of knowledge involve many layers of politics and contested power relations (see Garrick and Kirkpatrick 1998). These emerge because of the 'openness' of work-based learning, where the merging of the different discourses, of the different views on what is legitimate knowledge and of different agendas and expectations is, not surprisingly, a site of contest and debate. For example, while academics may understand that the development of critical thinking and reflective practitioners should be a central feature of study and of contemporary work, this may not be shared by the workplace management or by the learners' supervisors. Furthermore, a workplace supervisor may not have an interest in working with the employee in a learning arrangement.

But, in addition, work-based learning is also a site and exemplar of the new power relationships and resistant practices within the university itself. The radical nature of work-based learning encourages a degree of scrutiny of it by the university and by academics who are concerned about the quality and standards of university awards that are tied into organizational performance and productivity needs. Frequently in the development of more conventional courses, there is less scrutiny and therefore less need for argument about the quality or standards of the particular modes of learning, the 'content' of subject units or the appropriateness of assessment practices. Furthermore, the transdisciplinary nature of work-based learning awards at times provokes a disciplinary territoriality as a counter-reaction. This is manifested in several ways. One is at the practical level in the efforts, by some, to foreground a particular body of disciplinary knowledge in an individual's work-based learning programme. Another is at a conceptual level in the efforts to diminish the significance of the relationship between the mode of learning in work-based learning and the content of that learning. These struggles can be understood as part of a 'healthy' academic debate on what counts as academic learning. But they also have powerful material consequences – for example, on the kind of advice that academics provide on the 'content' of the learning programme and on the assessment of individuals' programmes where judgements are made about the level of the award based on its disciplinary content.

Together, the different positions of the participants, the flexibility of the programmes (in both content and mode), the changes in the discretionary practices of academics and the emerging complex power relationships all have implications not just for curriculum structures and practices but also for the macro-structures within which the curriculum is 'contained'. Chapter 4 deals in a more comprehensive way with these issues.

The origins of work-based learning

As indicated above and in Chapter 1, there are a number of educational antecedents to work-based learning. In one shape or form these programmes acknowledge the workplace as a site of learning and as a source for making the curriculum more relevant. As such they are a signal of the blurring distinctions between the university and the workplace. They are symptomatic of the increasing legitimization of learning (and knowledge) outside the academy and a general repositioning of the academy *vis-à-vis* the external world. This repositioning reflects as well as contributes to a general vocational-ization of undergraduate and postgraduate programmes, which has been accompanied by a privileging of contextual and experiential learning (see Symes and McIntyre 2000). Both phenomena can be understood as a con-sequence of the alliance between education and the economy which govern-ments have fostered in the past two decades, as an intervention either to improve the value of human capital or to bolster the knowledge economy.

These links between education and productivity relate to a number of macro-political and economic trends that are frequently either named as or attributed to 'globalization'. While globalization has become almost a cliché, it is, nevertheless, a concept that has useful explanatory power when it comes to understanding the new economic, political and cultural relation-ships in which we are all engaged.

So how do we understand what globalization is and how does its under-standing explain the reconfiguration of pedagogical practices that have produced work-based learning? In this chapter we do not provide a list of the characteristics of globalization, as these can be found in other writings (e.g. Waters 1995). Instead we draw attention to a number of factors that have helped to create those antecedent conditions in higher education that helped to position work-based learning as a seductive alternative, despite its difficulties and challenges.

Important to our understanding of the effects of globalization is an un-derstanding that it is not a 'thing' that is bearing down on universities in a prescriptive and deterministic way. Instead, it is a discursive practice; that is, it is a way of thinking, speaking and acting that interacts with changes in socio-economic and cultural structures, configurations and relationships (Edwards and Usher 2000). This view serves to highlight the potential of globalization to invoke spaces that challenge and disrupt certain assump-tions and binaries and in addition create a dynamic that allows for different and unpredictable consequences for the nexus between the global and local. This view offers a counterpoint to the notion of globalization as simply a homogenizing process. It positions globalization in a way that explains the emergence of similar cultural and political practices in differ-ent national contexts as co-existing with various local uptakes of these prac-tices as they are influenced by the existing cultural and political conditions (Featherstone 1995).

A significant shared global experience is the breaking down of national boundaries and the emergence of new regional and global trade and eco-nomic relationships. In educational terms this is experienced through a globalization of educational policies and the role of international bodies such as the OECD (Organisation for Economic Cooperation and Development) in policy transfer between nation states (Taylor *et al.* 1997; Ball 1998; Levin 1998; Dale 1999; Marginson 1999; Edwards and Usher 2000). Such transfer explains, in part, the common casting of education in economic terms, and the accompanying reduction in government resources and an increasing emphasis on standards and accountability – though not in nations that have resisted the policy prescriptions of the OECD (see Sennett 1998).

Another vital factor is the global spread of information and communication technologies. These have played a central role in the facilitation of the migration of ideas and in the compression of time and space – or, more accurately, the annihilation of space by time (see Harvey 1989). The speed of communication is such that the space between nations is now an irrelevant factor in sending information. These technologies have not only enabled instant global communication but also brought into focus the knowledge and information distinction. In particular, the acceptance that learning takes place in a classroom and that knowledge is produced within the academy (either in the classroom or by academic researchers) has been disturbed. Therefore information and communication technologies not only provide the mechanisms for enabling new modes of learning that connect learners outside an educational institution with 'knowledge' and with academics, but also have had significant consequences on the role of the university. The narrative architecture of knowledge and information is now more accessible than it was. Every home by the virtue of the Internet is a potential British Library or Library of Congress. Information and knowledge delivery has experienced the same space–time compression as travel and telecommunications.

Information and communication technologies have directly and indirectly contributed to a reconsideration of what is worthwhile knowledge. They not only 'enable' learning outside the institution to occur, but also legitimatize sites of learning and sites of knowledge production that are outside normal educational environments. This is leading to the deinstitutionalization of education (McIntyre and Solomon 2000).

Mode 2 knowledge and the new times university

When 'knowledge' and 'knowledge production' belonged to the academy, and when a key interest of knowledge was the pursuit of truth and human progress (Toulmin 1990), 'knowledge', as distinct from 'know-how', had only a minimal place in workplace discourses. However, since knowledge has become connected to the productivity and performance of employees and of the organization, 'knowledge' has developed a currency in workplace practices and language (Gee *et al.* 1996). Its new status can be seen in the emergence of knowledge industries, knowledge managers and knowledge workers. Indeed, in the contemporary workplace, knowledge has an internal place that is connected to organizational capability, innovation and creativity, and it has also a product to be produced and traded (McIntyre and Solomon 2000).

The foregrounding of knowledge then, not surprisingly, is related to the contemporary location of learning in workplace discourses – most notably the 'learning organization' (Senge 1992). Although this organization has many different incarnations, its principal feature is the learning capacity of its workforce. Within such organizations, learning at work is no longer understood as a discrete activity limited to a few, or as an activity that occurs only at occasional moments in one's career. Learning is considered to be a productive part of everyday work, embedded in the culture, structures, relationships and processes of the workplaces. Coexisting with the emphasis on internal learning processes is organizational interest in developing external relationships, and for some organizations these relationships are with universities. This interest in collaboration and participation in partnerships reflects the range of strategies that organizations deploy to 'add value' to their business in order to give them a competitive edge.

The new status of knowledge and learning in organizations is both a cause and effect of the alignment of employee and organizational goals in contemporary workplaces. While there are, no doubt, many mechanisms for bringing this alignment about, the use of organizational 'culture' as a management tool has been an important one. The use of the word 'culture' in the workplace signifies the way the workplace is being constructed as a site of 'belonging' (Wilmott 1993; Cope and Kalantzis 1997; Solomon 1999). With the foregrounding of culture, the primacy of the technical is becoming secondary to the social and the cultural – both of which are dependent on and accompanied by a 'humanizing' of the workforce. This humanizing can be understood as a technology for managing people and constructing particular kinds of workers (Garrick and Solomon in press). In management terms putting the 'human' into the workplace provides a mechanism for structuring the way employees think, make decisions and act in alignment with organizational norms, attitudes and values. Indeed, the emphasis on self and self-fulfillment is a way of maximizing capacities in the workplace (Wilmott 1993).

University as a workplace

We also need to give brief consideration to some other factors that have established the conditions leading to a reduction of the conceptual space between contemporary universities and other organizations. One of the most important of these is the change in government funding arrangements in many countries. These arrangements include the reduction in per capita funding to universities, government support for the establishment of non-government organizations as providers and accreditors of educational awards, and the encouragement by government of universities to forge alliances with business and industry.

These arrangements have had an enormous impact on the way universities are redefining themselves, in terms of their identity as educational institutions, their relationships with other universities and industries, their understanding of the composition of the target markets and much more. While these redefinitions are constantly unfolding, one sustaining feature is a set of discourses that construct higher education as an industry; that is, as a business involved in the commodification and marketization of education and learning. The university, as only one player in this industry, is being constructed as a workplace like any other. This construction is reflected in the utilization of the discourses of management in the practices of university administration. The mission statement, strategic planning, performance reviews and quality assurance have been appropriated as part and parcel of the wholesale corporatization of the university. Previously workplaces were of interest to academics mainly as sites of research or as a destination for their students. Workplaces were 'other'. However, in the contemporary university the 'other' has become the norm and the work practices that are familiar in other settings of work, notwithstanding the pockets of resistance to them, are now part of the prevailing work conditions of academics.

The conceptualization of the university as a workplace and the removal of the boundaries between universities and other organizations are therefore both cause and effect of the increased sharing of work practices and even discourses. Previously, in both sites, the language spoken may have been English but the particular discourses were so different that there was little exchange let alone understanding of the reciprocal gains that might be possible from working together.

The challenges of work-based learning

There are many challenges that universities are confronting in the design and delivery of work-based learning programmes. The challenges identified here draw upon the experiences of the writers in working with work-based learning in particular institutions, and as such may resemble or differ from the challenges experienced by others in other institutions – such as those described in Part 2. Perhaps though, not coincidentally, the challenges will have a resonance for academics not engaged in work-based learning, yet struggling with other initiatives such as the increased development of distance or flexible learning programmes. As indicated earlier in this chapter, work-based learning initiatives are symptomatic of a widespread university phenomenon. This phenomenon is to do with the new relationships between universities and other workplaces and the accompanying privileging of different kinds of knowledge and learning.

Many of the challenges that work-based learning practitioners are facing have already been indicated. Here we have organized them around three areas. The first relates to the challenge of *equivalence*, which focuses on the problems attached to the significance given to the contemporary need to inscribe academic standards at a time when universities are accountable to both internal and external audiences. The second area focuses on the different kinds of pedagogical *practices* that are central to the work-based learning experience. The third considers the challenges that these different learning experiences have on the *identity* of the university, the academic and the learner.

Challenge of equivalence

At a conceptual level, a major challenge that academics involved in work-based learning confront revolves around the notions of 'academic standards' and 'equivalence'. While these concerns are not confined to work-based learning practitioners, they are fuelled by a fear that work-based learning is contributing to a more general lowering of standards that has been set in motion through the massification and vocationalization of higher education and the accompanying competitive university market place. The concern with the lowering of standards is often voiced in terms of more general fears about the 'future' of the university.

The emergence of discourses around 'standards' is a relatively new one in universities. Previously there was little need to articulate the word 'standards' in relation to learning outcomes produced through or within the academy. The word 'academic' had enough status to suggest that the knowledge learned at university was worthwhile and legitimate. This was implicit and its value did not need to be inscribed. Levels of achievement were embedded in academic disciplinary cultures and were rarely made explicit. However, more recently, the word 'standards' has a currency in academic discourses. The reasons for this shift are numerous; some are related to the proliferation of sites of knowledge production and the new funding arrangements. As universities no longer have the monopoly on knowledge production, in part, the significance of academic standards comes from within the university itself in its efforts to (re)present the value of its own knowledge – as distinct from that other kind of knowledge produced 'out there' and as distinct from the rather opaque 'outcomes' implicit in the more recent discourses around 'learning' rather than disciplinary knowledge. But the term and the practices around 'standards' are also symptomatic of the increasing lack of distinction between universities and other workplaces. For several decades, these other workplaces have been operating with standards in one form or another. For example, the practices of organizations and industries have been influenced, to a greater or lesser extent, by international standards and/or competency standards and/or professional standards. Furthermore, in the context of current government funding arrangements that invariably link funding levels to productivity and performance levels, universities, like other workplaces in a competitive market place, have become accountable – accountable to the funding sources, both the government and the market place. This accountability requires an articulation of exactly what knowledge universities produce and how well they produce it. Therefore accountability is inscribed in 'standards' that make explicit the kind and level of knowledge that is produced in and with the university.

Academics working in work-based learning programmes are confronting the challenge of articulating not only conventional academic standards but also how the learning outcomes in work-based learning programmes are equivalent to those standards. In terms of the former, academics are only now developing frameworks that make visible and sayable what was previously invisible and unsaid. Perhaps ironically, the engagement with work-based learning, with its focus on similar but different knowledge, has further stimulated the articulation of the specifications about standards. For many academics, standards relate to a body of disciplinary or professional knowledge. This kind of knowledge is constructed within and accountable to a disciplinary or professional community that controls the curriculum content and entry requirements and thus controls the academic standards and its 'standing' within that community. One of the roles of the community is to maintain these standards and this in turn allows for predictability about the knowledge that is being learned/produced. However, as discussed above, increasingly this community is opening its borders. The movement to cross-disciplinary and transdisciplinary knowledge, the partnerships with organizations, the reframing of entry requirements that allow for, for example, non-graduate access to some postgraduate awards, mean that the predictability of knowledge learnt and the academic standard of that knowledge are no longer certain. This is particularly so in work-based learning awards. The 'standard' criteria cannot apply in a learning programme where the context of learning (that is, the workplace and the learners' work practices) is the source of the curriculum, and where the learning is linked to performance goals and the control of the curriculum lies with the three partners – the organization, the learner and the university.

It is little wonder that academics express their concern with questions such as 'How flexible can a degree be before it can no longer be regarded as a degree? Does it need to include subjects or units of study, which are otherwise taught in the university? To what extent does it need to meet the same requirements as other degree courses?' These questions could be understood as sites of resistance which aim to foreground more familiar conventional kinds of knowledge.

The challenge for academics is to work within an educational framework that recognizes and accredits learning that occurs outside the university. The framework needs to acknowledge that the work-based learning arrangement accommodates notions of academic learning and at the same time legitimizes 'working knowledge'. The challenge is not to apply the same criteria as one might for conventional awards. Nor is it to legitimize any kind of workplace learning. Instead it is to develop curriculum frameworks that 'count' for the academy, participating organizations and learners.

Challenges to practices

There is little doubt that the teaching and learning practices in work-based learning present a number of challenges to academics. At one level these challenges emerge through the different kinds of knowledge of work-based learning and a conceptual acceptance of knowledge that does not sit discretely within conventional course structures and understandings about academic learning. But at another level the challenge relates to the complexities of the different kinds of learning practices attached to this knowledge. When learning occurs outside the classroom and outside a disciplinary area, where learning involves many different relationships, and where the learning experiences construct a very different role for the academic, there are myriad challenges.

Academics are therefore facing the challenge of working with a curriculum that requires them to deal with the complexities of converting work practices into learning practices that have a legitimacy inside the academy and outside it. They are dealing with issues about the place of theory and critical reflection in an instrumentally driven programme and the place of generic versus context-specific learning. But they are also confronting the new skills required for negotiating learning with people who may have very different expectations of the relationship with the university and of the outcomes of the learning programme.

A related issue is the recruitment of staff into the work-based learning programmes. Perhaps not surprisingly this is an additional challenge. For quality assurance purposes, academics working with work-based learning need to have appropriate knowledge and skills, but this requirement itself raises a number of questions. The first is to do with the nature of this knowledge and these skills. For example, is experience in individual learning contracts the 'right' experience? Is experience in a consultancy capacity in organizations the 'right' experience? Does experience in recognizing and accrediting prior learning for other awards provide academics with the 'right kind of expertise'?

The second set of questions related to 'right kind of expertise' are to do with the 'right kind of professional development programme', and this is complicated by the uneven uptake of professional development activities by academics. Therefore, there is a dual challenge – the first is to develop a programme that meets the challenge of the new academic practices and the second is to encourage academic participation in the programme.

Perhaps the most successful professional development strategy, although a relatively costly one, is the establishment of mentoring relationships – where experienced and inexperienced work-based learning teachers work together through each of the stages of the design and delivery of a work-based learning partnership. Moreover, the possibility of offering work-based learning awards to staff within the university is an attractive one. With such a strategy, academic staff (and potentially non-academic staff) can work on individualized work-based learning programmes, drawing on their work practices and making claims for the recognition of current capabilities. In this strategy they are engaged in the work-based learning process as a learner rather than as a teacher. It is not a simulation or role-playing activity, but one that works towards a university award that acknowledges their current practice and professional directions.

Challenge to identity

The repositioning of the university, in general, and specifically in work-based learning initiatives, not only involves a reshaping of curriculum and knowledge structures, but importantly involves a repositioning of the academic. Indeed, academics engaged in work-based learning take on different 'subject' positions, with the word 'subject' referring to what is being learnt as well as the identity of those involved as they are 'subjected' to regulation in the university and in workplaces (Usher and Solomon 1999).

Conventionally, the subject position of academics is constructed by disciplinary practices associated with expertise in knowledge and curriculum structures. It was in acquiring these practices that many academics served a long apprenticeship (Boud and Symes 2000). However, in work-based learning awards, academics require a different expertise, for which their academic apprenticeship did not prepare them. This results in a shift from an identity that has been shaped by a particular disciplinary area and the academic community more generally. Their identity is now formed from their new role in the learning process – one of facilitator in learning rather than an expert in a discipline. Furthermore, the implicit surveillance of a disciplinary community gives way to a more explicit scrutiny as work-based learning often comes under the microscope by academics suspicious about the consequences of work-based learning programmes.

Moreover, as suggested above, the academic, at the same time, is subjected to a considerable amount of regulation by the participating organization, which can understand the academic as a kind of consultant and therefore, for the length of the programme, 'one of them'. The academic is at the intersection of these two sites of regulation (the university and the workplace) and this can result in a considerable amount of tension for the academic, whose identity is no longer clearly defined. It is not surprising that academics are confused about their role and identity when asked, for example, to ensure that the work-based learning projects add value to the company's productivity goals or to attend organization training sessions that remind the academic that this work-based learning is motivated by profit.

Taking up the challenge

This chapter began with a discussion of whether work-based learning was a radical pedagogy or not. At the end of it, it is clear that it is. While this may be a dramatic conclusion, we have argued that work-based learning is indeed a challenge to the academy and to the academy's view of the place of legitimate knowledge. And this has important consequences for academic practices. It is simply not possible to drop a body of disciplinary knowledge into a workplace and expect to sustain the same boundaries around it. Similarly, it is not possible to drop a body of workplace knowledge into a disciplinary culture and leave that unchanged. Knowledge in the work-based learning curriculum is of the socially distributed type (Gibbons *et al.* 1994) – specific, applied, pragmatic and certainly neither generated by nor only responsible to the academic community. Instead the workplace, the individual learner and the university have to work together to produce and validate a non-disciplinary yet still 'legitimate' knowledge.

This shift presents an unprecedented challenge to dominant conceptions of what a university education is, what university qualifications are and what 'legitimate' knowledge should be. And this has enormous implications for the identity of the university and of academics. Academics are struggling with the shift – both conceptually and in their daily practice. Work-based learning raises questions about their role and identity, and whether or not work-based learning is a vehicle for letting go of the very reason for their existence. Academics are confronting changes in curriculum ownership and the balance of power and control, and many are feeling deskilled, not to mention deschooled! The very notion of the workplace as a site of knowledge generation is new and one that many academics find it difficult to grasp.

At the same time, we cannot afford to underestimate how work-based learning also presents a considerable challenge for learners. On the surface work-based learning is a very seductive option. Its relevance is clear and it provides an opportunity to gain qualifications drawing on recent or current everyday work practices. It enables one to be responsible for, manage and timetable one's own learning and it is likely to require minimal university attendance. However, such freedom often presents its own problems. While some learners easily manage the work-based learning experience, many find the increased responsibility a struggle. For these learners it is not so easy to replace one's expectations of and experiences in academic courses in terms of the structure it provided in relation to content as well as learning routines and tasks. In work-based learning learners have to deal with the complexities of being both a worker and learner and of having an increased responsibility in the learning process.

While flexibility in both process and content is an important part of the appeal for both the organization and the learner/employee, flexibility has to be located and bounded. Learners, their organizations and academics are asking for such. But it is also in the interest of the academy to reconstruct boundaries within an educational framework that maintains 'standards' at the same time as providing guidelines and practices that make explicit the educational parameters within which work-based learning partnership awards are to be negotiated, organized and assessed.

References

Ball, S. (1998) Big policies/small world: an introduction to international perspectives on education policy. *Comparative Education*, 34(2): 119–30.

Boud, D. and Symes, C. (2000) Learning for real: work-based education in universities, in C. Symes and J. McIntyre (eds) *Working Knowledge: The New Vocationalism and Higher Education.* Buckingham: SRHE/Open University Press.

Cope, B. and Kalantzis, M. (1997) *Productive Diversity: A New, Australian Model for Work and Management.* Sydney: Pluto Press.

Dale, R. (1999) Specifying globalisation effects on national policy: a focus on the mechanisms. *Journal of Education Policy,* 14(1): 1–17.

du Gay, P. (1996) *Consumption and Identity at Work.* London: Sage.

Edwards, R. and Usher, R. (2000) *Globalisation and Pedagogy: Space, Place and Identity.* London: Routledge

Featherstone, M. (1995) *Understanding Culture: Globalization, Postmodernism and Identity.* London: Sage.

Garrick, J. and Kirkpatrick, D. (1998) Work-based learning degrees: a new business venture or a new critical 'business'. *Higher Education Research and Development,* 17(2): 171–82.

Garrick, J. and Solomon, N. (in press) Technologies of self-regulation in training, in V. Sheared and P. Sissel (eds) *Making Space: Reframing Practice in Adult Education.* San Francisco: Greenwood Publishing.

Gee, J., Hull, G. and Lankshear, C. (1996) *The New Work Order: Behind the Language of the New Capitalism.* St Leonards, NSW: Allen & Unwin.

Gibbons, M., Limoges, C., Notwotny, H. *et al.* (1994) *The New Production of Knowledge: The Dynamics of Research in Contemporary Society.* London: Sage.

Harvey, D. (1989) *The Condition of Postmodernity.* Oxford: Blackwell.

Heron, J. (1988) Assessment revisited, in D. Boud (ed.) *Developing Student Autonomy in Learning.* London: Kogan Page.

Levin, B. (1998) An epidemic of education policy: (what) can we learn from each other? *Comparative Education,* 34(2): 131–41.

McIntyre, J. and Solomon, N. (2000) The policy environment of work-based learning: globalisation, institutions and the workplace, in C. Symes and J. McIntyre (eds) *Working Knowledge: The New Vocationalism and Higher Education.* Buckingham: SRHE/Open University Press.

Marginson, S. (1999) Diversity and convergency in higher education. *Australian Universities' Review,* 42(1): 12–23.

Senge, P. M. (1992) *The Fifth Discipline.* Sydney: Random House.

Sennett, R. (1998) *The Corrosion of Character: The Personal Consequences of Work in the New Capitalism.* New York: Norton.

Solomon, N. (1999) Culture and difference in workplace learning, in D. Boud and J. Garrick (eds) *Understanding Workplace Learning.* London: Routledge.

Solomon, N. and Usher, R. (1999) Open plan? Reorganizing the space of knowledge, Conference paper presented at *Re-organizing Knowledge: Trans-forming Institutions – Knowing, Knowledge and the University in the XXI Century,* 17–19 September, University of Massachusetts, Amherst.

Symes, C. and McIntyre, J. (2000) Working knowledge: an introduction to the new business of learning, in C. Symes and J. McIntyre (eds) *Working Knowledge: The New Vocationalism and Higher Education.* Buckingham: SRHE/Open University Press.

Taylor, S., Rizvi, F., Lingard, B. and Henry, M. (1997) *Educational Policy and the Politics of Change.* London: Routledge.

Toulmin, S. (1990) *Cosmopolis: The Hidden Agenda of Modernity.* New York: Free Press.

Turpin, T., Aylward, D., Garrett-Jones, S. and Johnston, R. (1996) *Knowledge-based Cooperation: University–Industry linkages in Australia.* Canberra: DEETYA.

Usher, R. and Solomon, N. (1999) Experiential learning and the shaping of subject-ivity in the workplace. *Studies in the Education of Adults,* 31(2): 155–63.

Waters, M. (1995) *Globalization.* London: Routledge.

Wilmott, H. (1993) Strength is ignorance; slavery is freedom: managing culture in modern organisations. *Journal of Management Studies,* 30(4): 515–52.

3

Knowledge at Work: Issues of Learning

David Boud

The particular characteristics of work-based learning require a new focus on the notion of a course of study and the ideas about learning which underpin it. This focus arises from the different relationship between learning and knowledge that exists in work-based courses relative to traditional university courses. This relationship prompts a reappraisal of the ways in which learning is viewed in a work-based learning context and necessarily on the ways in which a programme of study is supported.

This chapter aims to provide a basis for framing the work-based curriculum in terms of ideas about knowledge and about learning. Following discussion of the challenges of learning while working and the different kinds of knowledge which might be explored in the curriculum, the question of how we learn for situations we have not yet encountered is examined. The specific concerns of this chapter are the features of the work-based curriculum, which are discussed and elaborated.

Learning and working

The defining characteristic of work-based learning is that working and learning are coincident. Learning tasks are influenced by the nature of work and, in turn, work is influenced by the nature of the learning that occurs. The two are complementary. Learners are workers; workers are learners. They need to be able to manage both their roles. The academy and the workplace need to operate together to ensure that they are not sending contradictory messages. The challenge for the work-based learning curriculum and those who support it is to ensure that the mutually reinforcing nature of work-based learning is effectively utilized and that conflicts between the exigencies of work and learning are minimized. This can only happen if all the parties involved – learners/workers, workplace supervisors and academic advisers – are mindful of the potentials and the traps, and they are appropriately resourced in terms of the materials and expertise needed.

While work and learning may be coincident, they are not the same. They may be reinforcing to each other, but they have different goals and are directed towards different ends. Work is directed towards producing what the organization is in the business of offering, or some related output, whether that is a tangible product or a service, either now or in the future. Learning is directed towards the acquisition of knowledge or the capacity to gain further knowledge. Many organizations are now adopting the idea of corporate capabilities, as examined by John Stephenson in Chapter 7, dealing with the capability envelope. The knowledge that is the object of learning may or may not be closely related to whatever the organization produces now or in the future. For example, there is always a need to orient new employees to their immediate work tasks and there is often considerable learning for them in this. However, most work-related learning involves the development of knowledge of use in improving present practices or processes or in developing practices or processes for the future. It may even involve knowledge to be used to transform the organization and lead it to new kinds of activity. Learning may be directed towards immediate or long-term ends.

Learning and working often take place at the same location, and to the external observer the activities associated with each may not be easily separated. Many work assignments require employees to engage in learning before the work can be effectively completed. Such learning is an intrinsic aspect of work and may not be differentiated from it in the minds of worker or supervisor. However, this aspect of learning is not the focus here. Work-based learning typically emphasizes learning beyond the immediate and necessary requirements of work completion. The employee takes on the additional and explicit role of a learner in the workplace and engages in activities that add to the normal work requirements of the position they hold. In many instances, activities of learning and working can be shared. The workplace provides a textbook from which the worker/learner draws problems, completes exercises and assignments, some prescribed, some not. For example, in the completion of a work assignment, the reading for and writing of a report may well be of benefit to work outcomes as well as other learning outcomes that can be formally recognized. There are therefore potential savings of time and effort on the part of the learner in work-based learning compared to similar tasks in an entirely educational environment. Not all these savings can be realized, as learning has additional demands of its own which may not be apparent to those new to work-based learning.

While they might share many interests in common, the roles of worker and learner do not necessarily sit easily together. When a worker is also a part-time student, there is a separation of activities in time and place that distinguishes learning from working. Classes may occur in the evening or at the weekend and course assignments are completed at home. In work-based learning, the activities or working and learning often take place in the same location at the same time. The learning involved is often multimodal. There may be no sign that a shift from one mode to another has taken place. This can create additional tensions and an extra process for the work-based learner to manage.

Work-based learners are students, but they may not feel like students. This raises identity questions that are dealt with elsewhere in this volume. That they do not attend an educational institution on a regular basis, if at all, compounds the feeling of identity ambiguity. They may not meet students other than those in their own workplace, who anyway are fellow workers. They do not follow an existing curriculum, and they do not sit examinations or complete set assignments. Many of the conventional attributes of being a student are absent. Learners have to manage their work and learning without the conventional boundaries that exist between them. They may even occupy the same physical space. Learners also have to manage the shift of identity from worker to learner and back again. They may not have the opportunity (luxury) of being able to devote themselves single-mindedly to one or the other role. They may have to explain to co-workers and supervisors what they are doing and why, and deal with the feelings which attending to learning in the workplace and the comments of others may provoke. All this can be managed, but the challenges are not necessarily obvious to the new learner. They also raise the aforementioned question of identity: is the work-based learner really a bona fide student at all or some type of hybrid student cum worker?

Knowledge and the work-based learning curriculum

Even though subject matter knowledge may not be the defining characteristic, the work-based curriculum must take into account a view of knowledge. Learning always has an object of attention. It is learning about something. It cannot be separated from knowledge in either the general or the local sense. What perspectives on knowledge need to be considered in developing the work-based curriculum?

A basic assumption of work-based learning is that knowledge is generated through work. All workplaces are potentially sites of knowledge production; similarly, universities and research institutions have traditionally been thought of as sites of knowledge production. Different workplaces will be differentially generative of knowledge production depending on the nature of the work undertaken and the particular expectations of productivity, which are placed on those who work there. These include the nature of the enterprise as well as the extent to which:

- work follows standard patterns and routines;
- the organization understands and represents its own knowledge;
- employees are given scope to exercise initiative to transform the nature of their work and that of others;
- there is freedom to pursue goals beyond those required for current work output.

The kinds of knowledge generated in workplaces may differ greatly from those generated and sustained by academic institutions. Knowledge production is driven by different imperatives. Different knowledge may well be valued in different sites. One way of contrasting the distinction between the kinds of knowledge valued in universities and that of other settings has been elaborated by a number of recent commentators. Gibbons *et al.* (1994) are among the most prominent of these and they describe two modes of knowledge production:

> in Mode 1 problems are set and solved in a context governed by the, largely academic, interests of a specific community. By contrast, Mode 2 knowledge is carried out in a context of application. Mode 1 is disciplinary while Mode 2 is transdisciplinary. Mode 1 is characterized by homogeneity, Mode 2 by heterogeneity. Organizationally, Mode 1 is hierarchical and tends to preserve its form, while Mode 2 is more heterarchical and transient. Each employs a different type of quality control. In comparison with Mode 1, Mode 2 is more socially accountable and reflexive. It includes a wider, more temporary and heterogeneous set of practitioners, collaborating on a problem defined in a specific and localized context.
>
> (Gibbons *et al.* 1994: 3)

Gibbons and his colleagues were focusing on research and did not appear to have in mind the kinds of work-based learning represented in this book when they developed these distinctions. However, such an analysis is helpful in identifying the ways in which knowledge may need to be treated differently in work-based courses relative to traditional disciplinary programmes of which most university work consists. As work-based learning develops there will no doubt be the need for more sophisticated conceptualizations of different knowledge modes in different settings. However, for present purposes the Mode 1/2 distinctions are helpful in pointing to some of the challenges that the work-based learning curriculum faces.

The focus of work-based learning is on the knowledge of practice, on what is needed to understand and develop the activities of particular work sites. The knowledge requirements and the knowledge outcomes of work-based courses will not necessarily coincide with those of disciplinary courses. This does not imply that Mode 1 knowledge is irrelevant to work-based learning, but that it may be subordinated to other, more pressing agendas. A work-based learning curriculum will not necessarily incorporate elements of existing university courses, although in many circumstances where these courses do provide for the kind of knowledge development needed for particular desired outcomes, they are included.

One of the major challenges of the work-based learning curriculum is how to reconcile the Mode 1 knowledge of the university and the Mode 2 knowledge of the workplace in ways that do not place an unrealistic burden on the individual learner. Academic advisers will typically be drawing on their background of Mode 1 knowledge, while workplace supervisors or advisers will be drawing on their understanding of Mode 2 knowledge. What Mode 1 knowledge they possess will be overtaken by the exigencies of work. While much of the vocabulary will be the same, they will not necessarily be speaking the same language. This means that there is a need for all parties to be explicit about what they are bringing to the encounter and what this offers to people who are availing themselves of the learning opportunity provided jointly by their organization and by the university.

Of course, knowledge derived from the university part of the work-based learning partnership is neither all Mode 1 nor only available wrapped up in standard course units. The university provides knowledge of learning and how it might be promoted. It provides access to an enormously wide range of expertise in many areas. It also has knowledge of knowledge acquisition over a wide range of fields of inquiry. Conventionally it has been assumed that access to such knowledge can only be gained by enrolling in standard units that are available in undergraduate and postgraduate degrees. However, this assumption will be increasingly tested. Universities will have to find ways of 'disaggregating' their courses and making them available in different ways and in different combinations as they move towards accepting the need for flexibility. The unit of study takes on a different complexion when it is not a part of a wider disciplinary framework. Additional items may need to be included and others removed when it is used in different ways and for different purposes. It is extremely unlikely that it will end up as being of the same magnitude as existing units that owe more to the amount that can be covered in weekly classes in a standard semester period. Well documented, smaller size, self-contained elements will be needed.

Work-based learning: beyond the present and the particular

Not only do new forms of learning and work require us to focus on what constitutes knowledge, they also require a new look at the notion of learning. When students are engaged in work-based learning, what are they actually learning? They are not learning existing knowledge from a standard curriculum. They are not engaged in research in the sense that someone undertaking a PhD is engaged in original research (unless perhaps they are engaged in doctoral level work-based learning). They are not learning how to do their existing job, though they may well be extending their present work. For the most part what they are doing is equipping them to be continuing learners and productive workers through engagement with tasks that extend and challenge them, taking them beyond their existing knowledge and expertise. Such continuing learning requires a fresher view of learning than that hitherto promoted in higher education.

Over the past 25 years or so there has been a transformation in understanding of student learning in higher education. A research base has been established where none existed previously and there is now a body of work that speaks directly to the concerns of academics. The most influential of this research has been that on qualitative conceptions of knowledge. This has been associated with the tradition of phenomenographic research associated with Marton among others (Marton *et al.* 1996). The much quoted distinctions between students' surface and deep approaches to learning are a result of research that belongs to this tradition.

In recent years Marton and his collaborators have moved on from phenomenography as such to a concern with a topic which lies at the heart of all education, that of what it takes to learn (Marton and Booth 1997; Bowden and Marton 1998). In particular they confront the fundamental problem of how we can learn in a way that enables us to deal with unknown situations. While they use this problem to explore curriculum and teaching issues for all university courses, their thinking is especially applicable to work-based learning. The reason for this is that in work-based learning most situations are unknown. Not only are they unknown to the learner, but unlike in conventional courses, they can also be unknown (at least in part) to their supervisors and advisers. The two features of Bowden and Marton's solution to the problem of learning for unknown situations are: first, to focus on discerning aspects of situations that vary from others; and, second, to integrate disciplinary and professional frameworks of knowledge. The first of these is less apparent, but it is probably of greater significance for work-based learning.

What do they mean by discerning aspects that vary and why is that important? They argue that one of the problems with existing curricula and approaches to teaching is that students are expected to focus on a particular issue or problem and practise solving it until they become expert. They then move on to another issue or problem type and repeat the process. When students are faced with a new issue or problem they try to decide which of the approaches in which they are expert is appropriate. When they find that it belongs to none of the sets they know, they don't know how to approach the problem. They have no experience in deciding what the problem is. In order for them to gain such experience, they must be exposed to novel situations with different kinds of problems. The important element that Bowden and Marton (1998) have added to this analysis is that students should go on to work out just what the problem really is. It is the understanding of what the problem really is that is the key to learning for the unknown.

Understanding what the problem is involves students in noticing the variation between one situation and another. They are required to draw on various aspects of their knowledge to make sense of and account for the particular features of the problem or issue with which they are confronted. Students learn variation by noticing differences in different problem situations. By comparing and contrasting these, they come to focus on salient features that will enable them to address the new problem. In this way of looking at learning, it is not just the solving of the problem which indicates learning, but the development of an appreciation of what was actually learned. Students need to stand back and reflect on their learning in order to understand what it is that they have learned that goes beyond the specifics of the situation in which they find themselves. It is this aspect of learning that enables them to face new situations with equanimity.

The second of Bowden and Marton's (1998) solutions to learning for unknown situations is the integration of disciplinary and professional frameworks of knowledge: Mode 1 and Mode 2 forms of knowledge. This is important for work-based learning, but potentially more problematic as work-related frameworks of knowledge are generally underdeveloped, or at least not well documented. Further, existing disciplinary knowledge frameworks are rarely constructed in ways that link directly with working knowledge. In particular, the ways in which disciplinary knowledge are represented in the conventional curriculum may not be accessible to those who have not progressed through a conventional disciplinary education. There are substantial challenges in making existing course units available within a work-based learning framework as Mode 1 and Mode 2 knowledge may be qualitatively different and cannot be translated from one to another. It is easier to imagine a dialogue between disciplinary and professional frameworks within a conventional course than in a work setting. There are a number of reasons for this. First, there is a degree of control and standardization of the curriculum possible within an academic framework. This means that work-based knowledge becomes subordinated to disciplinary knowledge. Second, there has been substantial dialogue between disciplinary and professional knowledge within universities, in some cases over very long periods of time. Traditional professions, such as law and medicine, have been represented in universities over many centuries and, while there have been tensions between academic and professional knowledge, both now are subject to research as the development of professional expertise is explored systematically. There is no equivalent investigation for most domains of work-related knowledge outside defined professional areas – though this is changing, particularly in areas such as nursing and teaching.

This does not imply that there should not be closer integration between disciplinary and work-related knowledge, but this remains to be undertaken. There is a need for new conceptual frameworks useful in interrogating Mode 2 knowledge. This is a prerequisite for the kinds of integration envisaged by Bowden and Marton (1998). There are, for example, many aspects of post-structuralist theory that can be deployed to this end, including Foucauldian analysis that can illuminate the power/knowledge dynamics of work settings (see Rose 1990; Gore 1997). However, by and large, there has been little systematic analysis of the kinds of conceptual and theoretical work of value for work-based learning. This is likely to be a fruitful area of research necessary for the further development of work-based learning.

Beyond the particular

A particular challenge for the work-based curriculum is the danger of trapping learners' understanding within their own work setting. That is, learners may well learn how to improve their immediate practice, but, constrained to that environment, they will be unable to move beyond it. Their under-standings and working knowledge become over-localized and cannot tran-scend the present and the particular. While this is an issue of much broader significance, in work-based learning it means that strategies for addressing it must be found if recognition of learning beyond the organization is sought.

Bowden and Marton's (1998) suggestions can also be used to address the problematic issue of the transfer of learning. That is, how can we ensure that students can apply their learning in situations other than the ones in which they developed it? The conventional way of phrasing this is: how can transferability of learning beyond the workplace be enabled? However, Bowden and Marton argue, following Smedslund (1953), that transfer is not needed as a concept. As they put it:

> Anything you learn, you must make use of in other situations. You can never re-enter the very situation, which gave birth to learning. Transfer is involved in every instance of learning; questions of transfer are simply questions of learning. And, if so, you do not need the concept of transfer of course. It is redundant.
>
> (Bowden and Marton 1998: 25)

They also challenge the framing of the problem in terms of transfer:

> Sorting situations into two categories – learning situations on the one hand and situations of application on the other – seems hard to defend. Every 'learning situation' includes the potential for application (of something learned previously) and every 'situation of application' implies the potential for learning (something new).
>
> (Bowden and Marton 1998: 25)

The difficulty that the notion of transfer seeks to address is still an import-ant one. They suggest that the idea of variation is sufficient to deal with the problems that 'transfer' was invented to deal with. They focus on the import-ance of the differences between situations of various kinds:

> There are differences between situations within educational institu-tions (this is one form of variation), there are differences between situations outside educational institutions (another form of variation) and there are differences between the two classes of situation (a third form of variation). Interesting issues are the extent and nature of these different sorts of variation, and the possible relationships between them.
>
> (Bowden and Marton 1998: 26)

Bowden and Marton thus shift the attention away from the notion of 'application' towards that of exploring the variations that exist in the objects of study and the relationships between them. It is only through experiencing variation in learning, discerning different sorts of variation and being able to draw upon this variation in new settings, that learners can successfully approach new problems or issues. This implies a greater emphasis on students appreciating what they are learning and what they have learned at the time of their learning. They need to disembed their knowledge from the particularities of context in which it learned so that it is available for use elsewhere (Donaldson 1978). In the work setting this will often involve an additional step beyond that needed for the immediate use of that knowledge. Developing an awareness of their learning is a necessary step that must be incorporated explicitly into the work-based curriculum. Such an emphasis helps to address the criticism of work-based learning that it lacks the feature of providing a 'critical distance' in the development of professionals; that is, that it does not enable learners to perceive what they are learning separate from their immediate context.

In terms of the language of approaches to learning, students must necessarily have engaged in a deep approach to learning if they are likely to be able to use their knowledge in a new situation. While there may be more potential for them to do so in the relevant and meaningful context of the workplace, pressure to cut corners and not fully process their learning are present too. Work-based learning in itself does not guarantee that a deep approach will be adopted.

While Bowden and Marton (1998) focus on what they term disciplinary and professional knowledge, they do not address the challenges of Mode 2 knowledge directly. They also draw most of their detailed examples from relatively simple science contexts. Professional knowledge has already undergone some degree of codification compared to the wider range of Mode 2 knowledge, and discerning variation is more demanding the more complex the situation considered. Nevertheless, their work provides the most useful starting point so far in dealing with the learning challenges of work-based learning.

Conclusions

In this chapter we have suggested that work-based learning represents a new way of organizing and learning in the academy. It does not arise directly from the disciplinary frameworks in which knowledge has been traditionally ordered within the university, and in many instances it exemplifies more local knowledge, flowing from the particular spatial and temporal circumstances of work contexts and situations. In the traditional university this knowledge was spurned, and the catchcry was to go beyond the present and the particular (Bailey 1984). Work-based learning celebrates the pedagogic significance of the particular and the present. As has been argued in the latter sections of the chapter, this could limit its transferability and trap the work-based learner in degrees that have a very limited shelf life. However, new theories of variation, most notably those espoused by Bowden and Marton (1998), could redress this, and offer the prospect of work-based learning being codified at source in such a way as to ensure that such learning transcends the present and the particular.

References

Bailey, C. H. (1984) *Beyond the Present and the Particular: A Theory of Liberal Education.* London: Routledge and Kegan Paul.

Bowden, J. and Marton, F. (1998) *The University of Learning: Beyond Quality and Competence in Higher Education.* London: Kogan Page.

Donaldson, M. (1978) *Children's Minds.* London: Fontana.

Gibbons, M., Limoges, C., Nowotny, H. *et al.* (1994) *The New Production of Knowledge: The Dynamics of Science and Research in Contemporary Societies.* London: Sage.

Gore, J. M. (1997) Power relations in pedagogy: an empirical study based on Foucauldian thought, in C. O'Farrell (ed.) *Foucault. The Legacy.* Brisbane: QUT.

Marton, F. and Booth, S. (1997) *Learning and Awareness.* Mahwah, NJ: Lawrence Erlbaum.

Marton, F., Hounsell, D. and Entwistle, N. (1996) *The Experience of Learning: Implications for Teaching and Studying in Higher Education.* Edinburgh: Scottish Academic Press.

Rose, N. (1990) *Governing the Soul: The Shaping of the Private Self.* London: Routledge.

Smedslund, J. (1953) The problem of 'what is learned?' *Psychological Review,* 60: 157–8.

4
Creating a Work-based Curriculum

David Boud

The structure of work-based learning has drawn upon many previous educational practices, which are discussed in Chapter 1: work placements and sandwich courses, independent and negotiated study, recognition of prior learning and the use of generic competencies and capabilities. However, while it has emerged from a number of these practices, the curriculum for work-based learning is not simply an amalgamation of them. It is driven, we would argue, by the logic of the context of partnership and the demands of new knowledge.

With the two key issues of knowledge and learning having been considered, this chapter examines implications for the work-based curriculum and how such a curriculum can be constructed. The focus is on elements necessary for it to operate effectively within the dual constraints of work and the educational institution in such a way that learners are provided with flexible and challenging opportunities; at the same time without creating such onerous demands that they are not able to operate effectively.

Unlike its widespread use in other education sectors, the use of the term curriculum does not have wide currency in universities. Course development has been a more popular term than curriculum development. One reason for this is perhaps that 'course' provides a stronger emphasis on the syllabus and subject matter content than 'curriculum', which encompasses a broader range of concerns, including those of educational process. Work-based learning challenges the idea of having a preset syllabus or content defined in advance by teachers. The older term 'curriculum' is therefore more appropriate for discussing the organization of work-based learning when the emphasis is placed on learning outcomes rather than knowledge inputs.

At present, most educational institutions organize courses around course units and credit points. Course units represent a discrete component of a course with specific learning outcomes and assessment processes. Work-based learning programmes have mostly found it necessary to adopt an apparently similar structure in order to fit alongside other courses and units of knowledge. The main difference has been that the course units in work-based learning programmes do not necessarily correspond to units of knowledge in the same way. Often they represent a mix of knowledge units and stages in the development of a negotiated programme. The discussion here is not dependent on the particular clustering of activities to form units, as these will vary over time. The focus is on necessary features of a work-based curriculum without which it would not be possible to operate effectively.

Work as the curriculum: educational implications

If work-based learning takes as a starting point work as the curriculum, a variety of implications follow. First, programmes must acknowledge the situatedness of the learner in the workplace, the 'present and particular' of Chapter 3. That is that the learner has a context in a particular setting at a particular time with various demands placed on her or him, with learning being only one of these.

Second, programmes must accept a great range of differences existing in this context. These include not only the range of individual learners with different aspirations, different cultures and different levels of knowledge. These factors are found in conventional study as well. There are different workplaces with different demands on workers with different opportunities for learning and different expectations of outcomes. Despite stereotypes to the contrary, most organizations are neither monolithic nor monocultural. Nor are they single-purposed. Different work (and therefore learning) environments exist within a single building or division of the organization.

Third, programmes will need to be flexible, not only for reasons of situatedness and difference mentioned above, but because work is ever-changing and learners change along with it. Unlike in conventional study in which the curriculum can be set de facto by academics and teachers – they control it – in work-based learning there are more influences over the content and process of study than can be captured or controlled by any one of the various parties involved.

Fourth, programmes will necessarily be contested at many different levels. Unlike in the disciplinary curriculum that tends to evolve gradually over time, punctuated by intense episodes of contestation about the inclusion of new knowledge, contestation in the work-based curriculum is ongoing and normal. There is rarely an authoritative source to define the necessary knowledge in the workplace. Not only is knowledge therefore questioned but those defining it are challenged. There is always a tension between workplace requirements and university requirements, between the short term and the long term, between Mode 1 and Mode 2 knowledge, between advisers and assessors.

What implications do these characteristics have for the construction of programmes? While they are obviously interrelated and demand a holistic design, for the sake of simplicity they will be considered in turn. First, a programme must accept and take account of the different types of knowledge represented when work is the curriculum. This means that Mode 1 knowledge must not be systematically privileged at the expense of Mode 2 knowledge. While the learning outcomes demonstrated must satisfy particular university criteria to gain recognition and accreditation, this does not imply that it is only knowledge represented in conventional university curricula that can be accepted. Unless frameworks of standards and levels are constructed in ways that acknowledge the legitimacy of other forms of knowledge, then work-based learning is doomed to marginalization. Such an acknowledgement, however, can be a major challenge to the university and what it stands for, as it implies that the academy is not the sole arbiter of what constitutes knowledge.

Second, the fact that there are different workplaces and different roles for employees within them means that work-based learning programmes must be flexible and responsive to the circumstances of the learner and of the work setting. This does not mean that group activities cannot be undertaken by learners engaged in similar projects or in similar work contexts or that programmes cannot be organized to provide peer support and development. It does, however, imply that designs in which the curriculum is defined in advance by anyone other than the learner cannot be readily envisaged.

Third, there needs to be a focus on an educational approach to the curriculum, not a narrow operational competency-based approach suitable for pre-defined learning outcomes. Competency-based frameworks that delineate the universe of outcomes – such as those used in vocational education and training derived from industry-based occupational standards – are unlikely to be appropriate except for relatively low-level work-based learning programmes. However, the more holistic approaches to competency (see Gonczi 1994; Hager *et al.* 1994), or the capability frameworks introduced by the Royal Society of Arts Capability in Higher Education initiative (Stephenson 1998, Chapter 7 in volume) are more fruitful.

Fourth, contestation needs to be embraced not as something which it is feared will tear work-based learning apart, but as a matter to be managed as a normal feature of daily practice. Contestation between parties occurs on two main occasions: at the time when the acceptance of a programme is being pursued and at the time when the assessment of the learning outcomes from that programme is being determined. These are the key stages at which contestation needs to be managed by the educational institution. During the programme the student will be faced with conflicting views throughout, but this is a normal part of any learning – in the conventional curriculum as much as the workplace – and responsibility for managing that is with the student and whoever is the adviser.

Key learning themes

Work-based learning not only focuses on the exigencies of work. It also provides an excellent example of a learner-centred approach to the curriculum. It could not be envisaged in any other way to meet its objectives. The focus is what students wish to learn, not what is provided for them to learn. It is therefore fruitful to set the features of the curriculum in the context of their relationship to learning.

The nature of work-based learning leads programmes to focus on four key learning themes. While some institutions attempt to relate these to particular units or modules of activity, they are more appropriately considered as ongoing motifs of work-based learning. Consideration of each needs to occur at more than one stage:

- *Learning identified.* That is, what knowledge does the learner bring to the programme and what is desired from the programme? Students engage in a process of reviewing what they have learned from their experience and how this relates to what they desire to learn. Their existing knowledge provides a starting point for study and locates them at a particular stage in a framework of qualifications (e.g. as equivalent to second year undergraduate level).
- *Learning added.* That is, new learning undertaken for the purposes of the programme. This is the core of any programme. It builds from existing knowledge to a new level of accomplishment. Learning comprises study which equips students for work-based learning, a planning task resulting in a learning agreement, work-related projects and self-monitoring of all these tasks. The learning added is not only with respect to particular work knowledge, but a contribution towards the lifelong learning skills of planning and evaluating one's own learning.
- *Learning recognized.* That is, the knowledge that the learner is able to recognize as having been acquired from study. Knowledge does not come already ordered and labelled. Addressing the question 'what has actually been learned?' is a substantial undertaking of central importance. Identifying what has been learned from engagement in the programme in terms of learning outcomes is needed.
- *Learning equivalence.* That is, what is the academic equivalent in terms of credit points and level of achievement of the documented learning outcomes? The outcome is not simply the 'content' or new knowledge required by work *per se* or the intrinsic knowledge gained by the learner. What is vital in work-based learning is consideration of what else is required to transform it into learning accepted for academic purposes.

As a programme of work-based learning study is necessarily unique, a curriculum cannot be predetermined. Neither can it be established on behalf of the learner. Learners within the same work setting are likely to be following different programmes depending on their prior knowledge, aspirations and expertise. However, creating a programme of study for a substantial course is a major learning achievement in itself and needs to be recognized as such.

Seven elements of a work-based curriculum

Work-based learning requires a different perspective on the notion of curriculum from that found in discipline or profession-based courses. The work-based curriculum cannot be established in advance, for it will not be the same for all students, and it cannot be created exclusively by the educational institution. All the curriculum elements may vary – aims and objectives, specific learning outcomes, programme of study, time for completion, relationships between staff and students and assessment practices. However, there are limits. One of the major challenges an educational institution faces is to establish what these limits might be. Without constraints anything goes and the programme cannot be regarded as constituting an educational qualification. With limits set too strictly, traditional courses become reproduced in an uncongenial environment.

There are many ways of potentially organizing a work-based learning curriculum. They all need to meet basic requirements that are driven by the dual exigencies of education and work. Some aspects of these have already been discussed above. The requirements include acknowledgement of the different kinds of knowledge requirements in work-based settings, appreciation of the requirements of learning no matter what the context may be, application of a range of learning technologies suitable for flexible, work-based programmes and the use of assessment practices taking account of the diverse outcomes of work-based learning and locating these in a broader educational framework.

While the central feature of a work-based curriculum will always be learning tasks undertaken in conjunction with work, in order that these learning tasks meet broader educational goals, it has been found necessary to include a number of other elements. These are required to:

1. Establish work-based learning as a learning enterprise that, while commonly undertaken at work, is not identical to work.
2. Address the diverse range of knowledge and skills possessed by students at the commencement of work-based learning.
3. Locate the outcomes of work-based learning in a framework of levels and standards of achievement.
4. Promote the development and negotiation of a programme of activities.
5. Support the ongoing learning of students in situ.
6. Encourage critical reflection throughout the programme.

7. Document learning in a form which can be assessed in terms of the frameworks previously established.

Corresponding to each of these purposes, there is a curriculum element. Careful thought needs to be given to the structures which will support the development of a programme, the ways in which it is carried out and how it is assessed and evaluated. A key concern is what is needed to assist the learner at each stage.

Establish work-based learning as a learning enterprise that, while commonly undertaken at work, is not identical to work

One of the reasons why work-based learning has an immediate attraction to employers and to employees is that it appears to offer the opportunity of gaining academic recognition for the learning that would have been undertaken anyway as part of normal workplace activities. This is true to some extent and there are potential savings of time and effort in many of the activities that involve learning. These include reading, developing new practices and writing reports, and may draw upon the same content and technical resources that are used at university. However, work-based learning programmes add value to what is needed to get the job done. They involve making learning explicit, appreciating existing achievements, acknowledging one's knowledge base, exploring desired outcomes, planning for knowledge acquisition, critically reflecting on understanding, learning cooperatively with others and documenting achievements. These are valuable outcomes that contribute to the development of lifelong learning in their own right. Being a work-based learner is about becoming confident that one's learning needs can be met, developing an identity as an active learner and taking a proactive stance towards the challenges that confront one in the workplace.

While work-based learning is a familiar idea, what is involved in doing it is not. Considerable effort in briefing prospective learners and orienting them to the demands of work-based study is necessary. Most of them are familiar from their school days with the organization of courses around academic disciplines, syllabuses and content. When confronted with a curriculum that does not follow this pattern, they may well be disoriented and confused. Some will welcome a release from a form of education in which they did not thrive, while others will feel that the props of learning have been removed. It is therefore necessary for them to understand the new curriculum structure and how it will assist them.

More than a simple briefing is required. Learners may have to shift their conceptions of what learning involves and what their role is in it. If students leave the orientation without a strong grasp of what work-based learning expects of them, they are unlikely to progress within it.

Address the diverse range of knowledge and skills possessed by students at the commencement of work-based learning

The recognition of prior learning (RPL) also known as the accreditation of prior experiential learning (APEL), has become established as a means of gaining entry and obtaining credit exemptions in higher education institutions in many countries (Mandel and Michelson 1990; Evans 2000). This involves students preparing a portfolio that documents the learning outcomes and evidence of the learning achievements that they undertook informally or in a non-accredited course. Such a portfolio is submitted and credit allocated on the basis of the extent to which it demonstrates equivalence to learning outcomes from formal courses.

Similar arrangements are important and necessary for work-based learning courses. Most learning developed in the workplace has hitherto been unaccredited, but it provides the foundation on which students will build their work-based learning studies. A process of portfolio development and assessment is needed for students to identify the point at which their formal work-based learning should commence. However, there are important adaptations needed for work-based learning.

First, the prior learning documented in the portfolio must relate directly to the proposed programme of study to be undertaken for work-based learning. Credits given must be allocated in terms of the actual curriculum proposed for work-based learning. The allocation of non-specific credit, common elsewhere, is inappropriate in this context. Second, it is important that current competencies only are recognized. As the knowledge identified in the portfolio is to be used immediately as part of the programme, it must be current and deployable. This implies that a stricter approach than that adopted in many courses for adult students must be implemented.

Locate the outcomes of work-based learning in a framework of levels and standards of achievement

The need for work-based learning to operate in the dual worlds of work and education means that a common language must be used to describe the outcomes of what is being undertaken. This language is represented in a framework of standards and levels. These standards and levels must be articulated in terms of educational achievements, which relate to well established qualifications and educational outcomes, and in terms which are meaningful in the work context. Examples used at Portsmouth and Anglia universities are discussed in Chapters 12 and 13. While each university has adopted its own framework, there have been many shared practices across institutions and various consortia of institutions have met to develop them.

Extensive discussion has normally taken place to clarify and make explicit the educational intentions embedded in levels and standards, and those people who have been party to these discussions have been involved in a valuable exercise to reach a common understanding of what is intended. This has not been the case for other staff and for students. While the language of levels and standards appears clear and self-evident to those who have developed them, there is a danger in assuming that this is the case for others. The framework of levels and standards has an equivalent function in some ways to the taken-for-granted core of conventional disciplinary courses. However, there is a major difference, which if not addressed directly can lead to major problems and the undermining of standards for work-based learning. It is this. When one grows within a disciplinary culture, the standards of that culture – what counts, what is valued, what must be included – are continually reinforced in subtle and incremental ways through all teaching, learning and assessment activities. A graduate from such a culture is imbued with a deep understanding of the cultural norms and values that is difficult to articulate to those in other cultures. While much maligned in current assessment discussions, it leads to observations such as staff being able readily to 'recognize', for example, upper second honours level work, without needing to work through long lists of criteria and standards (see Chapter 12 for more on this).

Such cultural conundrums do not exist in work-based learning. They will never exist in the same way as in disciplinary studies. When the curriculum is generated anew with each programme the same understanding of standards which is attached to codified Mode 1 knowledge is impossible. New ways of judging 'what counts' for what need to be established. These will develop over time for work-based learning, but they certainly do not exist in the early years of implementation as new staff are inducted into it and students fresh to the very idea of work-based learning enrol. The explication, sharing and analysis of frameworks of levels and standards are a major undertaking for new programmes. While sufficient attention is normally given at the institutional approval level to this, it is often not the case at the local level. Effort is required in all parties at all levels to understand and be able to use the particular framework that has been adopted.

Promote the development and negotiation of a programme of activities

The central feature of work-based learning is the programme of activities the student undertakes. This is equivalent to the programme of lectures, tutorials, practical work and placements undertaken by students on conventional courses. It can be even more diverse and complex, depending on the nature of the programme. The nature of the programme is driven by the needs of the learner and of the workplace, but it needs to satisfy the requirements of the university as manifest in the statement of standards and levels. Some curriculum elements are given because of the form of work-based learning. These include portfolio development and appraisal as well as elements discussed below. Others may draw upon aspects of existing courses; for example, units of study offered in flexible learning modes. However, the main emphasis is on the negotiation of a programme of study in the workplace.

Negotiated learning has become accepted in most higher education institutions, although it is far from pervasive. It commonly uses the form of a learning plan, often called a learning contract. A learning contract is a written agreement between a learner and others which sets out a range of activities that will need to be undertaken if certain learning outcomes are to be achieved. The typical components of a learning contract are statements about the learning goals to be pursued, the strategies and resources involved, what is to be assessed and the criteria for assessment. These are normally summarized in a short document and signed by the student and their advisers. In the case of work-based learning, as the programme needs to satisfy the student, the university and the employer, the contract is a three-way undertaking between the learner, an academic adviser and a workplace supervisor. The practicalities of the use of learning contracts are discussed elsewhere (Knowles 1975; Anderson *et al.* 1996).

Typically, a student drafts a contract and discusses this with their supervisor and adviser, before reworking it in the light of their comments and submitting it for final approval. In some institutions there is a process of registration of the plan after approval by a panel of assessors. This is of particular significance during the early stages of implementation of work-based learning in an institution or when a new partnership with an employer is formed, as it ensures that a common understanding of what is required is formed across students' advisers and locations.

Support the ongoing learning of students in situ

One of the valuable features of work-based learning is the potential richness of resources and support available to students. They can draw upon not only those of the educational institution, but also those of the workplace. Often the level of resources, reference materials and expertise is greater in the organization than in the university. The relationships available with work colleagues, colleagues elsewhere in the organization, managers, academic advisers and other academics create opportunities for learning which are not necessarily predictable, or readily manageable. Maintaining a focus requires a variety of forms of support.

Learning activities have to be sustained over time and through the many other pressures faced in the workplace. While academic advisers obviously have a vital role in support of learning activities, it is not normally possible to resource the more intensive supervisory relationships possible with, for example, doctoral students. Workplace supervisors have an important role, but their prime responsibility is to ensure that work gets performed effectively.

A number of different strategies can be used for students helping them-selves and each other. Some involve providing resources to students to assist them to monitor their own learning and their reflections on it. This can occur through the use of journals and ongoing learning portfolios. Others involve advisers, workplace supervisors, peers and students supporting themselves.

Role of advisers
If staff/student ratios are calculated, for example, on the same basis as those permitted by the funding levels of existing courses, the amount of contact between student and academic adviser is severely limited, especially if it occurs one-to-one. The time devoted to supporting work-based learn-ing can be effectively multiplied at a number of stages. Through careful preparation at the learning agreement negotiation stage, the provision of learning resources and the training of students in how to use them at the orientation phase, it is possible for advisers to set up activities which stu-dents can run for themselves. Valuable individual time should be used for those aspects that cannot be dealt with in any other way. These include working with students on ways of addressing unique problems encountered with their learning plans, assisting students to see how they can meet the requirements of frameworks of levels and standards and helping students to find ways of utilizing the wider resources of the university. As work-based learning programmes mature, information that underpins this advice can be codified and made available in various kinds of guides and manuals.

Role of workplace supervisors
While it is vital for workplace supervisors and managers to agree to the learning plans and to provide the conditions in which learning can take place at work, it is important not to expect too much of them with regard to facilitating learning directly. Recent research on the role of supervisors in facilitating learning has shown that employees are unwilling to reveal their learning needs to their immediate supervisors (Hughes 1999). Such revela-tions conflict with their need to portray themselves as competent workers. To admit to 'deficiencies' is to undermine one's position in the workplace. Skilful supervisors appear to understand this and devote their energies to those factors which can influence learning without getting directly involved in direct facilitation. The strategies which they employ involve building development into normal work through structuring jobs to involve chal-lenges for workers, engaging in job rotation, encouraging networking across the organization, setting appropriate targets for performance and so on.

Role of individual students
Planning and organizing one's own learning is a major undertaking and even students enrolled at postgraduate levels cannot be expected to be experts at it already, especially if they are the products of courses in which they were given relatively little responsibility for curriculum matters. They

cannot be expected to negotiate a learning plan to be conducted over six months or a year and implement it unaided. They will, of course, be given guidance in planning sessions about dividing tasks into manageable parts and producing intermediate products on which they can get feedback from both workplace experts and academic advisers. However, this is not sufficient.

A useful device is the journal or learning portfolio. It provides a forum for the ongoing keeping of records on learning and a prompt for reflection. It is equivalent to the diaries kept by writers or the laboratory notebooks kept by scientists. It is a place to note and speculate; it is a place to return to and review earlier ideas. The form in which it is kept is much less important than the need to make it one's own and to tailor it to one's purposes (Fulwiler 1987; Holly 1989). While there is sometimes resistance to the notion among some learners – to them it can be reminiscent of an adolescent diary – if it is explained thoroughly and the educational rationale for its use is justified, it can be implemented and changed as appropriate. A few students may still find it uncongenial. For them alternative mechanisms for building in reflective strategies must be devised.

Role of peers

One important benefit of studying within an educational institution is contact with other students. Sharing of perspectives and experiences, giving encouragement and other forms of peer learning often take place. Much of this is unplanned and not included as part of the formal curriculum. However, such informal learning is a feature of university life which is regarded as being of great value. It contributes to important educational outcomes as well as social and cultural benefits. Any programme of flexible study in which the curriculum for an individual is negotiated leaves open the risk of isolation and a loss of the benefits that derive from informal learning that occurs on campus. This is particularly unwelcome at work, as operating in collaboration with others, team development and leadership are key elements in the organization of effective workplaces.

While there is often a need to include specific activities involving other learners in a learning agreement, depending on the specific goals being pursued, there is often a need for other learning processes and activities to be incorporated into work-based learning. While peer learning is thought of as something to be left to students, responsibility for initiating the organization of such activities lies with advisory staff. If left to their own devices students will often realize the importance of these too late and may not be in a position to establish them effectively. In some ways this is no different from conventional study, where staff-initiated peer learning activities are finding a useful place in courses (Sampson *et al.* 1999).

One of the forms of peer learning very familiar in management settings is action learning (McGill and Beaty 1995) – not to be confused with action research. Action learning sets, in which learners meet regularly to spend time helping each other work on their learning problems, are a useful and legitimate feature of work-based learning.

Peer networking to form a real or a virtual community of learners that understand the challenges and demands of work-based learning is of particular importance in being able to share and articulate Mode 2 knowledge and to explore with others the interactions between this knowledge and university expectations. The use of computer-mediated communication, through either email or web-based discussion forums, is becoming common. In workplaces with extensive use of such forms of communication, not to use such facilities would be regarded as a limitation of the programme. While there are substantial merits in learners meeting face-to-face from time to time, when they are not co-located this becomes an arduous process to sustain. Having sufficient personal contact with co-learners to enable relationships to be continued remotely is the goal.

Encourage critical reflection throughout the programme

Work-based learning programmes are viewed with suspicion by some academics for the reason that they assume that the same kinds of critical capacities cannot be developed within the constraints of work as they can be in an exclusively educational environment. While this is clearly not a view accepted by work-based learning practitioners, there is a special obligation on them at this stage in the development of programmes of this kind to be very clear about how critical reflection is developed and how it is demonstrated.

Why should critical reflection be encouraged in work-based learning? What might it consist of? Critical reflection is important not because it is a means of demonstrating the intellectual prowess of students and impresses academic advisers, but because it is only through deeper critique that work situations can be improved, workplaces transformed and productivity significantly enhanced. It is about noticing and questioning the taken-for-granted assumptions that one holds and that are held by others. While it can be a discomforting process, it is necessary in all situations that do not involve perpetuating the status quo.

Although various reflective activities to support students in their ongoing learning have been mentioned above, in themselves they may not provide a sufficiently critical edge to promote the kinds of critical thinking characteristic of a university education. They may provide the vehicle and the form for critical reflection, but not the impetus or the desire. The journal or learning portfolio provides a forum for reflection, but it does not ensure that critical reflection takes place. To engage with this aspect of work-based learning we must return to the ideas about learning discussed in Chapter 3.

The centrality to learning of the notion of seeking variation provides a rationale for approaching learning tasks more critically. To seek variation learners must go beyond what is given and engage deeply with the ideas, concepts and practices that are central to their negotiated learning tasks.

T028249

They need to identify the structures of the knowledge they are working with so that they are not trapped by the specificities of their context. The development of awareness about what is actually being learned and the ability to articulate this convincingly are vital.

If learners are to be effective in noticing variation, they will need guidance for this in both general and specific ways. Formative assessment is just as important in work-based learning as it is elsewhere. However, the kinds of feedback that are provided cannot be assumed to be the same as those in disciplinary courses. Forms of sustainable assessment which enable learners to refine their skills of discernment in a workplace setting are required (Boud 2000).

Learners must also use disciplinary, professional or work-related frameworks as appropriate to interrogate their learning to appreciate its achievements and limitations. It is profoundly misleading to regard work-based learning as an entirely pragmatic and operational endeavour. It is as potentially theoretically complex and intellectually demanding as any form of education. What make it so are all the many elements working together. However, it is tested and manifest in the kinds of critical reflections in which students engage and the ways in which they present the outcomes of these for assessment. Brookfield (1987) has highlighted the value of problematizing one's own practice as a starting point for critical professional reflection and he provides useful strategies for prompting this with peers. Boud and Walker (1998) argue that reflective practices are highly situation-specific and are often misused because they fail to take sufficient account of the social and cultural context in which learners are operating. Their emphasis on examining the context of learning is of particular relevance in the work-based setting.

Of course, a focus on critical reflection poses challenges for those responsible for managing programmes. Encouraging critical reflection means that students, the programme and the staff involved in it, might also become the focus. Achieving a balance between critique and development is an important learning outcome.

Document learning in a form that can be assessed in terms of the frameworks previously established

Most traditional forms of assessment – the examination and assignment are typical – are based on the assumption that what is to be learned can be defined in advance and a suitable instrument devised for its demonstration. They are therefore singularly inappropriate in the new context. Luckily, there is now considerable experience available with forms of assessment suited for negotiated learning and acceptance that different learning programmes will result in qualitatively different kinds of product (Anderson *et al.* 1996). The key attribute of these products is that they must demonstrate that the student has met the requirements of the framework of standards and levels that underpin all programmes. In addition, experience from negotiated learning underlines the importance of the type and extent of documentation being agreed at the time of the acceptance of the programme by the educational institution. Without this latter agreement, students find it difficult to decide what to submit and disputes can arise when they provide documentation in forms that cannot be handled by the normal review processes.

Documentation completes the loop from programme planning to completion. It needs to address all the elements of the framework of standards and levels without being so voluminous that it becomes too demanding to produce and assess. These necessarily include products that manifest particular knowledge outcomes as well as demonstrating critical reflection on them. Very rarely indeed will the documentation of the educational outcomes be identical with a typical work output such as a report. The work product might be included as one aspect of the documentation of knowledge, but other material, which discusses and illustrates specific learning outcomes, would normally accompany it.

In most cases, depending on the outcomes agreed, there will be documentation of processes as well as products. This will be the case when educational goals such as collaboration, planning and monitoring learning and critical reflection are being addressed. Care must be taken in the use of raw, unprocessed material from journals and portfolios in final documentation. There are ethical concerns about representations of third parties, confidential business material and the exposure of students' personal encounters to be considered. One illustration of separating material for assessment from ongoing reflections in negotiated learning is the use of the student self-assessment schedule (Boud 1992). This involves a reconstruction and portrayal of learning goals and outcomes, which uses a portfolio as a source rather than as a vehicle for assessment.

Conclusions

Development of a curriculum for work-based learning requires an appreciation of different kinds of knowledge production as well as an understanding of the complexities of learning and the circumstances in which it can take place. While the core of the curriculum is workplace learning activities, these do not stand alone. Considerable preparation is needed if meaningful and worthwhile programmes are to be planned to suit the diversity of students. The university needs to equip students with conceptual and practical resources to enable them to identify and keep track of their learning and gain the support they need throughout their programme. In the series of case studies that follow in Part 2 – summarized at the conclusion of Chapter 1 – we shall the see the ways in which various universities have taken up the challenge of work-based learning and accommodated the problems that are faced when the culture of the university meets that of the workplace.

References

Anderson, G., Boud, D. and Sampson, J. (1996) *Learning Contracts: A Practical Guide.* London: Kogan Page.

Boud, D. (1992) The use of self-assessment schedules in negotiated learning. *Studies in Higher Education,* 17(2): 185–200.

Boud, D. (2000) Sustainable assessment: rethinking assessment for the learning society. *Studies in Continuing Education,* 22(2): 151–67.

Boud, D. and Walker, D. (1998) Promoting reflection in professional courses: the challenge of context. *Studies in Higher Education,* 23(2): 191–206.

Brookfield, S. D. (1987) *Developing Critical Thinkers: Challenging Adults to Explore Alternative Ways of Thinking and Acting.* San Francisco: Jossey-Bass.

Evans, N. (2000) *Expriential Learning Around the World: Employability and the Global Economy.* London: Jessica Kingsley.

Fulwiler, T. (1987) *The Journal Book.* Portsmouth, NH: Heinemann.

Gonczi, A. (1994) Competency based assessment in the professions in Australia. *Assessment in Education,* 1(1): 27–44.

Hager, P., Gonczi, A. and Athanasou, J. (1994) General issues about assessment of competence. *Assessment and Evaluation in Higher Education,* 19(1): 3–16.

Holly, M. L. (1989) *Writing to Grow: Keeping a Personal-professional Journal.* Portsmouth, NH: Heinemann.

Hughes, C. (1999) Facilitation in context: challenging some basic principles. *Studies in Continuing Education,* 21(1): 21–43.

Knowles, M. R. (1975) *Self-directed Learning: A Guide for Learners and Teachers.* New York: Association Press.

McGill, I. and Beaty, L. (1995) *Action Learning: A Guide for Professional, Management and Educational Development.* London: Kogan Page.

Mandel, A. and Michelson, E. (1990) *Portfolio Development and Adult Learning: Purposes and Strategies.* Chicago: Council for Adult and Experiential Learning.

Sampson, J., Cohen, R., Boud, D. and Anderson, G. (1999) *Reciprocal Peer Learning: A Guide for Staff and Students.* Sydney: Faculty of Education, University of Technology, Sydney.

Stephenson, J. (1998) The concept of capability and its importance in higher education, in J. Stephenson and M. Yorke (eds) *Capability and Quality in Higher Education.* London: Kogan Page.

Part 2

Case Studies

Part 2

5

From Once Upon a Time to Happily Ever After: The Story of Work-based Learning in the UK Higher Education Sector

Norman Evans

This story of the beginnings of work-based learning for academic credit in the UK is set in the context of rapid change in the social and economic and hence the educational life of the country during the 1980s. It covers the period from 1980 to 1988, a time when government was in a somewhat panicky frame of mind over the economy, and over the presumed inadequate skill and knowledge levels of the workforce in general. At the same time, it was putting great effort into expanding higher education while urging companies and higher education to be more active together through partnerships, collaboration, widening access and opening previously impenetrable boundaries.

The story is of a timely and pragmatic initiative to demonstrate the validity of the claim that learning at a higher education level can occur in the workplace. That initiative also sought to indicate the range of potential benefits for both institutions and employers when partnerships are formed to enhance the learning of employees. It was not concerned with far-reaching implications for the curriculum or for institutional structures. It is a story of action in an uncharted field with mistakes logged as well as successes, followed by reflections about some lessons learned. And it is a story told from the perspective of the Learning from Experience Trust, a small education charity based in London that seeks to influence institutional practice and national policy.

It follows that it is not a story that connects work-based learning with controversial relationships between vocational qualifications and higher education awards which arose after the establishment of the National Council for Vocational Qualifications (NCVQ) in 1986. Nor does it relate work-based learning to lifelong learning, as that was not part of the language in public policy at that time. Those come later as a partial reaction of the government to equip the nation to play a part in a more competitive and globalized economy.

Priority learning

The year was 1986. Then, under the leadership of its Chief Officer, Edwin Kerr, the Council for National Academic Awards (CNAA) established its Credit Accumulation and Transfer Registry. Before that, work-based learning for academic credit in higher education in the UK was off limits, beyond thought even. After May 1986 an almost limitless range of applications of the principles underlying the use of work-based learning within academic programmes were there for the enactment. Not that in May 1986 work-based learning was the prime target. As the story unfolds it gradually comes into view under the banner of the assessment of prior and experiential learning (APEL).

An understanding of the context for higher education in 1986 is vital. There was growing recognition that some students, probably older ones, were unable to find all the courses they wanted for a learning programme within one institution. The disappearance of a 'job for life' in an increasing number of occupations fuelled redundancy and unemployment, which meant that many people's domestic and economic circumstances dictated alternating periods of study with periods of work or at home. There was the possibility that students would want to move from one institution to another as they chose, without loss of time or academic credit and without some of the obstacles that were then encountered. In each case they needed to be able to collect credit, store it if necessary and take it across institutions if that was what they wanted to do. And students needed to be able to benefit academically from any knowledge and skill they had acquired previously, either informally or through formal study, where it met the necessary requirements. APEL was the means for doing so. It paved the way for work-based learning being admitted into the academic arena.

But between 1980 and 1986 a series of steps turned out to be highly significant. They were first taken under the aegis of the Policy Studies Institute (PSI). This group of academics drawn from most sections of higher education began meeting to explore the possibilities offered by what was then a brand new idea – the assessment of prior and experiential learning. They drew heavily on what could be learned from the USA about prior learning assessment, as it was called there. They were excited by the notion that informally acquired learning merited formal academic recognition, provided it met acceptable educational criteria.

Access courses for entry to higher education were then multiplying fast. This marked the beginning of a huge expansion in higher education that has moved participation rates from about 13 per cent then to around 40 per cent now, with a current government target of 50 per cent. Then there were expectations of increasing numbers of older men and women enrolling in award-bearing courses. So APEL for access was the obvious point to begin explorations for higher education, even though it offered little more than existed already. Possibilities were explored and documented in studies undertaken by the Trust for the Further Education Unit (FEU). Two studies were particularly important. The first was *Curriculum Opportunity: A Map of Experiential Learning in Entry Requirements for Higher and Further Education Award-bearing Courses* (Evans 1983) and the second was *Access to Higher Education: Non-standard Entry to CNAA First Degree and DipHE Courses* (Evans 1984a). The importance these publications had for work-based learning lay not only in the way they opened up discussion of APEL but also in their distribution. The FEU publication went to every higher and further education institution in the country and to a range of employers as well. It was reprinted in 1984, 1987 and again in 1988, making 10,000 copies in all. The CNAA publication went to every higher education institution in the country and to many further education institutions as well. Combined, these two publications served notice on the entire post-secondary education sector that APEL existed and was here to stay. Moreover, they suggested that it was being taken very seriously by two national bodies, one holding academic authority over and responsibility for about 50 per cent of the undergraduate provision in the entire country and a significant amount of postgraduate study as well. And although in the early 1980s no one was thinking about work-based learning, in fact it was lurking just round the corner.

At this point the FEU produced the first attempt to interest employers in what is now called work-based learning. On the back of *Curriculum Opportunity* aforementioned reports, the FEU published *Exploiting Experience*, which had a telling subtitle, *Recognizing What Has Been Learnt on the Job as a Starting Point for Retraining* (Evans 1984b). This report was distributed to employers throughout the country via the offices of Regional Development Agents. Whether it was also picked up by educational institutions is unknowable. For them essentially in 1984 work-based learning was not even on the horizon but in retrospect APEL for access can be seen as one small step forward for work-based learning.

The use of APEL for admission with academic credit towards diplomas or degrees seemed a richer vein to mine. But immediately this confronted a structural issue: how could it become possible to read off informally acquired learning against courses in degree programmes, which in the vast majority of cases were a full term in length if not longer? For most disciplines the answer was that it could not be done. All the experience from the USA showed that shorter rather than longer courses could facilitate the awarding of APEL for credit. Hence the PSI group came to try to grapple with the institutional consequences of converting academic programmes into what came to be known as modular and credit accumulation systems.

They were not alone. Some polytechnics, for reasons of their own, were moving in the same direction. Student choice was becoming a contentious issue. Modularization – organizing academic courses in smaller rather than larger units – looked like facilitating wider choice. So fortuitously some institutions were shifting in a direction that would make easier the adoption of APEL frameworks.

Puzzling over assessment, the group began to preach another sermon. If short courses facilitated APEL, writing those courses with learning outcomes attached to them would clarify the requirements for all concerned. Students would have a 'calculator' to help them to consider what claim, if any, they might make. Academics could use them as a first-line assessment tool.

All this preceded 1986 and the creation of the Credit Accumulation and Transfer (CAT) Registry in CNAA. However, most of it surfaced in its regulations (120 credits for each year of a three-year degree, with stop-off points at 120 for a certificate, 240 for a diploma and 360 for the degree). How many courses went into each year was a different matter. Generally it worked out at four courses of 30 credits each. But, and this cracked open the system and created an entry for work-based learning, the lowest amount of credit which was countable was four. That figure was settled on for four reasons. It seemed inappropriate for less than the equivalent of one week's full-time study to count academically at higher education level. The variety of short courses offered by professional bodies and companies and some in-service provision merited inclusion, provided that, as with all courses, they met the necessary criteria for content and assessment. This meshed with the government's interest in furthering collaborations between higher education and the world of work. Implicitly this opened the way for the academic validation of companies' own in-house courses, provided, that is, they met the necessary academic criteria.

All this was grounded in one vital provision: CNAA's CAT regulations that academic credit for APEL was authorized at both undergraduate and graduate levels. And by assuming, perhaps in a rather cavalier manner, that informally acquired knowledge and skill at work was experiential learning, work-based learning eventually came under the aegis of APEL.

Almost before the relevant regulations were published some polytechnics took them as a licence to develop their own schemes. And since they were operating under the academic authority of CNAA as a national body, there was no gainsaying them. The road was open, leading to all possible varieties of work-based learning. Coventry, Oxford, Sheffield and Wolverhampton polytechnics took it via the approach of Learning while Earning described below. Thames Polytechnic went along it working with the Trust on the validation of companies' in-house courses, leading to its own schemes with the Woolwich Building Society.

The Learning from Experience Trust

These important developments were signed and sealed in May 1986. The Learning from Experience Trust was also established that year. As a senior fellow I had been the instigator of work at the PSI, laying the foundations for work-based learning. By 1985 it was clear to Sir Charles Carter, chairman of the Research Committee at the PSI, and to me, that APEL was moving into a development phase nationally. Therefore it made more sense to create a small education charity as a vehicle for initiatives than to stay within a research institution. So with myself as Director and Sir Charles Carter as Chairman, the Trust set out its purpose to promote the theory and practice of APEL. Its self-imposed remit involved patrolling the frontiers between formal education and the world of work and life.

The CAT Registry gave the Trust the opportunity to pioneer work-based learning because the mechanism was available. It secured two projects funded by what was then the Manpower Services Commission (MSC) of the UK Department of Employment. One was 'Learning Contracts for Employees'. (Although 'learning contract' was in the official title of the project, its possible legal implications suggested that 'learning agreement' was a more appropriate label and it is that which is used throughout this chapter.) The other was the 'Validation of Companies' In-house Courses'. Both established the groundwork for subsequent developments in work-based learning.

Negotiations were not easy. They began with MSC officials in mid-1985. Through membership of the planning group the Trust knew intimately what CNAA's CAT was about to offer, and was anxious to strike as quickly as possible. For a start civil servants had to grasp the significance of the CAT Registry, about which they knew next to nothing. It was rather like trying to convince employers later on. The entire enterprise seemed so utterly different from their experiences of higher education, and it was hard for them to take in. The learning agreements being proposed, another new fangled idea, it was explained, had three requirements. First, employees had to undertake new learning; second, new learning had to be accessible academically; third, this learning had to benefit the employer as well as the employee and of course it had to be at higher education level. Moreover, to ensure that everyone involved knew exactly where they stood, each individual learning agreement would contain four sections: the learning intentions of the participant; the learning activities to be undertaken; the evidence to show that learning had been achieved; and the methods of assessment to be used. This highlighted what was probably the most significant element in the entire scheme. To satisfy all the requirements of a learning agreement, the three parties involved all had to agree. The employee learner, the employer and the academic, who would support and supervise the learner, not only had to agree, but all three had to sign off on the formal learning agreement. To meet the requirements for running academic credit through the CAT Registry, all learning had to be assessed by an external examiner as the ultimate verifier. This was all new thinking for the civil servants but without it there would have been no prospect of obtaining approval from the CAT Registry for the claims for academic credit which it was going to find itself having to handle.

Nor was that all. APEL came into the reckoning. There seemed no reason why, if some of the employee participants had acquired either prior or experiential learning or both, it should not be counted towards a higher education award. Such credits would then feature in the eventual result sheet for the learning agreement, as might another source of potentially countable learning: companies' in-house training and education programmes. This of course was the second project of the Trust: the validation of companies' in-house provision.

So the punch line for all these discussions was to assert that employers could be told that some of their employees were sitting on three sources of learning that could potentially count towards a higher education award, and they did not know it. Using that potential could be a significant contribution to the further education and training of their employees. The same applied to the employees. At the same time, the employees who were participants in a learning agreement scheme were set to improve their career chances as well as meeting their wider aspirations. The incentives for participation were compelling.

Having secured approval for the project, the next step was to recruit employers and pair them with academic institutions. The proposal instanced four, to cover as wide a range of employment as possible to demonstrate the viability of the scheme as a whole. Initial discussion suggested recruiting a high-tech company, a service/distribution/retail company, a building and construction company and the Manpower Services Commission (MSC) itself. For the Trust that was a delightful face-saver. The young civil servant who had the deciding voice calmly announced that while the MSC was vocal about training and employers, it did not do much of it itself. So it ought to be one of the employers. After protracted briefings and negotiations four pairs were announced: the MSC with Sheffield City Polytechnic for management and business studies; JBS Computer Services with Wolverhampton Polytechnic for information technology; Jaguar Cars with Coventry Polytechnic for engineering; and Wimpey International, the food and restaurant company, with Oxford Polytechnic.

An operational plan

The operational plan was simple on paper. Find six volunteers in each employing organization, appoint a supervisor for each and pair an academic from the partnering polytechnic. That trio was to hammer out the details of the learning agreement, oversee its progress, supervise its completion and agree on the final results. The academics found themselves having to deal with APEL, and where companies' in-house courses were relevant they had to try to juggle the three sources of academic credit to make best sense of the learning agreement itself.

There were two other important activities running simultaneously which widened openings for work-based learning. CNAA funded the Trust to do APEL for real in ten different higher education institutions covering the entire discipline range, which it did, except for mathematics and science. The results of this two and a half year project were published by CNAA in February 1988

(Evans 1988). This publication came to serve as a handbook for how to implement APEL. Principles, procedures, dos and don'ts were all set down with comments about the differences between the disciplines and questions of academic standards. Modularization of courses with learning outcomes/intentions attached were vital parts of the publication's message. And that message was spread through four regional conferences attended by some 150 people from all the different categories of higher education institutions.

Again it was issued as a 'freebie' by CNAA to all its membership institutions. So at the very time that some polytechnics were seizing the opportunity to develop their own CAT schemes, they had to hand a CNAA authorized publication. This enabled them to deal directly with some of the problems to be faced by introducing APEL and, with it, many different forms of work-based learning.

The second activity continued through those years and until 1996. This was an attempt to 'transfuse' APEL into the blood stream of higher education. It provided a strategic contribution to staff development to promote APEL, with a strong subtext on influencing institutional practice and national policy. The Trust organized week-long study tours to the USA on an invitation or nomination basis, for groups of four or five academics, senior civil servants and administrators, all from different institutions, to see at first hand the whys, hows and wherefores of the ways in which US institutions employed APEL. Among them were varieties of what in the UK came to be called work-based learning. The personnel from the four participating polytechnics overlapped with the CNAA project and the learning agreement project. Both Middlesex and Napier universities were well represented on those study tours. In 1983, Antony Turner, then admissions tutor for the modular degree at Middlesex, was on the first. He pioneered the procedural path for institutional support described by Derek Portwood in this volume (Chapter 6). Portwood was on a study tour himself in December 1986 while on the staff of Wolverhampton Polytechnic. The polytechnic's Director and Faculty Head of Information Technology followed within 12 months. In November 1987, Kathleen Anderson, Deputy Principal of Napier, joined in and then sent Iain Marshall on the October 1989 study tour. Altogether 160 academics and administrators participated. The 'study tour' story was published by the Trust in 1997 (Craft *et al.* 1997).

The validation of companies' in-house courses was the other arm of this first work-based learning endeavour. Again, negotiations were protracted. Like the aforementioned civil servants, employers found it hard to grasp that higher education could offer a facility that was light years away from their own university experiences. They were sceptical. That scepticism dissolved when they understood that in effect CAT was offering them two learning experiences for the price of one. Later on when the Trust undertook a second phase of its validation work, it was hugely disappointing and, indeed, puzzling to find that the trade unions did not jump at the opportunity of seeing how they could offer an additional service to their members. But that is outside the scope of this account.

Eventually, the list of employers included retail, computer and engineering companies. Academics in appropriate fields scrutinized the documentation of courses employers wished to submit for validation, and had to satisfy themselves on several issues. Was the content acceptable at a higher education level? Was the orientation of the course too company-specific to make it acceptable as formal higher education study – could it fit properly into a regular higher education curriculum? Were the assessment procedures rigorous enough to produce results that could satisfy academics in the field and also external examiners? How much credit could be awarded to a particular course – nothing less than four credits would do – expressed as a notional proportion of a formally taught course in a formal institution? Not surprisingly those questions led to some heated discussions between the companies' trainers and the academic scrutineers. Assessment was the most contentious. When everything was resolved satisfactorily both sides agreed that discussions had produced improvements all round for the employer while the academics gained better understanding of the companies' educational requirements. The recommendations were then put to the CAT Registry, and when approved became another acceptable source of credit for any employees who had completed the course satisfactorily. Some polytechnics were quick to validate the recommendations for credit themselves, so if an individual applied to a CAT unit in a polytechnic it could feature just the same.

Learning while Earning

The Learning while Earning project ran from November 1986 to October 1988. Gerald Dearden, Deputy Director of the trust that ran the project, converted the official report into *Learning while Earning* (Dearden 1989), a handbook with commentary published in January 1989. It was reprinted twice, so as a dissemination document it must have done its job. It was the first time work-based learning for academic credit had been introduced into higher education in the UK. Along the way there had been strenuous efforts to convert the periods of work experience in sandwich courses into sources of assessable learning, contributing to degree results. Unhappily most of that fizzled out; the timing was wrong. Apart from the result sheet, the most important sections of the report concerned lessons learned and a series of guidelines offered for employees, employers and academics. The project took everyone concerned into unmapped territory, so inevitably mistakes were made. It proved to be an exercise in learning through doing. For example, it was soon learnt that the time required for briefing employees, employers and academics was underestimated.

Naturally, employees found it difficult at first to grasp the full implications of the flexible nature of the scheme. How were they to determine their own preferred learning targets and how much new learning could they reasonably expect to undertake? Such self-diagnosis and the commitment required were daunting for most employees. In about half the cases the learning agreements were renegotiated. This had been foreseen and proved to be one of the key features and advantages of the scheme. If an employee's role within the company altered or home demands reduced the anticipated study time, renegotiation could accommodate alterations without penalty. Such compromises are difficult to achieve in normal undergraduate courses.

Some employees complained of a sense of isolation, wanting more contact with academic supervisors than had been allowed for. Assessment was the trickiest issue with which to deal. Understandably, most wanted to know, but could not be told, well before the completion of the learning agreement how much credit they would achieve. This was complicated by their desire to know before the beginning of the learning agreement how much credit they would obtain for their prior and experiential learning. This was entirely logical. How could they decide what to learn next unless they knew what they had accomplished already? Prior learning was relatively easy since it constituted formally completed courses taken for a different purpose. Similarly, the validation of companies' courses took in a second category of prior learning. Experiential learning was more difficult.

The fact that they could not have the information that they wanted was no fault of theirs. It was a design flaw in the proposal. Insufficient weight was put on that aspect of the work to be done. APEL should have featured in the first phase of the project from November 1986 to April 1987, which was devoted to recruiting the participants. Or it might have featured in the second phase from May 1987 to April 1988, when the learning agreements were negotiated, supervised and completed. As well as confusing the employees/students, it put additional work on the academic supervisors during the last phase from May 1988 to October 1988, which was allocated for assessment and monitoring and which obviously was not easy to accommodate.

The solution to all this was to offer interim indications for APEL and an interim assessment of the learning agreement as a whole, which could be either reassuring or a warning, and neither was official. This caused a number of problems that were compounded by others from a different source. Learning agreements were contributing credit to an award-bearing programme. It was left to an institution's CAT registry or CAT unit to determine the requirements of an award programme. Until that was done it was impossible to declare which elements of the learning agreement would carry credits into the final award. In the event none of this was a fatal deterrent. Most who completed their learning agreement either negotiated a further agreement leading to completion or enrolled in formal courses carrying their credits with them. Whether they went through the entire process or not, however, all claimed that the experience had been worthwhile. The self-analysis and job analysis had clarified their understanding of employer expectations and their own responsibilities, as well as their career prospects.

This represented a large body of unfamiliar information for employees to assimilate. Even if academic supervisors had spent more time in briefing their students it is doubtful if this would have allayed their anxieties. Part of the problem was that it was so early on in these developments that the institutions did not have student support services of the kind to which most of those involved in APEL or work-based learning now have access. Like the academic staff and employers, the students were pioneering new academic regimes.

The employers' experience

There were different lessons to be learned from the employers' experience. They had little difficulty in determining what new learning would be beneficial to the company. Most were uneasy about being asked to make assessments of that learning, let alone grading it, preferring to offer informal comment and evaluation. Line supervisors of the employee-participants were another matter. In retrospect, more attention should have been paid to their briefing. It became abundantly clear during the project and at its end that the motivation and accomplishments of employees as learners reflected the interest taken by their in-house supervisors. Lack of encouragement from line supervisors emerged as the prime reason for some withdrawing from the scheme. Unsurprisingly, line supervisor support was identified as a condition of success. Another problem for employers was the amount of working time they were prepared to allow as study time to their employees. It varied between half a day a week to nothing except for tutorials, according to company staff development policies. Naturally, employers were anxious about the costs they might incur if the programme were to continue after the funded project stopped. This raised the interesting question as to whether it could be cost-effective and educationally sound for group learning agreements to be arranged for those with similar learning programmes.

But as with their employees, employers were positive about the exercise. They instanced noticeable increases in self-confidence and work performance. One even said that to his surprise his strongest employees 'on paper' turned out to be the least successful in their learning agreements. This suggested that the company needed to review its recruitment policies. Another said: 'The advantages of learning agreements are that they are more flexible, relevant to work, geared to individual needs and are generally more attractive to employers than formal part time courses.' He was implying that it was a learner-centred programme. But he added, and this was another lesson learned, that seminars for line managers would be helpful to outline what is expected of them and to provide basic advice on coaching and tutoring.

Somehow the academic supervisors had fielded all those issues as they ventured into this new form of higher education when they had little idea of what the project might throw up next. No one had ever attempted to operate this style of adult learning within higher education before. On paper they had clear sets of tasks:

1. To make sure that they, the employees and their employers understood what they were undertaking.

2. To judge the suitability of the learning programme which evolved from the three-way negotiations.
3. To assess the likely level of that learning – whether it was level 1 for a certificate, level 2 for a diploma, level 3 for the final year of a degree or level M for a master's degree, all according to the regulations for the CNAA CAT Registry.
4. To estimate the likely number of credit points an employee might be awarded on completion of the learning agreement.

The problems encountered by the employees came thick and fast. They occurred as the academics were feeling their way as supervisors of learning agreements and trying to find an acceptable balance between the time and funds allowed for tutorials in the official contract from the Department of Employment and what it was obvious that the participants needed. It was not possible to renegotiate the entire contract to correct this imbalance because the calculations inevitably were guesswork. Some additional funds were allowed eventually to cover some of the costs incurred for APEL. But that did little to reduce the pressure on both employee participants and academics as the months passed.

Time was another pressure point, and another hard-won lesson. As was indicated above, the project was limited to a two-year period. That was a serious underestimate of the time required. In retrospect it was a source of the flaws already indicated in the work programme. However, the flexibility of the overall design meant that there was an escape route. There was no inherent difficulty about renegotiating a learning agreement, either to reduce its content or extend the time allowed for a section of it to be undertaken. Naturally this added significantly to the workload of the academics, as supervisors. On top of all this it was their responsibility to arrange for colleagues to act as examiners/assessors. It would have been utterly inappropriate for the supervisors to act as assessors. So in the event, as with most innovations and developments, the success of this first experiment in work-based learning depended on the willingness and generosity of the academics to act in true vocational style as professionals and continue with the project irrespective of its personal costs.

Discomfiture

At that time some of the problems raised in Chapter 6 of this volume were lurking in the background. These were causing us some discomfort, but no one had the energy or inclination to pursue them in the press of trying to cope with a new element in the higher education curriculum. Suffice it to say that from 1980 it was clear that taking APEL seriously threatened to put a bomb under the curriculum. Learning while Earning was not the place to explore that. However, it did help to clear the way for later explorations and analyses.

As it was, the four supervising academics were resoundingly successful in their endeavours. Seventeen out of the original 24 students submitted work for assessment. The majority wanted to continue with another end-on learning agreement or to enrol for part-time study to achieve an academic qualification in business studies, information technology, catering management or engineering. Most gratifying of all, it was clear that some that reckoned themselves as non-starters in 1987 were by 1988 on their way to a diploma or degree. Most surprising of all was to find four non-graduate employees who worked in the body design section of Jaguar Cars setting their target as a master's degree.

Their ages ranged from 19 to 46. Two were women and fifteen were men. At the undergraduate level they achieved numbers of credits ranging from ten with a grade D to 72 at grade B at level 1, from 15 at grade C to 60 at grade B for level 2. At M level, the four seeking master's degrees ranged between nine at grade C and 20 at grade B.

Eleven men made APEL claims, and two men and one woman intended to submit claims subsequently. At level 1 their credits awarded ranged from 30 to 120, at level 2 from 25 to 110, at level 3 one scored ten and at level M they ranged from ten to 50.

Learning while Earning represented a demonstration model of credit accumulation of learning derived from work. It established work-based learning as a legitimate element in the higher education curriculum. It was possible because some institutions had already adopted the modularization of their courses. It showed how the flexibility offered by modularization could extend the range of services offered to potential students. It served as an encouragement for the institutional change which would gallop along during the next 15 years. And it was important as an indication that higher education was capable of innovation to meet some of government's preoccupations.

The lessons from work-based learning

Among the many lessons to be learned from the project, two items for public policy stand out. The first is that it brought additional meaning to widening access and participation. It did so by enabling people to combine academic credits for APEL and from in-house courses with those from their learning agreements. Some employee participants were two-thirds of the way to the 360 credits they needed for graduation. Second, it added to the battery of modes of training and development at work and so helped to allay the rising anxiety about national economic efficiency and productivity. By putting into practice the theory that learning occurs in many different places and merits formal recognition when it meets required standards, the project showed that what is learned at work could become the foundation for further learning, benefiting both employee and employer. Work-based learning blazed a trail to be followed by other institutions and agencies. Government got the point.

The upshot of all this was that the Training Agency, the reincarnation of the MSC, instantly offered further contracts for work-based learning to the four participating polytechnics in the project, so keen was it to exploit what had been done. Since then the Department of Employment and its successor the Department for Education and Employment has poured scores of millions of pounds into hundreds more work-based learning projects in an almost bewildering variety. Employability of graduates is all the rage. So is collaboration between higher education and industry and commerce. Work-based learning has proved to be a catalyst for both.

It took several years for the Trust to get funds for another pioneering variation on work-based learning. This was Work Based Learning for Academic Credit for undergraduates on non-vocational first degrees in three very different institutions – Liverpool University, Liverpool John Moores University and Chester College of Higher Education – all working to a common programme of learning intentions and assessment procedures. That too was a pioneering success story. It has been told elsewhere (Evans 1993).

Twenty years after its rather halting beginnings, it is obvious that recognition of the significance, actual and potential, of work-based learning is part of a far wider, if sometimes grudging, acceptance by academics that in the contemporary world there is an extensive range of learning opportunities available to individuals. For higher education the need is to convert acceptance into understanding. But to be true to its historic role and to safeguard its academic integrity, higher education must translate that understanding into imaginative programmes that promote additional learning. After all, learning is its purpose.

References

Craft, W., Evans, N. and Keeton, M. (1997) *Learners All – Worldwide.* London: Learning from Experience Trust.

Dearden, G. (1989) *Learning while Earning: Learning Contracts for Employees.* London: Learning from Experience Trust.

Evans, N. (1983) *Curriculum Opportunity: A Map of Experiential Learning in Entry Requirements to Higher and Further Education Award-bearing Courses.* London: Further Education Unit.

Evans, N. (1984a) *Access to Higher Education: Non-standard Entry to CNAA First Degree and DipHE Courses.* Publication 6. London: CNAA Development Services.

Evans, N. (1984b) *Exploiting Experience.* London: Further Education Unit.

Evans, N. (1988) *The Assessment of Experiential Learning.* Publication 17. London: CNAA Development Services.

Evans, N. (1993) *Work Based Learning for Academic Credit.* London: Learning from Experience Trust.

6

Making It Work Institutionally

Derek Portwood

Universities have few problems with work-based learning until they contemplate its institutionalization. In the meanwhile it can be marginalized as work-based projects in management courses, work placements for social science students, teaching work-related skills across the board and so on. It can be absorbed into areas of curriculum development or educational experiment. Academic ideologies remain intact, systems require minor tinkering and the university proudly exhibits another example of its commitment to working with industry. Institutional innovation of any kind is invariably a messy business and institutionalizing work-based learning is no exception. Standards, regulations, systems, practices and even the epistemological map of the university are challenged. Inevitably, proponents and opponents emerge and engage with each other at decision-making levels of the institution. The university is clearly exposed as a political arena. Why then should a university subject itself to such upheaval? What is there about work-based learning that warrants it? The case of Middlesex University is used to explore these questions and the matter of what is involved in making work-based learning work institutionally is deliberated.

Capitalizing on developments

Middlesex University has 25,000 full-time students located in seven major campuses spread over 120 square miles of north London. Its academic programme consists of 4000 modules, combined mainly for academic planning purposes into subject areas which are allocated primarily for staffing, resource and quality assurance purposes to eight schools. By the mid-1990s, Middlesex University was ready to capitalize on major educational developments undertaken while it was a polytechnic. Of these, the creation in 1991 of a total institutional model of a credit-based modular academic system was the most significant. By then many polytechnics and universities had made limited use of credit accumulation systems (Robertson 1994) but Middlesex was the first to adopt a full constitutional model (Portwood 1990; Chapter 6 in this volume). This allowed full exploitation of earlier developments in modular degree courses and the accreditation of students' prior learning. Mainly practical arguments over the multi-purpose use of modules (not just for specialized programmes) and references to widening access through flexible programming overcame resistance to the introduction of this common academic framework. Misgivings over the fragmentation of learning experiences and assessment overload provoked occasional dissenting voices that subsided when it became clear that old practices need not be altered radically. Attention switched to logistical problems of implementation, particularly in relation to administering student records and tracking. The critical point is, however, that the full expression of the cardinal principle of the academic credit system – that learning whatever its source and location may be given academic value – depended on the emergence of work-based learning initiatives.

The impetus for this initiative came mainly from a two-year research project funded by the Department of Employment as part of a series of projects concerning the development and use of work-based learning in higher education (Brennan and Little 1996). In Middlesex's case, interest centred on the learning opportunities, provisions, resources and achievements by individuals and organizations and whether or not these constituted a curriculum in the workplace. The researchers experienced plenty of surprises. Not so much in how the workers learned – they listened, consulted and conversed with each other, read books and manuals, took special notice of experts, in fact much like students on campus except with a heavier emphasis on 'learning by doing'. What the workers learned also bore many of the characteristics of on-campus study, although the emphasis in both knowledge and abilities was heavily loaded towards the applied and the useful. What the researchers learned was more about the formation, development and demonstration of the workers' knowledge and abilities. Context rather than content became the crucial originating and organizing concept. The expectations and performance of actual work roles emerged as the focus for auditing, analysing and assessing knowledge and skill in the workplace. Above all, the clustering of such roles helped to explain the genesis, nature and uses of knowledge and skill in that context and thereby comprised a curriculum, albeit of an unconventional and informal kind.

The dramatic development occurred some time after the project ended. Backed by the newly appointed vice chancellor and deputy vice chancellor, a development team was commissioned to institutionalize the findings of the project. Thinking through the notion of the curriculum in the workplace, the members of this team perceived that it was self-evident not only that the workplace is a classroom but that workers learned as well as students. But most revolutionary of all was the perception that the university may helpfully be understood as a workplace; or rather, because of the boundaries that are drawn around its various departments, a federation of workplaces.

However, the team noted that, unlike a company whose departments are distinctive for functional purposes within a total enterprise, the university's departments are perceived as separate from one another even though operationally they are connected. Thus the question of the relationships between the curriculum in the workplace and that on campus was a complex one with many facets and dimensions. For while particular aspects of roles within the workplace clearly had affinity to specialized subjects within the university, the development team was aware that all work-based roles must necessarily be interdisciplinary to some extent.

Hence, the team faced the problem that while the mechanics of accreditation (whereby academic value is accorded to learning derived and developed outside the university) provided a means to interrelate the curriculum in the workplace with that on campus, there could be no easy fit between the two. And even more fundamentally, the aspiration to produce programmes customized to the needs of individuals within the interests of their organizations would demand changes in the structures, attitudes and practices of the university and its members, especially in the composition of its curriculum and the status of its various parts.

The battle of the prepositions

The academic community found the implications of all this hard to swallow. It had few problems with work-based learning as a mode of study. It was readily prepared to concede that parts of its programmes might benefit if undertaken at work. But the team of developers was not talking about programmes *by* work-based learning but programmes *in* work-based learning. Its arguments were that work-based learning is a new form of the curriculum, combining the workplace and the university campus. This meant new knowledge and understanding, which in the team's view constituted a field of study capable of producing new analytical concepts, theories and methodologies, as well as drawing on, using and enhancing concepts, research and study techniques from existing subject areas. The battle of the prepositions began ostensibly between those accepting 'by' only and those advocating 'by and in'. In truth, the struggle was only on 'in work-based learning'; that is, the claim that work-based learning is not simply a different type of learning but an educational field in its own right.

Debate raged from crude denials that work *per se* could produce academically valid learning – in essence a restatement of the alleged dichotomy between vocational learning and education – to, at a more sophisticated level, work-based learning being perceived not only as an intruder into the academy but as a usurper. Opponents noted that it laid claim to a pan-university role because it could selectively use elements of other subjects within the university's programmes. This challenged the autonomy and authority of those subjects. More fundamentally, they foresaw that the monopolistic power of the university over the content of its programmes could be compromised, if not relinquished, once learning from other sources was legitimately included. Related questions were raised as to who teaches and who assesses. Underlying the whole controversy (although not often articulated) was unease about the implications for the university as the gatekeeper if not the builder of knowledge. Who can study what from where? Ultimately the issue became the nature of the relationship between the university and other providers. The team of developers argued that if those providers were producing learning that could be credited, the partnership must be one that is equitable.

Rightly, both supporters and opponents of work-based learning as a field of study asserted that the developers must make an academic case for their proposal, particularly as its implementation would involve a total institutional curriculum model. All said that this was not possible. Arguments about the new business that could be gained by using the currency of academic credit and the unit of measurement of modularity carried little intellectual conviction for the field of study approach. In any case, with Middlesex undergoing rapid expansion, did the university need this new (doubtful) innovation? Nor were many persuaded by the political claims about widening access. And many argued that the same ends could be achieved by adopting work-based learning as a mode of learning within existing programmes.

Academic credibility

The development team had little to draw upon. The proponents of experiential learning had never made a convincing academic case for work-based learning. Perhaps this was because of their preoccupation with the learning of the individual and the self-directed features of that learning (Knowles 1996). Or, possibly, it was because the proponent of experiential learning usually conformed to the rules and lines drawn by academic disciplines in the assessment of experiential learning rather than seeing its essential interdisciplinary nature, whereas work-based learning is essentially a social activity involving colleagues and employers as well as tutors. It is learning which is derived from and directed within a company or professional community (Eraut 1994).

Taking their cue from the nature of work, which is a social activity involving sets of relationships, networks of communication and ranges of skills and knowledge, the development team asserted the primacy of interdisciplinarity in work-based learning. It stressed that work is a cooperative enterprise, involving intellectual as well as commercial partnerships between members of the workplace and the academic community. Implications for action learning and the relationship between theory and practice were then examined. The most profound argument rested on some of the major purposes of higher education, particularly the production of intelligent scepticism (the critical thinker) and focused intelligence (the skilled expert). It was contended that work-based learning not only treats these concepts in terms of groups and teams as well as individuals but relates them in a different way, thereby producing new knowledge and capabilities (Portwood 1995). However, assertion outweighed argument and experience has shown that to maintain credibility in a university, it is vital that the development of this intellectual argument continues.

The first vital lesson from the Middlesex experience is therefore that if work-based learning is to work institutionally, a persuasive academic case must be made for it in the first instance and carried forward if the implementation is to be effective.

From prepositions to propositions

The contention that work-based learning is a field of study or subject was specially pertinent to Middlesex's academic programme, which is organized on the basis of clusters of modules comprising subject areas which themselves are clustered to form schools for staffing, resources and quality assurance purposes.

Intensive consultation and intensive debate processes took place between 1991 and 1993. They involved the senior management team and board of governors, and concerned the introduction of a work-based learning subject area. This was achieved by adopting the title 'Work-based Learning Studies', which while an admission of the weakness of the academic case (Barnett 1997), none the less elicited the distinctive characteristics of work-based learning. These were expressed in a set of propositions, which the university's academic board was given to consider. The propositions included the following:

- That the work-based learning subject area would produce programmes to all levels of university 'taught' qualifications, from foundation certificates through diplomas and bachelor degrees to master's degrees.
- That an entire programme of study could be work-based and not restricted to the current regulation that at least one-third had to be under university control on campus.
- That the established honours classification system was inappropriate for work-based learning because of the incorporation of ungraded accredited learning but the postgraduate classification of fail, pass, merit and distinction could be used for all degree programmes at bachelor and master's levels.
- That the programmes within this subject area could be customized (including the actual title of the award) to meet the requirements of the student, the employer (or head of organization) and the university. This would be accomplished by adding a bracketed title of the focus of the programme to the normal protocol of award and title of subject area (e.g. BA in Work-based Learning Studies (Curriculum Development)).

- That the incorporation of accredited prior and work-based learning would be the normal starting point for the construction of a programme of study.
- That the subject area would draw relevant subject expertise from across the entire university on a contract basis.
- That the subject area would be pan-university in scope and not tied to one school.
- That the target population would be adults in paid or unpaid work.
- That where programmes are developed with companies and organizations, the university would be related to them on the basis of an equitable partnership involving them as fully as possible in the design, delivery, assessment and quality assurance of programmes.

The academic board was notified that the newly created National Centre for Work-based Learning Partnerships (NCWBLP) at Middlesex University, which was headed by the first professor of work-based learning in the United Kingdom, would be responsible for preparing appropriate documentation for approval of the subject area and subsequently for managing its implementation. Lengthy debates at three meetings of the academic board, during which (most significantly) the senior executives of the university fully supported the proposal, resulted in approval of work-based learning studies.

The second vital lesson from the Middlesex experience, therefore, is that if work-based learning is to work institutionally, approval by the supreme academic authority of the university is vital. This necessarily involves extensive consultation, unambiguous propositions, clear presentation of thorough planning and backing by senior management.

Tools of the trade

In practical terms, the academic board's approval of the propositions for introducing work-based learning meant that the proposal could proceed to institutional validation of the scheme itself. Documentation was needed on a range of implementation issues concerning management and administration of the scheme, contributory modules, criteria of assessment, quality assurance procedures, staff development – in fact everything relating to the design, delivery and assessment of work-based customized programmes for individuals and groups and the attendant support systems.

In so far as work-based learning studies was now accepted as a subject area, it could deploy all normal university structural and procedural arrangements for registration and assessment of students, costing of programmes and quality assurance of its work. Little more than technical modification to the university's systems was needed. Any additional activities with employers concerning accreditation and customization of programmes was costed on approved hourly or daily rates and specified in contracts.

The crucial issue was the development of enabling learning instruments fitted to the various levels of customized programmes. The development team had previously designed and used a set of modules to produce portfolios of prior and work-based learning for accreditation, learning agreements, work-based research methods and work-based projects. All were enabling frameworks rather than content-based courses. The latter were available from the vast store of the university's modules. The immediate problems, therefore, were: first, how these enabling instruments would produce the customized programmes which needed to take account of the past, current and future learning of individuals and groups; and, second, what criteria would be used for assessing the parts and the whole of such programmes.

While Middlesex University required all modules to be assessed in terms of learning outcomes relating to knowledge and skills, it had not described these outcomes in generic terms. The development team confronted this task not least because they were conscious of suspicions about the quality of work-based programmes and requests from employers regarding this subject. They were far more interested in this matter than any issues of money.

The team proposed that the achievement of learning outcomes would be through the satisfaction of what were called level descriptors. There were six of these:

- action planning, leading to effective and appropriate action;
- identification, use and evaluation of sources of knowledge and evidence;
- justification of approaches to tasks;
- analysis and synthesis of work-based information and ideas;
- application of learning;
- effective communication.

These elements were then related descriptively to the expectations of the differing levels of qualifications: level 1 certificate; level 2 diploma; level 3 degree; level 4 master's. Action planning, for instance, was described as follows:

- level 1 will tend to be within a prescribed context and probably not impact greatly on others;
- level 2 is likely to be within a prescribed context but may be wide-ranging and may involve the work of others;
- level 3 is likely to be complex and impact upon the work of others;
- level 4 will be complex and is likely to include the work of others.

Apart from enabling consistency in assessment standards across a potentially huge variety of programs, the level descriptors solved the thorny problem of the classification of bachelors and Master's degrees. Merit, for instance, would be achieved at the level of master's if there was excellent performance in analysis and synthesis and at least two other areas; distinction if there was excellent performance in all areas.

The earlier development of work-based learning modules within an independent learning subject area proved invaluable for the validation process.

They had not only been tried and tested but they had been used in negotiations with employers to produce customized programmes. A model for such programmes was thereby beginning to emerge.

All this preliminary work, as much as the academic board's stamp of approval for the idea itself, convinced the validation panel that Middlesex University through its National Centre for Work-based Learning Partnerships was ready to open for business in work-based learning.

The third vital lesson about making work-based learning work institutionally is, therefore, the need to develop and test learning instruments and models capable of producing customized programmes to defined standards.

Paying its way

While the university's academic authorities wrestled with establishing the academic case for work-based learning because they realized its potential to impact substantially on the academic profile and direction of the university, the financial authorities prompted by the board of governors increasingly questioned the business case for this innovation. What scale of investment would be involved? What would be the likely return within the medium term?

The team of developers accordingly needed to produce a business plan. The decision by senior management to give the National Centre for Work-based Learning Partnerships responsibility for the institutional development and management of work-based learning helped to simplify this difficult task. The centre's experience in operating the university's accreditation services and its own business planning as a cost centre had developed some commercial expertise. In any case it was bound to use the normal costing and charging structures of the university. As an approved subject area, for instance, work-based learning had to use the same module tariff as other subjects. Fees for accrediting an individual's and companies' learning were already agreed, as were hourly and daily rates for additional services. The business question, therefore, rested on the scale of student recruitment. Experience with the delivery of modules and the accreditation of prior learning had shown that cost-effectiveness could be achieved only on a group basis.

Accordingly, priority needed to be given to work with organizations which would guarantee groups on an ongoing basis. This, of course, fitted the thrust of the National Centre's activities, which focused on partnerships.

Experience had already shown that working with organizations has many benefits. As will be seen shortly, reputation figures highly among these. The economic benefits are also considerable, not least because the resources of the workplace (physical as well as educational) are available free of charge. Employers consider this a small cost compared with the time away from work usually required for university courses. Indeed, employers appreciate the time and financial advantages in the form of lower charges and reduced periods of study brought about by accrediting prior learning as opposed to teaching parts of the programmes. Consequently, the track record of the National Centre's team of developers in winning and servicing contracts served their cause well and gave additional credibility to their business planning.

None the less, the university recognized that student recruitment and contracts with organizations would need to be built up and allowed a three-year period to achieve a break-even balance, adding an incentive of a reduced rate of the university overhead charge. In fact, break-even was achieved after one year.

Opening for business: the importance of centralization

The decision to operate the work-based learning scheme centrally brought several strategic and administrative benefits. For instance, the portfolio of activities of the NCWBLP, which included national conference and workshop programmes, publications and consultancy practices, deepened and extended its teaching role. The centre's responsibility for all the accreditation services of the university also meant that it could discuss and negotiate the use of accreditation within customized programmes when dealing with companies and other organizations. Perhaps the main benefit was the refinement of the model of customized programmes. The model is portrayed in Figure 6.1.

The model highlights not only how various interests are satisfied and the clear ownership of the programme by the learner but also how various learning experiences are connected. The emphasis is on the whole programme, which essentially is about personal and professional development. This is a matter of linking individual and organizational interests (Critten 1998), achieved primarily through research and development activities.

Figure 6.1 Academic work-based learning programmes

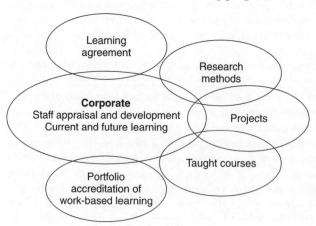

Taught courses are seen as (and are used only if they are) complementary to that approach.

A further advantage of the centralization of work-based learning (although a headache to set up because of the non-conformity of work-based learning practices) came with the development of an efficient administrative system. This was vital not only for providing an appropriate service for a dispersed student population, many of whom rarely if ever attend sessions on campus, but also for all the contractual work arising from accreditation of companies' programmes, using the specialized services of academic colleagues throughout the university.

Finally, centralization proved invaluable for staff development. Central team members were expected to undertake award-bearing work-based learning programmes themselves. Apart from gaining insight and practising what they preached, such programmes offered project activities that were helpful to the advancement of the centre's work. An apprenticeship approach was used to train the centre's staff in negotiating academic programmes with employers, and they, in turn, acted as role models, advisers and tutors for other university colleagues to undertake their own programmes. Indeed, approximately 15 per cent of work-based learning students are drawn from Middlesex University and other educational institutions, mainly academic staff but also administrators and technicians.

The professional development of university colleagues has supported, if not initiated, the spread of work-based learning studies to other schools in the university. Often their work-based projects have produced modules, programmes and schemes within their professional areas. Hence, while the National Centre remains the test-bed of work-based developments, its modules are increasingly being used and supplemented by other schools as they engage in work-based programmes relevant to their professional partners. A pattern of the devolution of work-based learning is, therefore, beginning to emerge. Schools use it for general staff development purposes, thereby building up a body of expertise. This is followed by the secondment (part-time) of a member of staff for apprenticeship purposes and development work to the centre. As a portfolio of work for the school emerges from this and other sources, the secondee becomes the school's coordinator and is given appropriate support to develop the school's own initiatives in work-based learning. This may include joint work with the centre in programmes organized on the basis of joint majors or majors and minors where specialized taught professional courses are linked with work-based learning studies programmes.

To date, more than 1200 students have engaged in the scheme at Middlesex and recently the work has spread overseas (especially in the Middle East and Asia), using a very similar development model to that at Middlesex. The participating population is fairly gender balanced and, while covering all age groups from 25 onwards, is concentrated in the 35–45 grouping. About 60 per cent engage in postgraduate programmes, mainly drawn from public and private organizations.

As always, the proof of the pudding is in the eating and the testimony of participants and partner organizations has been very important for establishing the credentials of work-based learning. Indeed, it has been deliberate policy at Middlesex University to use only word-of-mouth marketing for this scheme. This especially applies to work-based learning because of the business, professional and community networks to which participants and partners belong.

However, curriculum innovation of this radical kind needs other support to quell lingering doubts in the institution. At Middlesex this has taken two forms. One is the confirmation of the quality of its work from the national body commissioned to undertake quality audits. 'Imaginative' and 'rigorous' were key words in the Report of the Higher Education Quality Council (1996).

The other endorsement is that work-based learning at Middlesex has been valued nationally and internationally. In 1996 the Queen's Prize for Further and Higher Education was conferred on the university for its innovation in work-based learning, which was described as 'world class'.

The final vital lesson of the Middlesex experience is that making work-based learning work institutionally requires ringing endorsement primarily from its participants and partners but also from external authorities.

Conclusions

This account of the introduction and operation of work-based learning at Middlesex University has described a number of factors that contributed to its success. Many of these would apply to any form of institutional curriculum development, such as determining the resources, especially appropriately qualified staff, that are available, or how it will advance the institution's reputation and economic interests. And so on.

Work-based learning, however, involves radical change. It changes institutional regulations, redefines the institution's curriculum, reconfigures learning relationships and introduces new practices. It affects directly the institution's other areas of work and redraws its epistemological map. Little wonder, therefore, that winning the intellectual argument for its introduction and continuation is critically important. Nor is it surprising that, when implemented, the ultimate test remains a qualitative one in terms of fitness for purpose. Are its programmes truly customized? The achievement or otherwise of this is a matter for judgement by the partners as much as by peers and participants. The continuing success of work-based learning and whether or not it continues to work institutionally depend crucially on their verdict.

References

Barnett, R. (1997) Beyond competence, in F. Coffield and B. Williamson (eds) *Repositioning Higher Education*. Buckingham: SRHE/Open University Press.

Brennan, J. and Little, B. (1996) *A Review of Work Based Learning in Higher Education.* London: DfEE.

Critten, P. (1998) From personal to professional development, in A. Cowling and C. Mailer (eds) *Managing Human Resources.* London: Arnold.

Eraut, M. (1994) *Developing Professional Knowledge and Competence.* London: Falmer Press.

Higher Education Quality Council (HEQC) (1996) *Collaborative Provision Audit Report for Middlesex University.* Subject Area No. 35, Work Based Learning. London: HEQC.

Knowles, M. (1996) Androgogy: an emerging technology for adult learning, in R. Edwards, A. Hanson and P. Raggett (eds) *Boundaries of Adult Learning.* London: Routledge.

Portwood, D. (1990) *Intellectual Models of CATS.* News No. 5. London: SEEC.

Portwood, D. (1995) Learning from work, Inaugural Professorial Lecture, Middlesex University, 23 June.

Robertson, D. (1994) *Choosing to Change.* Report of the Higher Education Quality Council CAT Development Project. London: HEQC.

7

Ensuring a Holistic Approach to Work-based Learning: The Capability Envelope

John Stephenson

This chapter examines a holistic approach to work-based learning, based on the concepts of individual and corporate capability. Capable individuals and the organizations within which they work, it is argued, have a mutual interest in continuous development within changing environments which can best be served by a shared commitment to autonomous learning. The better the individuals are at addressing their own developmental needs in the context of their work the more likely it is that the organization itself will prosper and develop. In these circumstances, it is the role of the organization's management to provide a culture of support within which autonomous learning can take place. The 'capability envelope' is proposed as a model for encompassing individual learning activities within an overall learning strategy, which reconciles the learner's needs with the interests of the organization and the constraints of formal accreditation. As a considerable bonus, the learning processes involved in using the capability envelope enhance and reinforce the personal skills and qualities increasingly prized by employers of graduates.

Individual and corporate capability

The concept of capability – of individuals and organizations – has emerged in the past 20 years as a useful construct for examining a range of issues related to education, training and business success. In the UK, New Zealand and Australia it has contributed to debates about the nature of learning, the design of the curriculum and our understanding of the basis for effective performance in the workplace.

Individual capability

Individual capability (Burgess 1979) as an educational concept appeared in 1980 when the Royal Society for the Encouragement of Arts, Manufactures and Commerce (RSA) launched a national campaign to redress what it identified as a harmful and unnecessary imbalance between 'education' and 'training'. The RSA argued for a system which did not give higher status to the development of people who 'know' and who are not expected to 'do', and lower status to those who are expected to be proficient in practical things but who are not expected to be 'cultured' and knowledgeable. Stephenson (1992) elaborated on the concept of capability developed by Burgess and suggested that it was:

> an all round human quality, an *integration* of knowledge, skills, personal qualities and understanding *used appropriately and effectively* – not just in familiar and highly focused specialist contexts but in response to *new and changing* circumstances.

This emphasis on 'taking effective action in unfamiliar and changing circumstances' places the person in an exposed position, being reliant on his or her own initiatives in order to take effective action. Accordingly, Stephenson argued, to be capable, people need justified confidence, based on successful autonomous demonstration of their:

- specialist knowledge and skills;
- ability to manage their own learning and to learn from experience;
- power to perform under stress;
- ability to communicate and collaborate effectively;
- capacity for dealing with value issues – their own and other people's.

In Australia, Hase *et al.* (1998) have formulated a similar definition of capability as an integration of specialist skills, self-efficacy and 'appropriate' values, and have identified three key elements: mindful openness to change, self-management of learning potential and a problem-solving approach.

These elements of capability expose some of the limitations of the related notion of 'competence'. In the context of work-based learning, competence often refers to the possession of specialist knowledge and skills relevant to a specific context. Components of competence – often referred to as 'competencies' that can be measured – are used as predetermined learning outcomes for vocationally oriented training programmes. The governments of Australia, New Zealand and the UK have established national frameworks of vocational qualifications based on industrial standards of competence. These are welcomed by some major companies as a way of benchmarking the standards of their own workforce (CBI 1997), rather than seeking ways of enhancing overall levels of performance through the learning of new skills. The application of competency-based ideas and epistemology has, in the fields of work and training, been largely based on narrow definitions of specific tasks and in outcome terms on identifiable and tightly defined performance criteria (Harris *et al.* 1995; Smith and Keating 1997). There has been some broadening of the competence concept (Chappell *et al.* 1995), in which complex combinations of attributes in performance criteria are brought together and written at a reasonable level of generality, taking into account generic competencies.

Personal qualities associated with capability – such as courage, risk-taking, intuition, sharing, acceptance of personal responsibility, flexibility, initiative, self-confidence and values – are easier to describe than to measure and so, in a competency-based scenario, tend to take a back seat. Competence is about delivering the present based on past performance; capability is about imagining the future and bringing it about. Competence is about control of standards; capability is about learning and development. Competence is about fitness for (usually other people's) purpose; capability is also about judging fitness of the purpose itself. A capable person also has culture, in the sense of being able to 'decide between goodness and wickedness or between beauty and ugliness' (Weaver 1994).

Corporate capability

The concept of personal capability can be extended to organizations. After an extensive review of the literature on corporate capability (Kanter 1984; Senge 1992; Beddowes 1993; Sadler 1993; Stahl *et al.* 1993; Bloom *et al.* 1994; Mayo and Lank 1994; Pedler *et al.* 1996), it was concluded that:

> an organization can be described as capable if it embraces the intrinsic, conscious and continuing capacity to survive, grow, improve and transform, achieved through a positive commitment to developmental learning and relationship with its environment. It is a synthesis of process, outcome and culture, encompassed in the notion of flexible capacity.
>
> (Williams *et al.* 1997: 6)

This list of key characteristics of a capable organization reflects those of the capable individual: a concern for values, flexibility, openness, responsibility and continuous learning. Williams *et al.* concluded that as long as it is currently surviving, an organization can be considered capable, even if it is not currently as effective or successful as it might be, as long as it is 'consciously building its collective capacity to be successful and effective in the future'. In their extensive review of capable organizations in Australia, Hase *et al.* (1998: 14) describe such an organization as one that is 'dedicated to fostering learning in both its individuals and its corporate sense'.

The capable organization, like the capable individual, has an all round quality, an integration of technical expertise, belief in its capacity to perform in changing circumstances, confidence in its ability to learn and the capacity to make appropriate judgements within an explicit and relevant set of values.

Synergy through learning

The defining characteristic of being capable as an individual and an organization is the capacity for autonomous learning and development within the context of change. One way of looking at this is shown in Figure 7.1, which shows the world of actions in terms of the familiarity of the context in which people and organizations find themselves and the problems with which they have to deal. In position Y, both can refer to 'the manual' of past experience, or bring themselves up-to-scratch according to external benchmarks or standards. In position Z both are exposed, having to learn about the new situation, formulate any problems to be addressed, plan actions without being certain of outcomes and learn from the experience.

To take actions in position Z both need confidence in their own identity, values against which to judge appropriateness of actions and confidence in their own ability to perform. When an organization is in position Z, so are its employees. The capacity of the employees to learn to cope with Z is the best guarantee that the organization as a whole will also cope.

This synergy between individual and corporate capability was recognized by Mayo and Lank of ICL Ltd, who suggested that:

> survival in a rapidly changing world is dependent on . . . the capability to learn; and that capability is dependent on the motivation for continuous learning of everybody in an organization within a supportive learning environment.
>
> (Mayo and Lank 1994: vii)

Senge (1992: 139) has drawn a similar conclusion and suggests that 'Organizations learn only through individuals who learn. Individual learning does not guarantee organizational learning. But without it, no organizational learning occurs.'

Figure 7.1 Positions Y and Z in the world of actions

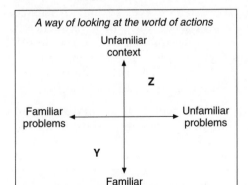

Herein lies the challenge and the opportunity for work-based learning. If individual learners and organizations need the same qualities to survive, grow, improve and transform, a common approach to work-based learning based on openness, responsibility and continuous learning would appear to make sense for both parties. A top-down control model based on measurable predetermined learning outcomes might meet short-term needs (a feature of position Y) but may have the effect of disabling through neglect those qualities which are most useful for longer-term growth and survival (in position Z). A more productive approach would be for the organization to concentrate on creating a culture that recognizes and supports the autonomous work-based learning of all of its members.

From the above it is apparent that a capability-focused work-based learning programme should aim to achieve synergy between the employee's need to explore and prepare for their own future (their personal position Z) and the organization's needs to survive and grow within a changing environment. Such a programme would aim to achieve the following outcomes for employees/learners:

- confidence in their ability to manage their own learning in response to changing circumstances in the workplace;
- belief in their power to perform effectively under conditions of risk;
- the ability to engage effectively and constructively in the formulation and solving of operational problems related to the organization's business;
- the habit of sharing ideas and learning with others;
- the ability to judge the effectiveness of their own performance and its contribution to the performance of the organization;
- a capacity to contribute to the shared values of the organization.

Process as outcome

The above learning outcomes are additional to the development of specialist skills and knowledge. Since confidence in the ability to manage one's own learning is an intended outcome, the experience of having to manage one's learning is likely to be a useful process by which that confidence is enhanced. When those responsible for formal training and education disregard the significance of outcomes from the process, preferring to focus only on the achievement of their predetermined learning objectives imposed at the outset, a number of negative consequences might follow:

- managers of the system might believe that because their predetermined specialist outcomes have been met the workforce is well prepared for the future;
- valuable personal skills and qualities might not be explicitly developed and recognized;
- a culture of top-down control of standards, which precludes bottom-up development of potential, might be reinforced.

The nature of learning through work

A learner-managed approach to work-based learning would be consistent with the informal processes by which people learn through work. Eraut *et al.* (1998) show that formal education and training provide only a small part of the preparation for work. Achieving personally set goals formulated within everyday workplace problems also contributes to both the work itself and the vocational development of the learner (Hager and Beckett 1998; Slotnik 1999). In informal learning situations, goals are achieved by 'a combination of self-directed learning and exploiting learning opportunities as and when they appear' (Slotnik 1999: 1). When specialist information is required, 'the most common form of learning from other people takes the form of consultation and collaboration within the immediate working group' (Slotnik 1999: 2).

Much of the knowledge gained through informal learning is tacit in nature – meaning that it cannot be taught in the normal sense or rendered explicit (Polanyi 1967). Learners unconsciously or incidentally accumulate specialist knowledge and skills through experience. This tacit knowledge can take three forms: situational understanding; routinized procedures based on experience of what normally works well; and intuitive decision-making, usually in response to 'hot action' under pressure (Beckett 1996; Eraut 1999).

If informal work-based learning is 'normal' and leads to relevant tacit knowledge, how can those of us with responsibility for work-based learning 'go with the flow'? How can we make more visible the process by which tacit knowledge is accumulated so that we might facilitate its acquisition and development, help to improve the quality of people's performance, spread valuable knowledge throughout the organization and prepare new recruits for a career of effective learning? How can we recognize such learning (Hager 1998)?

In Eraut's (1999) terms, we could make the process more explicit to the learners themselves if we helped them to move towards a more deliberative informal approach to learning in which the learner reviews past actions and experiences, engages explicitly in current problem-solving activities and plans future learning goals. In Schön's (1983) terms, we should help learners to reflect on their experiences and learn from both the process and the outcomes of that reflection. In Kolb's (1984) terms, this would mean helping people to manage and manipulate the experiential learning cycle for their own benefit. What these approaches have in common is a focus on metacognition, the process of building a mental map or framework within which one can locate one's learning and to which one can make explicit reference in subsequent situations. Understanding the map by participating in its construction, it is argued, will assist people to manage their own learning more effectively.

But effective performance in the workplace is as dependent upon how one feels about oneself as a learner as it is upon what one knows about work. Alderton (1999) found in her interviews with 120 professionals in

12 working environments that critical factors of success included a willingness to respond to challenges and confidence in one's ability to perform effectively under stress. Stephenson (1990), in his study of the impact of independent study on subsequent life experience, found that deep underlying personal needs (e.g. survival, respect, personal identity, commitment) are major factors in helping people to decide to engage with learning. Situations are 'challenging' when one's underlying personal need is being put at risk. Subsequent successes attributable to one's own actions can lead to enhanced self-image and self-efficacy, which in turn encourages further learning initiatives, enhanced aspirations, increased belief in one's capacity to learn and increased self-efficacy (Bandura 1982).

The research conducted into learning through work consistently emphasizes the importance of interaction with others and support from supervising staff and significant others. Alderton (1999) identifies the importance of a 'micro-culture' of friends and colleagues that supports the taking of responsibility and translates 'failures' into opportunities for learning and the improvement of quality. Williams *et al.* (1997) describe how the informal 'learning milieu' of social contacts stimulated by the competency-based programme made a larger contribution to the overall capability of the organizations than the mastery of the competencies themselves. Both Alderton and Williams *et al.* emphasize the crucial role of the organization itself in providing space, time and recognition for informal learning, particularly through the formal management structure.

From the above it is apparent that a successful work-based learning strategy would be one that uses processes which:

- are consistent with informal patterns of learning through work;
- help people to be explicit about their learning goals and experiences;
- relate to people's longer-term personal development needs;
- engage people with the learning potential within the problems they face at work;
- accommodate and exploit informal networks of support;
- build people's belief in their power to learn and perform;
- engage people in exploring value issues in the work they do;
- provide an informal culture of support and official recognition of achievement.

Exposure to such processes in real work situations under conditions of challenge or risk will help people to develop those same characteristics as learning outcomes.

One experience illustrating the impact of such an approach is reported by the Director of Personnel Policy for Sainsbury's Supermarkets Limited. Describing the processes and value of self-managed learning within a fiercely competitive industry, supermarket retailing, Evans concluded:

> self-managed learning has given us much more than a traditional training course. As well as people with more skills, it has given us more

confident and able individuals who have the courage to tackle the many tough issues brought about by a changing organization.

(Evans 1997)

Challenges posed by certification

One feature that differentiates informal from formal work-based learning is certification. This can take the form of internal certificates of completion of training programmes, and can be used for internal audits, personal port-folios and performance appraisal systems or externally recognized awards such as diplomas, degrees or vocational and professional qualifications. Those who invest in learning – including governments, companies and learners themselves – need affirmation that learning occurred. As companies become more conscious of the value of their intellectual capital, entries will appear in annual balance sheets. Inevitably, comparisons will be made along the following lines:

* by recruiters (is this candidate's skill and knowledge comparable to that of others?);
* by companies (are we up to scratch with our competitors?);
* by providers (are we as effective as alternative providers?);
* by learners (how am I doing compared with others?);
* by clients (is this company up to the job?).

In the UK, public funds are channelled to programmes that comply with national standards – to protect the interests of the taxpayer. These are the drivers towards the use of standardized competencies tested by common means in the interests of fairness and accountability.

But as we have seen, an informal holistic approach to work-based learning is not as easily containable within a standardized framework. Learning is individual, circumstances are distinctive and the rhythm or cycle of learning is determined by opportunity rather than annual assessment schedules. Capability is easier to describe than to measure. If we make explicit that which is implicit so that we can make explicit provision to support informal and autonomous learning, are we inevitably diminishing the features we are trying to sustain? Atkins *et al.* (1993), Boud (1995a, b) and Yorke (1995) have addressed the inherent contradictions between assessment as an aid to enhancing performance and assessment as a basis for standardization of performance and accountability.

Formal assessment for external awards presents the biggest challenge of all. One solution which is gathering momentum in work-based learning partnerships is the use of generic level indicators to ensure comparability of outcomes while accommodating the maximum range of individualized content, format and mode (Foster 1998; Osborne *et al.* 1998; Shaw *et al.* 1998). Another is to allow learners themselves to negotiate their own learning goals and the basis on which they will be assessed, activities which have the

Figure 7.2 The capability envelope

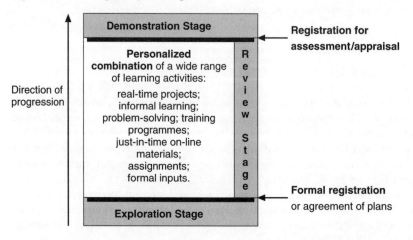

bonus of also improving the quality of learning and strengthening the commitment of learners to complete them satisfactorily. A third solution is to establish formal procedures for reconciling in advance the needs of the learner with the external requirements of certification, usually by some form of learning contract (Laycock and Stephenson 1993; Anderson *et al.* 1998). A fourth is to assess the meta-learning and skills development that occurs through the process of self-managed learning and self-assessment, irrespective of the content or format of the work (Laycock and Stephenson 1993). A fifth is to allow learners to present for assessment their own account of their learning experiences, to be judged in the manner of a behavioural event interview (McClelland 1968) against criteria which indicate capability in action. All these approaches can be brought together in what Stephenson and Yorke (1998) have called the 'capability envelope'

The capability envelope

The capability envelope provides a structure of support to enable people to relate their work-based problem-oriented learning to their own longer-term goals and development. It has three interrelated stages that wrap around, engage and integrate with the person's specialist programme of work; hence the descriptor 'envelope' (see Figure 7.2). Each stage provides a structure within which learners/employees can engage in discussion with other employees/learners, their employers and, if necessary, the awarding bodies, to ensure the eventual programme has internal coherence and is relevant to all parties.

The process of working through the envelope is consistent with the styles of learning relevant to the development of capable individuals and organizations articulated above. By focusing on the relevance of the overall strategy of the programme to the needs of both the employee/learner and the employer, the field is open for the specific content to be as varied as the individual circumstances require. This allows for the inclusion of any combination of real-time projects, informal learning, training programmes, just-in-time online materials, assignments or even formal inputs. The three stages are:

1. *The exploration stage.* This occurs at the very beginning of the process and ends with an agreement on what will be done – perhaps only with oneself but preferably an agreement with others. In formal relationships with universities, these agreements can take the form of three-way learning contracts negotiated by the learner with the university and the employer. People are helped to reflect on and make sense of their prior experience and learning, articulate their aspirations, explore possibilities and establish an overall strategic plan for their own development through work. Particular opportunities for learning through everyday routine and projects can be articulated into learning activities as part of the overall development strategy.
2. *The progress review stage.* This stage runs through and alongside the main learning activity phase. Learners are helped to monitor and review their progress in the light of their agreed plan, share learning with others and judge their own progress and further needs. This provides an opportunity for articulating their work-based learning, which is informal and tacit.
3. *The demonstration stage.* This stage occurs towards the end of the learning episode. Learners are helped to articulate not just the specific achievements related to the problems or tasks in hand, but also their personal learning and their plans for continuing development as a result of their experience.

The sequence can be repeated many times, with each iteration taking the learner forward. Support for the learner in each stage can be provided formally (e.g. within a modular structure) or informally, with notes for guidance, online materials and (as in the Sainsbury example cited above) self-managed learning sets. At all times, each stage operates in the context of the person's learning programme.

For those seeking formal certification, the envelope has two further components:

1. *Formal negotiation and registration of plans.* This takes place at the end of the exploration phase. Formal negotiation and registration usually takes the form of a three-way learning contract between the learner, the employer and the awarding body. It secures the assent and support of key stakeholders for their overall plans and the general nature of the final certificate being sought (e.g. awarding body, title, field and level). Through this procedure, learners are able to engage colleagues and line managers in their planning, secure commitments of support, set out their own learning goals and be reassured that once they have achieved

according to the generic standards of the awarding body they will receive their intended external certification.

2. *Registration of final assessment.* This takes place at the beginning of the demonstration stage. Learners are in a position to articulate, more precisely than was possible in the exploration stage, the outcomes they have achieved in terms of the generic level requirements for the award that they are seeking. The success of the envelope in supporting holistic learning as described in this chapter will depend on the participation of awarding bodies (universities, professional bodies etc.) willing to express their awards in generic terms.

The scope of the envelope can vary according to needs. For major awards such as university degrees, it can encompass work-based learning in conjunction with a full period of study with reviews on a semester or annual basis. The envelope can also be used with work-based real-time projects, provide an agenda for annual performance appraisals or become an informal habit to help experiential learners manage, make explicit and share their tacit knowledge as urged by Eraut (1999).

In a work context, the envelope enables people to share their thoughts, experiences and plans with fellow learners within a mutually supportive micro-culture, integrate their immediate task-related learning into their longer-term development and engage the active and purposeful support of their immediate line managers. The envelope provides an opportunity for people to make their tacit learning explicit within a deliberative mode, and provides the opportunity to set personal learning goals within a generic external awards structure. The public commitment to a personally negotiated external award adds challenge, exposure and risk. This opens up the probability that a successful outcome will enhance not only the person's specialist expertise to the benefit of the company but also the person's self-confidence, self-efficacy and belief in their power to learn and perform. If all members of an organization are helping each other to address their own learning needs in the context of the needs of the organization, then the organization as well as the members can be said to be capable.

The capability envelope and the development of personal skills

The capability envelope as described above provides the learner with challenges which, when addressed successfully, will help to develop skills and qualities relevant to personal capability and effective performance at work. These skills are outcomes from the processes of learner-managed work-based learning – planning, negotiating, implementing, demonstrating and reflecting. They can, of course, be cited as predetermined learning outcomes, in which case they will help those who wish to locate learner managed work-based learning

Table 7.1 Opportunities for skills development through learner-negotiated learning contracts

Process	Skills, understanding and personal qualities
Planning	Self-appraisal, context awareness, target-setting, scheduling, creativity, decision-making, problem formulation
Negotiating	Communication (oral and written), awareness of others' needs, justification of relevance to self and external context, clarity of purpose, resource awareness, competence in formal procedures
Implementing	Self-organization, monitoring skills, adaptation to experience, application of knowledge, working for a purpose, working with others
Demonstrating	Presentation, communication (oral and written), evaluation of performance, dialogue with experts (clients, assessors), self and peer assessment
Reflection	Conceptual development, understanding (knowledge, self, external context), problem reformulation, awareness of personal needs (knowledge and skills) for further development

Source: adapted from Laycock and Stephenson (1993: 173).

within a national framework of qualifications. On the basis of 20 examples of learner-negotiated learning contracts used in UK higher education, Laycock and Stephenson (1993) summarized the processes associated with skills, understanding and personal qualities. These are identified in Table 7.1.

Similar evidence has come from the USA, where the Weatherhead School of Management discovered that encouraging MBA students to formulate goals and learning plans appeared to be significantly related to the development of 'efficiency orientation, planning, self-control, empathy, networking, self-confidence, systems thinking – i.e. cognitive abilities, personal confidence and effectiveness, initiative, flexibility' (Boyatzis *et al.* 1995: 194–5).

The capability envelope in practice

In 1997, the Leeds Training and Enterprise Council (TEC) sponsored a work-based learning scheme in association with local small and medium-sized enterprises (SMEs) and the two universities in the city (University of Leeds and Leeds Metropolitan University) based on the capability envelope. In the 'Learning Power Scheme' (Stephenson 1998), the SMEs provided the focus, projects and in-house support, the universities provided specialist supervision and accreditation. The programme was almost entirely work-based except for some group sessions on campus and occasional one-to-one support for work-based projects from tutors. By the end of year one, the

Table 7.2   Components of the University of Leeds generic level criteria

Field of work-related activity	University level variables
Formulation of the problem	Complexity of concepts, variables, influence
Generation and design of possible solutions or responses	Autonomy and control
Implementation of solutions or responses	Relevance and impact
Evaluation of outcomes	Abstractions, generalizations and transfer
Organization and persentation of all activities	Creativity and innovation

scheme had attracted 100 learners interested in work-based learning in the fields of business, computing, health care and multimedia.

Learning Power was based on an earlier scheme at the University of Leeds that addressed some of the assessment issues described above. By making explicit the underlying assumptions about the level of a University of Leeds degree, and by expressing those assumptions as generic level criteria, it has been possible to accommodate a wide range of individually negotiated specialist programmes. A full account of the generic criteria and how they were established can be found in the final report of the project (Foster 1996), but a brief summary is presented below. Similar articulations of degree-level generic criteria are being developed in Australia as well as elsewhere in the UK (Foster 1998; Osborne *et al.* 1998; Shaw *et al.* 1998). The Higher Education Quality Council of the UK explored the notion of 'graduateness' as a way of teasing out generic qualities for graduates as a whole (HEQC 1997).

The University of Leeds's generic criteria were devised as a matrix between five fields of activity related to work-based learning and six key variables that indicate the levels at which university students' achievements are recognized (see Table 7.2). The resultant generic level indicators bridged the interests of both the employers and the university. In the matrix, each field of activity can be defined at each university level (e.g. year 1, year 3, postgraduate). For instance, problem formulation at level 1 would show less complexity, autonomy etc. than would be expected at level 3. Since the level indicators were drawn from the tacit understanding of key university academic gate-keepers, it was possible to argue that work-based learners presenting work which met those levels were comparable to though different from, campus-based students working at the same level.

In their preliminary evaluation of Learning Power, York Consulting (1999) concluded that, despite some teething troubles related to the initial unfamiliarity of the procedures and culture shock for some university tutors, 'Learning Power has made a very worthwhile local contribution to the development of new forms of delivery of higher skills to the workforce.' Despite frustrations – most of which were related to the mismatch between the fixed lock-step pace of the university calendar and timetable and the more varied pace of work-based learning – students remained 'enthusiastic' about their participation. Employers reported high motivation of their employees, satisfaction that the content was directly relevant to their own needs and, overall, found, as one participating employer reported, that 'The programme offers excellent value for money; accreditation of prior work is very important – from my limited experience of the program I have been impressed; flexibility is very important' (York Consulting 1999: 8).

Despite the euphoria (manifested by demands from neighbouring areas to be included in the scheme), there are still problems to be resolved, mainly related to the rigidity of the university's schedules and the difficulty of providing ease of access to specialist materials and advice on demand. Stephenson and Yorke (1998) spell out some of the basic features of the university culture that need to be in place to support the capability envelope in full. The authors demonstrate that many universities already display some of these features, so progress is being made. Despite its difficulties, the Learning Power Scheme in Leeds has demonstrated that individual learners can use the capability envelope to help them to plan, negotiate and complete their own work-based learning programmes – in association with their employers – within a formal accreditation regime.

Prospects and trends

The main difficulties encountered by the Learning Power project concern access to advice, control of access to specialist material, the different rates at which learners can progress compared with the normal academic cycle and the apparent complexity of procedures. Despite these concerns the participants remain enthusiastic. What will it be like if information and communication technology (ICT) can minimize these frustrations? The UK government is investing heavily to find the answer. Its University for Industry project (UfI Ltd) is a national online service aimed at, among others, work-based learners. At the time of writing, UfI is putting together an online capability envelope template to provide ready-to-desk specialist interactive support for self-managed work-based learners – in partnership with the major quality assurance and funding agencies for launch in mid-2000. Time will tell if it fulfils its promise.

Probably the most significant development, however, is the rapid growth in the use of ICT for learning. One immediate and obvious effect is that 'just-in-time' access to specialist material in support of work-based problem-solving is greatly enhanced. But ICT has the further potential to provide

• a smoother engagement with the formal process of negotiation and registration of programmes;

- online demonstration of performance;
- immediate access to personal specialist support;
- interactive learning materials designed to facilitate reviews;
- experience, planning and monitoring processes;
- access to an online lifelong learning portfolio.

A holistic approach to work-based learning, as explored in this chapter, presents many difficulties. The implications of giving learners greater responsibility for their learning through work, and providing the necessary support for them to do it well, require teachers, line managers and external agencies to adjust the way they operate and the services they provide. To traditionalists, a holistic approach may be unwelcome because it appears to be difficult to predetermine and control the outcomes. A culture change within the universities and companies from one of control of learning to one of negotiation, potential and development will be needed if holistic approaches are to be more widely adopted in academic contexts. The trends, however, are driving in that direction (Foster and Stephenson 1998). New understandings of the nature of corporate capability and the role of personal capability in its achievement will translate into new demands on how universities should service the work-based learning needs of their industry and business partners. New learner-centred approaches to teaching are beginning to proliferate in universities and will encourage further experimentation and innovation.

References

Alderton, J. (1999) Factors which facilitate workplace learning: confidence, challenge and support, Conference paper presented at the Annual Meeting of the American Educational Research Association (AERA), Montreal.

Anderson, G., Boud, D. and Sampson, J. (1998) Qualities of learning contracts, in J. Stephenson and M. Yorke (eds) *Capability and Quality in Higher Education.* London: Kogan Page.

Atkins, M., Beattie, J. and Dockrell, W. B. (1993) *Assessment Issues in Higher Education.* Sheffield: Employment Department.

Bandura, A. (1982) Self-efficacy: Towards a unifying theory of behavioral change, in M. Rosenberg and H. B. Kaplan (eds) *Social Psychology of the Self-concept.* Arlington Heights, IL: Harlan Davidson.

Beckett, D. (1996) Critical action and professional practice. *Educational Theory,* 46(2): 138–50.

Beddowes, P. (1993) Europe in the 1990s, Ashridge Management Research Paper.

Bloom, H., Calori, R. and de Woot, P. (1994) *Euromanagement: A New Style for the Global Market.* London: Kogan Page.

Boud, D. (1995a) Assessment and learning: contradictory or complementary?, in P. Knight (ed.) *Assessment for Learning in Higher Education.* London: Kogan Page.

Boud, D. (1995b) *Enhancing Learning through Self Assessment.* London: Kogan Page.

Boyatzis, R. E., Cowen, S. S., Kolb, D. A. and Associates (1995) *Innovation in Professional Education.* San Francisco: Jossey-Bass.

Burgess, T. (1979) New ways to learn: education for capability, Cantor Lecture III. *Journal of the Royal Society of Arts*, 127(5271): 143–57.

CBI (Confederation of British Industry) (1997) Reasons to be cheerful, *Human Resource Brief*, August.

Chappell, C., Gonczi, A. and Hager, P. (1995) Competency-based education, in G. Foley (ed.) *Understanding Adult Education and Training*. St Leonards, NSW: Allen & Unwin.

Eraut, M. (1999) Theoretical and methodological perspectives on researching workplace learning, Conference paper, AERA.

Eraut, M., Alderton, J., Cole, G. and Senker, P. (1998) *Development of Knowledge and Skills in Employment*. Brighton: University of Sussex Institute of Education Research Report No. 5.

Evans, J. (1997) Key Skills for Tomorrow's World. *Capability*, 3(2): 11–14.

Foster, E. (1996) *Comparable but Different: Work-based Learning for a Learning* Society. Leeds: University of Leeds.

Foster, E. (1998) Can higher education deliver capability?, in J. Stephenson and M. Yorke (eds) *Capability and Quality in Higher Education*. London: Kogan Page.

Foster, E. and Stephenson, J. (1998) Work-based learning and universities in the UK: a review of current practice and trends. *Higher Education Research and Development*, 17(2): 155–70.

Hager, P. (1998) Recognition of informal learning: challenges and issues. *Journal of Vocational Education and Training*, 50(4): 521–35.

Hager, P. and Beckett, D. (1998) What would lifelong learning look like in a workplace setting?, in J. Holford, C. Griffin and P. Jarvis (eds) *International Perspectives on Lifelong Learning*. London: Kogan Page.

Harris, R., Guthrie, H., Hobart, B. and Lundberg, D. (1995) *Competency-based Education and Training*. South Melbourne, Vic: Macmillan.

Hase, S., Cairns, L. and Malloch, M. (1998) *Capable Organisations: The Implications for Vocational Education and Training*. Brisbane: Australian National Training Authority.

Higher Education Quality Council (HEQC) (1997) *Graduate Standards Programme: Final Report*. London: HEQC.

Kanter, R. M. (1984) *The Change Masters*. London: Unwin Hyman.

Kolb, D. A. (1984) *Experiential Learning: Experience as the Source of Learning and Development*. Engelwood Cliffs, NJ: Prentice Hall.

Laycock, M. and Stephenson, J. (1993) The place and potential use of learning contracts in higher education, in M. Laycock and J. Stephenson (eds) *Using Learning Contracts in Higher Education*. London: Kogan Page.

McClelland, D. C. (1968) *Measuring Behavioral Objectives in the 1970s*. Boston: McBer and Co.

Mayo, A. and Lank, E. (1994) *The Power of Learning: A Guide to Competitive Advantage*. London: Institute of Personnel and Development.

Osborne, C., Davies, J. and Garnet, J. (1998) Guiding the student to the centre of the stakeholder curriculum: independent and work-based learning at Middlesex University, in J. Stephenson and M. Yorke (eds) *Capability and Quality in Higher Education*. London: Kogan Page.

Pedler, M., Burgoyne, J. and Boydell, T. (1996) *The Learning Company: A Strategy for Sustainable Development*. Maidenhead: McGraw-Hill.

Polanyi, M. (1967) *The Tacit Dimension*. London: Routledge and Kegan Paul.

Sadler, P. (1993) The talent intensive organisation, Ashridge Management Research Paper.

Schön, D. (1983) *The Reflective Practitioner: How Practitioners Think in Action.* New York: Basic Books.

Schön, D. (1996) Learning through reflections on conversations. *Capability,* 2(2): 12–16.

Senge, P. M. (1992) *The Fifth Discipline.* London: Century Business.

Shaw, M., Stoney, C. and Green, H. (1998) Reconciling quality and standards with diversity, in J. Stephenson and M. Yorke (eds) *Capability and Quality in Higher Education.* London: Kogan Page.

Slotnik, H. B. (1999) How doctors learn in the workplace, Conference paper presented at the Annual Meeting of the American Educational Research Association (AERA), Montreal.

Smith, E. and Keating, J. (1997) *Making Sense of Training Reform and Competency Based Training.* Wentworth Falls, NSW: Social Science Press.

Stahl, T., Nyhan, B. and D'Aloja, P. (1993) *The Learning Organisation: A Vision for Human Resource Development.* Brussels: EUROTECNET.

Stephenson, J. (1990) The student experience of independent study, Unpublished PhD thesis, University of Sussex.

Stephenson, J. (1992) Capability and quality in higher education, in J. Stephenson and S. Weil (eds) *Quality in Learning: A Capability Approach to Higher Education.* London: Kogan Page.

Stephenson, J. (1998) Learning power: a learner managed work-based learning programme for regional development. *Capability,* 3(3): 4–37.

Stephenson, J. and Yorke, M. (1998) *Capability and Quality in Higher Education.* London: Kogan Page.

Weaver, T. (1994) Knowledge alone gets you nowhere. *Capability,* 1(1): 6–12.

Williams, R., Cunningham, L. and Stephenson, J. (1997) *The Use of NVQs as a Means to Develop Corporate Capability.* Coventry: OCR.

York Consulting (1999) *Evaluation of Learning Power: Executive Summary.* Leeds: Leeds TEC.

Yorke, M. (1995) The assessment of higher order transferable skills: a challenge to higher education, in M. Yorke (ed.) *Assessing Capability in Degree and Diploma Programmes.* Proceedings of a conference, Liverpool, 8 February. Liverpool: Centre for Higher Education Development, Liverpool John Moores University.

8

Working with Partners to Promote Intellectual Capital

Jonathan Garnett, Alison Comerford and Neville Webb

This chapter draws on the experience of Middlesex University, Bovis Construction and Webb Associates in designing, delivering and assessing customized programmes in work-based learning studies for managers in the construction industry. The resultant partnership is presented as a case study and the matter of how the development and operation of the partnership contributed to the intellectual capital of the employer and the university is explored.

Background

In 1995 Middlesex University validated programmes in work-based learning studies at undergraduate and postgraduate levels (see Chapter 6 in this volume). The programmes offered through the university's National Centre for Work-based Learning Partnerships (NCWBLP) have proved to be highly successful, winning national recognition and expanding rapidly. In 1998/9 Middlesex had 850 students enrolled in work-based learning programmes, including major schemes with over twenty organizations spanning the public, private and voluntary sectors.

The Middlesex approach to work-based learning focuses on the use of work-based programmes as a process for recognizing, creating and applying knowledge through and for work rather than simply at work. This approach challenges the position of the university as sole validator and evaluator of high-level knowledge. For not only does a work-based programme have to satisfy the academic scrutiny of the university, it also has to embrace fully the complexity of the specific context. It also has to demonstrate 'fitness for purpose' at the level of the individual, the immediate community of practice and in some instances the wider professional community. Work-based learning demonstrates alternative and equally valid ways to acquire and exhibit higher-level learning by recognizing the intellectual and hence academic legitimacy of critical thought leading to critical action (Barnett 1997). A solution to a real-life problem may not have been 'fully researched' but sufficient insights may be present within the confines of the time and resources available to take critical action based upon critical thought. In work-based learning a vital part of critical thought is the exploration and consideration of the 'bounded rationality' provided by real-life situations. The real challenge to the university is not that work-based learning provides a novel alternative route to university qualifications but that such learning should also have to meet the needs of employees. We need to remind ourselves that they are students as well as employees and are also owners and users of the high-level knowledge incorporated in and generated by the work-based programme.

In the age of the 'knowledge-driven economy' and the 'corporate university' the creation and evaluation of knowledge is too important to be left to academic researchers. This is well articulated by management gurus, chief executives and stock market analysts seeking to evaluate the 'intellectual capital' of organizations (Stewart 1997). The clear challenge to the university is to be not only a learned but also a learning organization, able to transform the curriculum and to develop new ways in which individuals and organizations can engage with higher education (Portwood 1993).

The approach to work-based learning at Middlesex University is based upon partnership in the design and, as appropriate, the delivery and assessment of the programme with employers and other providers of high-level learning. The university provides a quality assured framework within which individual employees, their organizations and NCWBLP negotiate programmes of study which meet the personal development and career needs of individuals, the developmental objectives of the employing organizations and the academic requirements of the university. The framework consists of a sequence of core modules focusing on the recognition and accreditation of learning, programme planning, methodology for work-based research and development and at least one major work-based project. Throughout this set of core modules is threaded a reflective element designed to enable participants to become increasingly aware of, and able to articulate, the links between their own work experience and what it means to learn as professionals within the context of their organization.

Development of a partnership

The partnership described here involved a relationship between Bovis Construction, Webb Associates and Middlesex University. Bovis Construction is a global company providing consultancy and construction management expertise to clients. The European headquarters is based in Middlesex, and oversees 2500 of its 5000 staff around the world. Bovis has long been committed to the training and development of its staff, and has a long history of apprenticeship and employee development. Bovis works with a number of universities and training providers to provide opportunities for employees to engage in personal development and achieve degree and postgraduate qualifications. Bovis pioneered the first in-house masters in construction management in 1990.

Webb Associates is a 'virtual organization' consisting of 15 self-employed consultants who network together to provide tailor-made interventions for a variety of organizations. The philosophy that permeates their work is summed up by the axiom 'teach a man to fish, and feed him for life'. This means that the consultants at Webb include a high degree of process transfer within their approach. They do not give direct answers and solutions, they set up scenarios that ask questions and invite participants to determine their own thinking. In this way a high level of participation and ownership is ensured.

Bovis originally approached the university in order to gain accreditation for its management development programme. The programme had been developed over a period of two years in conjunction with Webb Associates in order to develop the general management skills of technical managers. The specific aims were to raise awareness of the role of the manager, examine team dynamics and develop leadership skills. The programme culminated in a project based upon a workplace problem. Following the established Middlesex University accreditation procedures the programme was evaluated by staff from the University Business School and NCWBLP, leading to a credit point and level rating agreed by the central University Accreditation Board. Middlesex was able to accredit the programme as carrying academic credit points at the postgraduate level.

Further discussions about the development of a postgraduate scheme for Bovis managers identified the Bovis core competencies as a potential key source of organizational learning that the company wished to be incorporated into the programme. The Bovis core competencies are a set of behavioural indicators that are common to all staff within the organization, are part of the performance management process and underpin all learning and development activity at Bovis. NCWBLP worked closely with the Bovis Training Manager to identify the knowledge and skills required for appropriate performance in the Bovis competency areas. Thus each competency area had underpinning learning outcomes which could be accredited by the university. This approach challenged existing thinking and practice in relation to the accreditation of prior experiential learning (APEL). APEL had previously focused on the learning of the organization, as described in the areas of learning based upon the organization's competency framework, rather than the learning of the university, as described in validated university modules (see Garnett 1998 for more on APEL and competency frameworks).

Bovis and Webb Associates believed that Middlesex demonstrated a number of characteristics that helped to develop the partnership. These included:

- flexibility of approach in encompassing and enhancing existing programmes and inputs;
- did not seek to impose a standard pedagogic approach;
- showed a willingness to focus on the practical application of theory in order to meet the needs of the individual and the organization.

An initial pilot programme in 1996 convinced Bovis of the potential value of the Middlesex University work-based learning approach and it was swiftly followed by several groups of previous and new management development programme participants. This intensive start forced Webb Associates and NCWBLP to establish quickly a joint working pattern that was then progressively refined in the light of experience. Cohorts graduated in 1996 at postgraduate certificate level, in 1997 at postgraduate certificate level and master's level and in 1998 at master's level. In 1998/9 there were some 45 participants on the programme, almost all of whom were working towards a master's degree.

Partnership programme

The development of the partnership ensured that Bovis (through its central education and training department and Webb Associates) played a full part in the design of the postgraduate scheme. This was because some of Bovis's training activities had already been accredited by Middlesex (e.g. the management development programme and Bovis competencies). These activities became central features of the scheme. As NCWBLP work-based learning programmes are always designed on a partnership basis, within the validated framework approved by the university, this did not represent a challenge to existing university procedures or practices. As always, the crucial part of the joint development was developing a common understanding across all the partners of what each wished to gain from the programme and what each could contribute. Neither Bovis nor Webb Associates had experience of a university willing to work in this way and which was able to offer such a high degree of customized provision. Once they grasped the potential of the Middlesex framework they rapidly became adept at suggesting innovative ways in which it might be utilized.

The key to success of the programme is the learning agreement to which the individual participant is contracted. This began as the standard NCWBLP learning agreement between the individual, their employer and the university. It soon became apparent that in order to ensure employer commitment to the programme at operational level the signature obtained from the central Bovis Education and Training Department had to be supplemented by the signature of the Head of the Bovis Local Business Centre. It was vital for the growth and standing of the programme within Bovis that it was regarded positively by the Local Business Centre Heads, who, in effect, owned the work time of the participants. Participation in programme design (covering duration, timing and content) ensured that the Local Business Centre Heads had the opportunity to become full stakeholders and hence major beneficiaries of the programme. This refinement of the use of the learning agreement emerged as a significant strength as it widened the pool of stakeholders and reinforced the relevance of the programme at the operational level.

It is a requirement that participants negotiate their own programmes and gain agreement for them via completion of a learning agreement. A typical programme includes:

- *Programme planning*: a standard university module that is a compulsory part of all Middlesex negotiated work-based learning programmes. It challenges the individual to negotiate their own programme with the university and their employer. The outcome of the negotiation and the product assessed and considered for approval by the university is a learning agreement.
- *Management development programme*: management input devised and delivered by Webb Associates. The outcome is a course file, assessed via two reports on the application of the learning gained.
- *Core competency development*: selected competencies are related to the individual's work role and evidence is gathered which exhibits the knowledge and skills required to demonstrate competent performance. The output is a portfolio of evidence and a reflective essay linking the areas of learning based upon the Bovis core competencies.
- *Work-based research and development*: a validated university module developed by NCWBLP that results in a portfolio of work-based research approaches, data collection techniques and a specific proposal for the work-based project. This is seen as a vital part of every programme by the university but was not initially perceived as relevant by many programme participants. NCWBLP and Webb Associates had to work hard to devise strategies for presenting this module in an accessible and relevant way. Perceived relevance was achieved by the development of the concept of the worker as researcher and by enabling participants to relate this concept to their management roles.
- *Work-based project*: the main focus of the programme is on the delivery of a major work-based project (on an individual or collaborative basis) which addresses real-life issues and has the capacity to have an impact on the organization. As most participants were engaged in work that was heavily task-oriented it was not natural for them to stand back and take the more reflexive approach advocated by the university. In order to be effective it was necessary for the university to be flexible in the timing of project work and the provision of supervisory support.

The core modules are designed with Kolb's learning cycle at the heart of the educational experience (Kolb 1984). Participants were introduced to the concept of this cycle and presented with opportunities for reflection upon the learning process of the programme and how it related to their personal and professional development. This approach was in keeping with the philosophy of Webb Associates and key members of the Bovis Education and Training Department.

Patterns of delivery

The partnership programme adopted the same pattern of delivery favoured by Bovis for its management development programme. In order to reduce disruption to work and enable participants to travel from across the UK, delivery typically took the form of three- or five-day blocks at a residential centre. This concentrated pattern of delivery challenged existing university practice as it meant that the boundaries between modules were often blurred, as a session would routinely include input and supervision relating to more than one module. Delivery took the form of group activity, seminar and individual or small-group tutorial. Input on management development was provided by Webb Associates, input on the development of accreditation claims was based upon the Bovis core competencies and programme planning was shared between NCWBLP and Webb Associates. As an experienced industry specific provider, Webb Associates played a major role in relating the requirements and inputs of the university to the Bovis context. NCWBLP led in the research methods input and supervision of project work. Subject expertise from other areas of the university was available to support project work. The teaching styles provided by the university and the independent training provider have evolved, with planning from experience, and have proved to be highly complementary. Both providers share a firm ideological commitment to learner-centred and learner-managed education and a belief in a partnership approach to individual and organizational development.

Employer involvement

The scheme was constructed with the full involvement of the central Bovis Training Department and the Bovis Training Manager acted as the coordinator and key point of contact within Bovis for the scheme. This high-level point of contact is a common feature of successful NCWBLP work-based partnerships. Bovis administered the scheme, and the university administered the assessment. Initially there was some confusion among participants concerning the nature of the programme and the respective administrative roles of Bovis and the university. This was resolved by providing fuller information to the participants at the outset of the programme. Bovis contracts with Webb Associates to participate in the delivery of the programme. Webb Associates undertook the assessment of the management development programme, with the university having a monitoring role. Research proposals and final project presentations were assessed jointly by Bovis, Webb Associates and the university. All other assessment tasks were a university responsibility.

Generic work-based learning academic level characteristics, approved by the university as part of the validation of work-based learning, provided a basis for joint development and understanding of assessment criteria. Bovis and Webb Associates tended to focus on the practical application and potential impact of the project, while the university was equally concerned with the project methodology and the development of critical thought. Through the joint consideration of work and assessment criteria, assessment capability was enhanced over time.

The learning agreement produced in the programme-planning module was the key mechanism for securing employer involvement and commitment at operational level. The active involvement of Bovis Local Business Centre Heads in the negotiation of the agreement was essential if precious time was to be won away from work to attend block sessions. The major incentive for the local manager was the potential of the major project to address an issue of current concern and thus provide a local benefit within a relatively short timescale. With a real stake in the programme, Local Business Centre Heads have often emerged as effective champions of the programme by winning access to the participants' information and resources. However, their inclusion in the negotiation process has not always been unproblematic, as they represent yet another interest group for the participants to take into account. This has occasionally led to Webb Associates and/or the university having to argue for the holistic value of the programme rather than the immediate potential gain from the project stage.

Participant, employer, provider and university outcomes

The Bovis managers who participated have consistently rated the scheme highly. The work-based and practical focus of the programme, coupled with flexibility, has been much appreciated by participants, as is the effectiveness of the Webb Associates/Middlesex input and support. The emphasis the programme places on enabling participants to take responsibility for their own learning has had a lasting impact. The academic recognition of work-based learning was also ranked as one of its strengths.

Bovis values the customization of the scheme to reinforce and develop further knowledge and skills that are at the heart of the Bovis performance management scheme. The Bovis Training Manager (Comerford 1998) identified the following benefits for the programme's participants:

- a clear sense of purpose for work-based projects and the personal rewards that can come from them;
- an understanding of the concepts of academic research methods and how to apply them to the workplace;
- a greater sense of responsibility for personal and continuing professional development;

- an enhanced and more participative role in personal performance appraisal and consequently an improved dialogue with line managers;
- a greater sense of self-esteem, especially as the result of gathering evidence of competency;
- a clearer understanding of the role and expectations resting upon them as managers.

In addition, the work-based projects provided Bovis with a significant in-house research and development capacity, which can utilize university support. These projects add to the intellectual capital of the organization and have the potential to improve performance and thus produce a direct bottom line benefit through improving reporting and the ability to learn from construction defects.

Being part of a university master's programme has given Webb Associates a level of credibility and status within Bovis. This is apparent not only when new programme groups are starting on their first few days of training, but also in other non-allied training and consultancy events within the company.

The scheme has provided the university with a model of partnership that is based around organizational core competencies. This has provided NCWBLP with a significant model of curriculum transformation. The NCWBLP approach to APEL has been radically changed to allow for a corporate dimension to what was previously a highly individualistic process (Garnett 1998). The scheme has also demonstrated how the university can benefit from the client knowledge and industry expertise of an independent training provider. Thus the partnership not only embraces the employer, university and individual participants; it also includes Webb Associates as one of the major providers of learning.

Partnership in the development of intellectual capital

The Bovis case study illustrates how the development of intellectual capital (Stewart 1997) drew the partners together and became central to the work-based programme that was developed. Bovis and Webb Associates originally approached the university seeking accreditation for their management development programme. They were seeking to enhance its structural (the course) and human (course participants) capital via the use of client capital (accreditation structures) of the university. The intellectual capital analysis of work-based learning programmes highlights the importance of the project as it results in knowledge creation within bounded rationality enhancing the human as well as the structural capital of the organization.

The scheme has enhanced the intellectual capital of Middlesex University by providing a model of partnership which is based around organizational core competencies and a model for accreditation which focuses on achievement while on the programme rather than prior to programme entry (Garnett 1998). The scheme has also demonstrated how the university can benefit from the client capital (knowledge and industry expertise) of an independent training provider.

Conclusions

The project with Bovis and Webb Associates illustrates a number of essential employer requirements of a university in order to develop an effective and sustainable work-based learning programme:

- recognition and enhancement of high-level learning where it already exists within the organization (e.g. training courses, the experiential learning of individual employees);
- flexibility in the pattern of delivery, pace of the programme and approach to pedagogy;
- willingness to work with other providers of high-level learning utilized by the employer (e.g. independent training providers);
- customization of programmes to meet the needs of the individual and the organization;
- tangible outcomes which have the potential to enhance the intellectual capital of the organization;
- provision of a quality-assured and flexible route to reliable and internationally recognized qualifications.

The case study also illustrates how a university might effectively satisfy these requirements by the use of accreditation coupled with the learning agreement as key instruments in constructing customized programmes. It also highlights how the partnership approach can be extended to embrace not only the employer and individual participants but also other providers of high-level learning. The Middlesex approach to partnership illustrates the potential of work-based learning to challenge the deficit model of higher education by recognizing and then extending the intellectual capital of not only the employer but also the university. This has profound long-term implications for the role of the university, transforming it from a monopoly supplier of high-status and privileged knowledge to an active partner with the employer and the student in the creation and application of knowledge within the learning context provided by work.

References

Barnett, R. (1997) *Higher Education: A Critical Business.* Buckingham SRHE/Open University Press.

Comerford, A. (1998) Building on capability: learning to learn at Bovis Construction. *Capability*, 3(4).

Garnett, J. (1998) Using APEL to develop customised work-based learning programs at postgraduate level, in D. Croker, D. Ellis, Y. Hill, J. Staran and I. Turner (eds) *Beyond Graduateness*. London: South East England Consortium for Credit Accumulation and Transfer.

Kolb, D. A. (1984) *Experiential Learning: Experience as the Source of Learning and Development*. Englewood Cliffs, NJ: Prentice Hall.

Portwood, D. (1993) Work-based learning: linking academic and vocational qualifications. *Journal of Further and Higher Education*, 17(3): 61–9.

Stewart, T. (1997) *Intellectual Capital: The New Wealth of Organizations*. London: Nicholas Brearley.

9

The Possibilities in a Traditional University

Lynne Caley

To remain viable in an environment characterized by uncertainty and change, organizations and individuals alike depend upon an ability to learn. Knowledge and skills are vulnerable to obsolescence, and future success depends upon flexibility, responsiveness and new capabilities acquired through ongoing learning. To be effective, this learning needs to take account of the particular circumstances within which it is applied. One solution has been a move towards siting learning in the workplace itself, making learning not just 'for' work (the conventional 'frontloaded' approach) but either 'at' or 'through' work (Eraut 1998). Work-based learning is a slippery concept, not given to straightforward definition. However, since the generation, transmission, and utilization of knowledge at work are becoming increasingly recognized as important components of professional development, we have to make some attempt to understand precisely the nature and limitations of such knowledge.

At the Cambridge Programme for Industry (CPI) I work with private and public sector organizations, both nationally and internationally, in support of the university's commitment to professional development, executive education and lifelong learning. CPI's activities reflect the diversity of ways in which organizations and individuals learn, encompassing support for both non-formal and formal learning. The former we have defined as continuous and lifelong, as occurring in workplaces, as being personalized, relevant and transferable. The latter provides formal learning opportunities through courses, seminars and workshops which are bounded by time and place, require attendance with predefined sets of relationships and obligations, and usually culminate in an award or reward.

In developing and managing programmes of learning, CPI act as part of a triumvirate of interests. We work closely with organizations, recognizing them as important stakeholders within the relationship. The context within which any programme is set will directly influence the optimization of non-formal learning opportunities. But it is the individual learning that we are recognizing when making an award, and so our relationship with the individual has to be a direct one. This places significant stresses on those involved, and has implications for what can be achieved. In this chapter I shall recount some of the background to the particular form of work-based learning that we practise at the CPI. Taking as an example one of the programmes that we have developed and deliver I hope to illustrate the possibilities and limitations of work-based learning within a traditional university context.

New approaches to learning

In developing our programmes we start with the premise that professional development is about more than the straightforward acquisition of knowledge and skill. It is crucially also about building on the confidence of professionals by offering challenges and transmitting values of lifelong learning, about supporting and reinforcing formal learning and about enabling non-formal work-based learning. Significantly, we also believe that work-based learning is best done collaboratively; and that the socio-technical circumstances that operate within the workplace, at both macro- and micro-organizational levels, are crucial in maximizing the benefits of work-based learning.

Debate within several communities of interest has led to a change in what can be recognized as 'knowledge'. While academia may be appropriate to the development of propositional knowledge, this is just one of many forms of what is necessary but not sufficient for the world of work. It is argued (see Sternberg and Kolligian, 1985; Boud and Feletti 1997; Eraut 1998) that knowledge is context specific, and that the academic environment is just one of many contexts.

When one is describing occupational knowledge, broader definitions are called for, incorporating the procedural as well as the propositional, and the tacit as well as the explicit. Academic knowledge is generally considered to be located within a collective school of thought, related to previous epistemology, and 'seeking abiding truths'. By contrast, personal context-bound experience is likely to be more significant for the accommodation of practice-based forms of knowledge that are encountered at work. At the same time what is recognized as valid in these forms of knowledge will be more dependent on the circumstances within which they are acquired and deployed.

The traditional view of learning as the acquisition of information from an 'expert' ignores the fact that learning has its roots in everyday activities and experience. Importantly, this approach does not conceive of knowledge as being what is stored in books, databases or even a person's head. Rather, 'To know is to be capable of participating with the requisite competence in the complex web of relationships among people and activities' (Gherardi *et al.* 1998: 274). Learning, then, is about finding out 'what to do, when and how to do it and why it was done', and it 'takes place among and through other people' (Gherardi *et al.* 1998: 274).

We are beginning to understand the different roles of formal and non-formal learning (Eraut 1998) and the importance of the latter in the workplace, where 'the distinctions between working, knowing, learning and innovating get rather blurred' (Araujo 1998: 328). Eraut *et al.* (1998) have identified a number of non-formal routes through which people learn: collaborative work, personal reflection, dealing with challenging projects, consultation, activities external to the workplace. Planned, formal learning has an important role in providing 'concepts and theories ... to make sense of ... experience and understand issues and alternative perspectives more clearly' (Eraut *et al.* 1998: 8). However, additional non-formal support is essential if the learner is to develop the capability of using the knowledge.

Traditional professional development relies on what Lester (1995) describes as the 'technocratic' model. This is built around the acquisition or updating of a fundamental knowledge base that can then be related to well defined problems. This is achieved through formal learning programmes, which are built around someone else's idea of the learner's needs in terms of curriculum and timing, and frequently do not take into account the contextual needs of the professional. In particular, they do not acknowledge the stock of personal experience and knowledge adults bring to any learning situation. Such an 'input-based' model is appropriate for 'maintenance learning', but does not address our need for 'innovative' or 'generative' learning (Botkin *et al.* 1979; Senge 1992).

What, then, is the key to successful work-related learning in organizations today? How can we help organizations to respond both to their own needs and to those of their employees? To what extent do the needs of both converge? If the CPI is to offer successful work-based programmes then these questions have to be addressed.

Cambridge and the Programme for Industry

At the CPI these questions underpin the continuing professional development (CPD) provision that we offer. We were set up ten years ago, as part of the UK government's drive to broker closer links between industry and university research. We were located within the Board of Continuing Education of the University of Cambridge, which for more than a century has had responsibility for part-time 'extra-mural' provision. The board is one of four senior bodies directly answerable to the university's senate.

During its first decade the CPI has worked with academics from departments and faculties within the university. We initially focused on configuring high-level research into CPD 'products'. These usually took the form of short residential courses held at Cambridge on university and college premises during vacation periods. For a number of reasons we have had only limited success with this formula. First, the research undertaken at Cambridge is highly specialist, and is of only direct relevance to a very small number of professionals. This has meant that for any one short course subject area we can never achieve economies of scale; each course has to be unique and targeted at successively narrowing markets. At the same time, academics who might be persuaded to give their time once or even twice are not amenable to the idea of repeat teaching of similar material. Second, it has become apparent that a supply-led model of development is not always appropriate. We have found that fascinating as some of the research is to the academic involved, it is often impossible to 'sell' to industry, where the ability of the researcher to communicate their enthusiasm may be limited.

External changes in perception about CPD and lifelong learning have impacted on Cambridge as well as elsewhere. We began to realize that professionals are reluctant to spend more than the briefest of time away from their workplace, unless that time could be justified in terms of direct relevance to the job. Thus we began in general to question the transferability of classroom-based learning into the workplace for the majority of professionals. And, finally, the rise of part-time award-bearing programmes in vocational areas began to impact. Our client organizations started to ask if they could have their learning recognized – could they have a certificate?

Our growing realization that formal learning provision might be inadequate as a response to professional CPD needs was fuelled by a series of funded action research projects undertaken within the CPI. The profile of our provision began to alter in 1997, and although we feel that these are still early days, we are already learning significant lessons about how adults learn and about the crucial relevance of the context within which their learning occurs. Initially our relationship with clients was brief and two-way; essentially we sold places on courses to individuals who worked for a wide range of organizations or were members of specific professional groups. Now we foster three-way relationships with the organization (in the form of line and senior managers) as well as the individuals undertaking the learning experience. These relationships are longer, deeper and consequently more friable, and the cost of them not surviving is greater to all parties.

We are a small unit within a traditional university and this puts particular constraints on what we are able to achieve. As more of our programmes are award-bearing (within the UK CAT framework) provision has to be made for the assessment of the outcomes of learning. Successful participants are awarded undergraduate or master's level certificates or diplomas. We are able to offer these awards (proportions of undergraduate degrees and/or proportions of master's) as well as full master's degrees by part-time study. We are not as yet allowed to offer a full undergraduate degree by a part-time route, because of the particular emphasis placed by Cambridge on college residence. Any proposal for a programme of study leading to a board award undergoes the same high level of scrutiny afforded to other new university initiatives.

Given our size, we are allowed to operate with a high level of independence from the university central structure. While this enables us to be responsive to organizational need, it also means that we have to meet all of the attendant costs of our operations; in effect we act like a small private sector business within public sector imperatives. Accreditation and its attend-ant bureaucracy places strain on our ability to deliver. Therefore we work with a limited number of client organizations to craft tailored responses to the CPD needs of their employees, which we establish by undertaking a detailed needs analysis early in each relationship. The organizations tend to be large and well resourced, although we continuously work to foster links with small companies. We place a great deal of emphasis on the necessity for non-formal learning as part of each learning programme and we work with a range of stakeholders from the client organization to negotiate optimal conditions for this, drawn from our experience in this field.

Issues relevant to the context of a traditional university

The CPI operates within a traditional university that is widely acknowledged as a centre of excellence for research and teaching. This reputation affords both an opportunity and a threat for us. We find that we are welcomed at the highest levels within major companies, and we are generally afforded an audience when we seek one; indeed, we are very often sought rather than seeking. The drawback, however, is that we spend an inordinate amount of time demonstrating that, as an institution, we are no more or less flexible than the majority of higher education institutions in the UK; that 'traditional' does not necessarily mean 'hidebound'. This university has a very devolved decision-making mechanism, and can be rapidly responsive when called upon. Our programmes undergo close scrutiny, but decisions are not over-long in coming. Occasionally we find ourselves in the position of Jenny Onyx at UTS (see Chapter 10): everywhere the business culture is one of rapid turn-around, and our pace can appear sedate to the chief executive officer culture. But we can usually contain this by emphasizing the need to ensure 'fitness for purpose' in all that we do; hasty decisions can be regretted later.

At the same time, Cambridge is renowned for the emphasis that it places on the context of learning; the communities of practice and the collabor-ative environments found in the college system are precisely what we are attempting to mirror in our work-based learning programmes. This is fully understood and acknowledged by our scrutineers, making them sympathetic to our models of collaborative learning.

We have arguably more of an issue with the curriculum. The academic paradigm of 'scholarship as discovery' rather than of application means that the way that occupational knowledge is built into the curriculum can be idiosyncratic. Traditional universities such as Cambridge sometimes have problems in adapting to current ideas about what should be the outcome, and how demonstrated, of work-based learning programmes. There is un-doubtedly a dichotomy between the interests of the library-based academic and the knowledge interests of the academic engaged in work-based learning.

Whereas the academic experience is founded on a recognized canon, work-based learning is founded on experience, problem-solving and action-based approaches. Many have suggested that this dichotomy is more of an issue with the 'traditional' rather than the 'new' universities in the UK. At the CPI we have skirted the issue by developing a model which encompasses academic and work-based outcomes, and programmes which marry a formal, residential element with work-based, non-formal implementation of learning.

University senior academics have spoken of their commitment to professional development and to the concepts of lifelong, work-based learning. However, there is a desire to guard the standards and the 'brand name' associated with Cambridge. Therefore, the CPI is required to maintain a close monitoring relationship with programme delivery and to undertake directly on behalf of the university the assessment of learning which results from any work-based learning programme.

Thus we are not permitted to 'validate' the programmes of other providers, where this may mean that assessment is done by others in our name. The remit of the CPI is to assess and recognize the learning of the individual, in direct communication with the learner. Again this can be seen as an opportunity and a threat. We have been privileged to form relationships with a wide range of people taking part in our programmes, and the experience of helping them to identify and benefit from their learning has been professionally very satisfying. But occasionally there has been discord between the needs of the learner and those of the organization; where the learning needs of the individual are more likely to be long-term and developmental, while those of the organization are primarily short-term and business-oriented.

Issues relevant to the organizational context

We believe that the context within which formal and non-formal learning occurs is pivotal to its success. Therefore we spend some time at the early stages of any new client relationship in discussing such things as the organizational systems in operation. The degree to which organizational objectives are known and understood and the extent to which they articulate with learning objectives are significant. We think that the way that work is organized, the speed and manner with which change is handled and the levels of control and accountability within the organization are also crucial to the success of any work-based learning programme.

We are concerned about the level of support offered to learners, encompassing people (supervisors, mentors, workplace 'experts'), time allocated and received, documents available (IT access, manuals, learning contracts and so on) and the level and form of assessment and feedback offered to learners at work. In broad terms, the organizational culture is a matter of interest to us, as is the extent to which its espoused theory is close to the theory-in-use. Do members of an organization do what they say they do? For example, the degree to which people are socialized into the organizational norms, its generative metaphors, its rituals and routines is germane to the optimization of effective work-based learning.

Equally, we seek to understand the extent to which individuals who are registered on our programmes are volunteers or co-optees on to the programmes, and whether the outcome of their learning will influence their career pattern within the organization. We know that this affects the attitudes of learners, and we are concerned that people undertaking a significant learning programme with us are enthusiastic, autonomous learners who will rise to the challenge and feel confident to grasp opportunities that are presented to them. This presupposes that the programme is set in a no-blame environment where mistakes are acknowledged and dealt with appropriately.

Work-based learning in practice: a case study

Although we are quite late in the business of work-based learning we have a number of programmes which employ this approach. As an example, I would like to describe a programme that evolved to meet the particular requirements of a group of already well qualified professionals, who most needed an opportunity to share their existing knowledge as well as remain current within a rapidly changing field.

The CPI was approached by a non-profit making social business that was seeking both to improve the performance and to raise the professional standing of project managers. Their 'front line' role entailed them in negotiation with and mediation between a diverse range of professionals. Although much of the required knowledge and experience was present across the organization, the individual project managers had only their own professional background to draw upon. The pressures of time and geographical distance, as well as the autonomous nature of the work, offered little opportunity for the sharing of expertise across the organization.

Both central, strategic staff and the project managers themselves were keen to increase the diffusion and understanding of widely diverse professional issues within the context of their particular area of operation. They were also concerned that they had not sufficient credibility in the eyes of the people with whom they dealt, and were conscious of the need to improve internal communications and support mechanisms. The nature of the project managers' work made it difficult for them to follow a normal course of study, even one using flexible, distance learning methods.

The organization

The organization is a medium-sized social business that has been in existence for ten years. This business, which is non-profit making, nevertheless employs a business ethos in its operations and has a national presence with regional centres throughout the UK and a central office near Cambridge. Like many medium-sized enterprises, it is in the throes of rapid change and is undergoing reconfiguration by its chief executive officer, to alter the core business of the organization. This is being necessitated by political imperatives that require economies of scale in such organizations. At present the organization offers human resources in a specialist area, but is moving towards becoming a consultancy in its specialist area, that of working with the disadvantaged. The organizational structure is quite flat, with much control and accountability vested in one or two senior managers who make all significant decisions. It might be described as team-focused, with an emphasis on people management rather than knowledge management. These two foci are necessarily counterposed, for there is a case for saying that the first is about systems and learning with the emphasis on people and career management, whereas the second is about organizational competence and the codification of knowledge to benefit the organization.

Senior managers offer a high level of support to employees. They place great emphasis on retaining staff, and see learning as vital for the achievement of business objectives. They allocate time and resources to learning, providing both formal and non-formal learning opportunities. The organization is structured towards vertical support through line management, and teams work cooperatively rather than collaboratively. By this I mean that although project managers work closely and offer a high level of peer support, they have a peripatetic job pattern and take sole responsibility for their projects, working in some isolation from each other. There are formalized appraisal and feedback mechanisms in place.

As is the reality in most companies, we discovered an inevitable division between espoused theory of workplace behaviour and theory in use (Argyris 1994). There are gaps in the extent to which people are effectively socialized into the organizational norms. The organization's geography and the distance that exists between its centre and periphery are factors making communication difficult. Organizational rituals and routines were evident to us; the generative metaphor (Schön 1987) is that of the maverick professional, operating alone on the front line, tough and independent. As a result, the team culture is more assumed than real, making collaborative learning a novel concept.

The learners

We detected a high level of challenge available to learners, not least because of the dynamic air of change surrounding the company. Possibilities for formal and non-formal learning abound, although support structures for this were not necessarily in place before we started to work with the organization.

Among the groups of learners that we have met, confidence levels and their degree of self-awareness vary. Generally speaking, participants come from different educational and professional backgrounds, but are predominantly graduates, young, female and of empathetic personality. Although they are competent professionals, they are fairly insecure learners.

All the learners with whom we have worked so far could be described as having a positive attitude to their job, career and professional development. Although they are not all volunteers on the learning programme, for the majority it is an opportunity of which they want to take full advantage. On the surface, we are working with four groups of sociable, flexible professionals, amenable to our ideas about shared lifelong learning and peer support. As the programme has progressed there have been some tensions around deadlines distance and uncertainties about standards and assessment of learning. But, to date, the programme has experienced no major difficulties with either the curriculum or the outcomes of learning which have been assessed.

The programme

We conducted a 'scoping' exercise over a period of six weeks, comprising regular day-long meetings with reflective periods between, and involving a small team of the organization's strategic and operational staff. The outcome was a proposal for an accredited programme, which was accepted by both the organization and the university. Over the following six months we worked with specialists from the university who formed an Academic Reference Committee, alongside managers and potential participants from the organization, to flesh out the proposal into a one- or two-year accredited work-based, collaborative learning programme. Learning outcomes were specified at two levels, and there were two exit points (i.e. a two-by-two matrix) to take account of the wide range of educational and professional background of participants.

The delivery of the programme was designed to make use of and build on the project managers' monthly regional meetings, which were extended in order to run a series of workshops based on commissioned materials leading to projects produced by several groups. These projects were based on predefined 'problems', each of which included a trigger paper, possible sources of information and issues to be addressed. Although the groups were facilitated by the writer of the trigger paper, their various members were responsible for allocating tasks among themselves, finding and analysing information between meetings and ensuring that the issues contained in the paper were addressed in an appropriate way.

The programme was designed to raise awareness both within the group and among those professionals working closely with them about the socio-political issues that impact on the role of project manager in this context. Locating interaction in the workplace, and extending responsibility for learning to the individual as a group member, reinforced the concepts about experience and judgement, action and illumination that appropriate work-based learning can achieve.

The pilot programme was run with 16 participants, in four groups geographically dispersed throughout the UK. Each group met monthly; alternate workshops were managed by the groups themselves taking responsibility for the discussion and 'tasked' to reach a consensus view on the topic under examination. Each member of the group took responsibility for providing a written response to one of a series of questions embedded in the trigger paper, and one person took charge, on a rotating basis, of managing the process and producing a synthesis report for each assignment. In total each participant undertook five pieces of written work per module/year over the two years that the programme ran.

Successful participants are awarded an undergraduate level 3 certificate or M level certificate following completion of one module of the programme; but it is hoped and intended that they will continue to a second year resulting in an undergraduate level 3 diploma or an M level diploma.

Evaluation of the programme

We are now at the mid-point of this programme and have undertaken an evaluation of what has been achieved so far. The maturing relationship between stakeholders (the learners, the providers and the organization) has given rise to two interesting areas for further investigation:

- the difficulty of finding convergence between the needs of the organization and the individual;
- the inevitable emergence of previously hidden – or poorly understood – aspects of the organizational culture and structure, frequently not recognized by the organization itself.

Considerable change has happened within the organization in the eighteen months of our collaboration. We are essentially dealing with a different set of needs from those that we uncovered at the beginning of our relationship. The socio-political environment within which the business operates, and the impact that this has had on the objectives of the organization, has resonated within the programme. Given that our prime purpose is to match closely need to result, this is a real issue for us. This particular organization has undergone an extreme change, but has caused us to recognize that we need to make some provision for discussion of any issues that might be involved in the early stages of the client relationship.

Equally, we cannot expect that we shall ever fully understand the deep layers of meaning embodied in a complex organization. Despite every effort our scoping study has proved only partially effective at drilling down into what is and was really required by this organization.

Participants on the programme are overwhelmingly positive in their appraisal of the outcomes, in terms of what they have learned and their ability to do their job better as a result. Senior managers are more circumspect in their praise. The result is that the second half of the programme will need to respond to this in a way that could not have been anticipated initially. Given our need to remain within the boundaries of what was agreed by the university 18 months ago, our degree of flexibility is somewhat limited. Negotiations continue.

Unresolved issues in the case study

Our evaluations have also focused on the intended outcomes for both the individual and the organization, and the extent to which these have been achieved. This has led us to ask the following questions.

First, what is work-based learning for? Should the purpose be to enhance organizationally specific skills – a short-term quick fix – or should the focus be long-term individual development? On the one hand the longer-term personal agenda is likely to be closer to the university's conventional interest in the liberal-humanist paradigm; but on the other hand the organization is paying the bill.

Generally universities would categorize their role as educators in the liberal-humanist tradition. They would consider themselves as facilitators of the development of a broad understanding within the individual, enabling a 'reflective, critical life-view'. They would see education as an entitlement and would argue that educational enquiry should be in the cause of the disinterested pursuit of truth. But is this what the government and others intend when they press for 'lifelong learning' for all to become the norm? The reality is that organizations wish to grow or maintain flexibility on the basis of the competencies of their workforce. The development of occupational knowledge, general or specific, remains central to programmes of work-based learning.

Second, who is the client? Is it the individual whose learning is assessed, or is it the organization that pays the bill? This has particular relevance for curriculum specification, but it also has implications for the knock-on effects on people's careers. What happens if they fail the course? Will this inhibit their progress within the company? Questions such as these need to be raised at the negotiation stage, not least so that the senior managers can confront the possibility of failure.

Third, should these programmes carry an award? Assessment and credit carry messages about completion, they have a beginning and an end. How does this sit with the suggestion that we should all be lifelong learners, which by definition suggests that learning is continuous? We hope to foster skills of learning to learn and informal reflective activity in the workplace. The extent to which this can be incorporated into an award-bearing framework is problematic. Yet it is one that is sought by individuals and organizations alike, and so the necessary tension has to be faced and accommodated.

Fourth, how do we manage these complex relationships? All these issues influence the nature of the three-way relationship that this model of work-based learning implies. On the one hand lie potential tensions concerning the desire of organizations to dictate curriculum specification and assessment. Transparency of goals and detailed negotiation is required to ensure that trust and understanding exists on all sides in confronting these matters. Since these negotiations often take place at the early stages of relationships, they require particularly sensitive handling. At the same time these discussions take place against a backdrop of our concern about conditions for learning in the workplace.

Neither the organization nor the university is accustomed to intervention by the other in what each perceives as its territory. Access to information and open negotiation are necessary to ensure that the imperatives for work-based learning are appropriate. The degree to which organizations accept these imperatives varies. The reality of meeting expectations is occasionally hard to achieve for senior managers in both the company and the university. So managing the relationship and keeping it a positive one is perhaps the greatest challenge for all involved.

Conclusions

As we have worked with various organizations we have found a number of ways to conceptualize emerging ideas, none of which completely conveys the complex interplay of the different factors which influence learning in the workplace. Work-related learning cannot be separated from business, structures, people and culture, of which the organization as a socio-technical system consists. Broadly, however, the factors critical to the success of work-related learning would appear to be the need for an organization-wide understanding of the role and value of learning. At the same time, individuals need to have a sense of their own value and how learning can enhance it. These things presuppose that a work-based learning programme is set within an organizational culture that encourages learning and is underpinned by appropriate managerial support and communication.

At the CPI, we are naturally wary of stepping into the swamp of organizational theory, preferring the high, hard ground of well defined programmes. But in working closely with organizations to uncover and respond to the development needs of their employees, we are drawn into that swamp despite ourselves. Our current challenge is to translate our ideas as described here into pragmatic guidelines for improving the effectiveness of both formal and non-formal work-related learning.

Acknowledgements

I would like to thank my colleagues at the CPI who have made comments on drafts of this chapter; they are Elaine Hendry, Christopher Padfield, Stuart Reid and Mark Waltham. However, any opinions, errors or omissions are entirely my own.

References

Araujo, L. (1998) Knowing and learning as networking. *Management Learning*, 29(3): 317–36.

Argyris, C. (1994) *On Organizational Learning*. Oxford: Blackwell.

Botkin, J. W., Elmadjra, M. and Malitza, M. (1979) *No Limits to Learning: Bridging the Human Gap. A Report to the Club of Rome*. Oxford: Pergamon Press.

Boud, D. and Feletti, G. (1997) *The Challenge of Problem Based Learning*. London: Kogan Page

Department for Education and Employment (1998) *The Learning Age: A Renaissance for a New Britain*. London: Stationery Office.

Eraut, M. (1998) Non-formal learning, implicit learning and tacit knowledge in professional work, Unpublished paper.

Eraut, M., Alderton, J., Cole, G. and Senker, P. (1998) *Development of Knowledge and Skills in Employment*. Brighton: University of Sussex Institute of Education.

Gherardi, S., Nicolini, D. and Odella, F. (1998) Towards a social understanding of how people learn in organisations. *Management Learning*, 29(3): 273–97.

Lester, S. (1995) Beyond knowledge and competence. *Capability*, 1(3): 56–67.

Schön, D. A. (1987) *Educating the Reflective Practitioner*. London: Jossey-Bass.

Senge, P. M. (1992) *The 5th Discipline: The Art and Practice of the Learning Organization*. New York: Doubleday.

Sternberg, R. J. and Kolligian, J. (1990) *Competence Considered*. New Haven, CT: Yale University Press.

10

Implementing Work-based Learning for the First Time

Jenny Onyx

This chapter offers a reflection on the experience of establishing a work-based learning programme in the Faculty of Business at the University of Technology, Sydney (UTS). In terms of the conceptual structure developed by Barnett (1994), the introduction of work-based learning (WBL) has created a dramatic juxtaposition of two rival versions of competence: the operational competence of the workplace, and the academic competence of disciplinary knowledge. The resulting contest has created a dialogue in which the nature, ownership and development of knowledge are re-examined.

As the first programme in work-based learning in Australia, it is breaking ground both within the university and more broadly, within the context of Australian universities. In the process of implementation the Faculty of Business has had to engage with the demands of a high-profile commercial client as well as its own academic standards and the rigidities of its bureaucratic processes. It can be argued that there was no necessary contradiction in the introduction of work-based learning within the Faculty of Business, or within UTS as a whole. Indeed, in many ways, work-based learning is an extension of an existing commitment to the delivery of flexible, practical learning. None the less, the introduction of work-based learning created a number of significant tensions that are still in process of resolution.

As Head of the School of Management, Chair of the Faculty WBL Programme Committee and member of the university WBL Board of Studies, I was well positioned to experience many of the issues discussed below. However, those positioned differently will necessarily have a different perspective on events. For another view of work-based learning at UTS, it is useful to consult Chapter 11 in this volume. While others within the faculty have offered comments and suggestions, this chapter does not represent an official statement and the views expressed are those of the author.

The first part of the chapter reviews some of the precursors to work-based learning within the faculty. The second part provides an account of some of the key events involved in the implementation of work-based learning. The third part then explores some of the tensions involved in this process.

These are discussed in the hope that the lessons learned may prove useful to others embarking on a similar path.

Precursors within the faculty

The University of Technology, Sydney provides a setting that is conducive for work-based learning. The university holds a general commitment to professional and work practice as an integral aspect of the learning environment in all its faculties. The Faculty of Business, in particular, has long had a large part-time student cohort, with the majority of students, particularly at the postgraduate level, studying while maintaining full-time employment. For these students, practical relevance of course material has always been a prime consideration. The majority of subjects include as assessment items an applied project or case study application of content material. In addition, several small courses have been designed specifically to engage the workplace. These include the bachelor of accounting, manufacturing management and community management programmes.

The community management programme encompasses undergraduate and postgraduate courses, the first of which was the diploma in community organizations, established in 1987. Both postgraduate and undergraduate courses rest on the fundamental principle of bringing theory and practice together. An analysis of the original programme noted:

> A problem-centred approach brings theory and practice together. The organizational context in which the learner works generates real problems. In grappling with those problems, the learner searches for information. She seeks to develop personal skills or practical competencies that will help her deal with the problem. But the problem must also be theorized. It must be analyzed and identified, and related to a wider class of similar problems. The learner draws on a range of resources to do this: peer discussion, facilitator guidance, objective knowledge sources in the form of readings and expert resource people, in order to develop a broader theoretical understanding and to develop insights into the likely causes and effects of the problem in question. Those theoretical insights are brought to bear on the generation of practical strategies or solutions to the problem at hand. The learner then applies and extends this knowledge through the unit assignment. In that assignment the learner addresses a practical problem within the organization, analyses it and develops practical solutions for implementation.
> (Onyx 1992: 104)

While the community management programme depends on the existing employment of students, the manufacturing management programme did not. This was a highly innovative undergraduate programme (now defunct) for full-time students, the majority of whom had no industry sponsor. The curriculum was explicitly interdisciplinary in nature, again with a strong emphasis on problem-oriented learning:

> Innovative concepts of curriculum design using experiential learning theory, 'hands-on' training in workshop technologies, a simulated factory environment for teaching CIM cell and FMS technology, self-directed computer-based learning techniques for guiding students' industry training periods, and matrix teaching structures for linking streamed theoretical subjects with practical case study material, place the degree at the leading edge of cooperative education design.
>
> (Sheather *et al.* 1993: 5)

In this case, student learning was integrated and applied through two formally constructed industry placement projects in which students were required to research, analyse and resolve actual industry problems under the joint supervision of academics and industry supervisors. The resulting projects were made public and had to reach the required criteria of relevance and academic rigour. The programme operated with the financial support of the Foundation of Australian Manufacturing Enterprise (FAME) and the cooperation of individual companies. However, the 'contract' essentially remained between the university and the individual student.

The initiation of work-based learning in the faculty signalled a significant shift in the basis of learning. For the first time, the employer was an explicit partner in the learning contract with the employee/student and the university. The employer, as partner, was to co-determine the design, supervision and outcome, and bear the financial cost of the programme. The launch into this new terrain required considerable courage, skill and resources on the part of both the faculty and the industry partner.

Key events in the implementation of work-based learning

The implementation of work-based learning occurred in stages, through a number of key events within the partner or client organization, within the university, within the Faculty of Business (and other faculties) and between the client organization and the faculty. Apart from the faculties, a key UTS player was the commercial arm of UTS, the Insearch Institute of Commerce (IIC). IIC is incorporated as a separate, though wholly owned entity of UTS. As part of its brief, IIC provides vocationally accredited courses, generally with direct articulation for successful candidates, into mainstream UTS courses.

The impetus to the initiation of work-based learning came in 1996 with an approach by a large Australian commercial organization (henceforth referred to as Company Z) first to IIC and later to the Dean of the Faculty of Business. The project began formally with a UTS statement of understanding that was lodged with Company Z in October 1996. At this point, Company Z began to badge its internal core and business leadership programmes as a Company Z/IIC/UTS partnership. There was a joint selection of UTS and external training partners. The issues under discussion at the time included: whether UTS/IIC was a sole supplier or not; the role of IIC/UTS in the management of educational quality and accreditation; levels of participation of Company Z staff; remuneration for course providers; and copyright.

Most of 1997 involved detailed 'behind the scenes' negotiations between the client, IIC, various faculties and the central administration of UTS. The university established a taskforce to oversee the initial development of work-based learning. Derek Portwood of Middlesex University was invited to visit in May 1997, and provided workshops and individual advice to senior executives of Company Z and those responsible in UTS. Portwood identified five key objectives for UTS in relation to work-based learning:

1. To establish UTS as the national leader of work-based learning partnerships in Australia.
2. To develop and implement institutional systems, procedures and practices which enable work-based learning partnership initiatives at UTS.
3. To initiate and test work based learning partnership developments through a leading agency comprising the Faculties of Business and Mathematical and Computing Science in collaboration with IIC.
4. To develop and quality test curricular frameworks, subject modules and learning instruments through pilot developments by the leading agency, especially with Company Z.
5. To engage in appropriate staff development, building teams and individual expertise in work-based learning at UTS.

In the meantime a small working group of three was formed to conduct much of the detailed negotiation with the client, while developing a set of procedural protocols. They were assisted in this process by further consultation with Portwood and his colleagues at Middlesex University. Much of this development work was 'commercial, in confidence' and therefore not available to the wider university community.

As the detailed negotiations with the client continued, the university set in place a set of formal structures and protocols for dealing with work-based learning courses. In recognition of the differences in learning and in the partnership relationships that would be demanded for the new awards a separate Board of Studies covering work-based learning was established by the Academic Board with a university-wide accreditation and quality assurance role. The inaugural meeting of that board was held in October 1997. The Board of Studies held a formal role within university governance structure. In addition, an *ad hoc* working group of senior managers was formed from a variety of faculties, with resources, to guide the development of work-based learning as a strategic initiative of the university.

The Faculty of Business also established a work-based learning Programmes Committee whose inaugural meeting was held in October 1997. The terms of reference for the committee included:

- advising Faculty Board in Business on all matters pertaining to the offering of award courses in which a significant proportion of learning occurs in the workplace;
- developing and recommending to Faculty Board an accreditation framework that recognizes various forms of learning which occur in organizations external to the Faculty of Business;
- considering proposals for the introduction of new courses and major changes to existing courses which result from work based learning partnerships with organizations external to the faculty;
- approving individual portfolios and proposals and approving every negotiated learning contract;
- approving recognition of learning on behalf of individual clients.

There were thus set in place a number of structures within the faculty and the university, with overlapping roles in the development process. The inevitable confusions and tensions resulting are discussed later in the chapter.

Some confusion was evident in the accreditation of the initial course accreditation proposal for work-based learning. This had been developed by the faculty coordinator in preparation for the subsequent signing of a memorandum of understanding with Company Z. The draft course accreditation proposal was first considered by the newly formed university-level Board of Studies for work-based learning. While making detailed comment, the Board of Studies required that the proposal be amended and returned for consideration by the Faculty Board of Business. The faculty board required a recommendation from the newly formed faculty-based work-based learning Programmes Committee. In fact the course accreditation proposal for work-based learning was finally approved for a one-year pilot. This approval from Academic Board, on recommendation of the Board of Studies, occurred in November 1997 after several rounds of meetings involving the work-based learning Working Group, Faculty of Business work-based learning Programmes Committee, Faculty Board and the University Board of Studies. Although the inter-faculty working group prepared a generic manual for the establishment and implementation of work-based learning for all partnerships, the Board of Studies never approved the manual. Each individual course accreditation proposal was required to stand alone in terms of justification of process and structure.

Following the approval of the course accreditation proposal, the university and Company Z signed a memorandum of understanding in February 1998, thus officially launching the new programme.

The pilot proposal

According to the proposal, Company Z employees are able to obtain a university qualification that comprises up to four key components. The mix of learning is summarized in Figure 10.1.

Figure 10.1 Work-based learning award structure

Proposal and portfolio (compulsory)		
Recognized learning	Formal subjects	Advanced performance improvement activity (APIA)

The participant may seek a sub-degree award through IIC, or a postgraduate degree through the Faculty of Business. The Graduate Certificate in Business (work-based learning), Graduate Diploma in Business (work-based learning) and Master of Business (work-based learning) all follow the above pattern. In each case the proposal and portfolio is awarded nine credit points of study out of 24 credit points (certificate), 48 credit points (diploma) or 72 credit points (master). The proposal and portfolio provides the compulsory core of the programme, and is completed before the employee is formally enrolled as a student in the substantive course for which they were seeking entry. At this stage employees negotiate their learning goals with their workplace manager and an academic adviser from UTS. The proposal sets out individuals' learning programmes, specifying the activities they wish to undertake to complete the award. The associated portfolio enables employees to demonstrate, through past formal study and experiential learning, their current capability in relation to their learning objectives and level of award sought. Each proposal and portfolio is independently assessed before the total learning package is approved and the student is officially enrolled in one of the above courses.

Recognized learning (similar to recognition of prior learning (RPL), but linked specifically to current usage of that prior learning) refers to those relevant activities and awards that have been previously achieved by the participant, and are recognized and accredited by UTS. They may include university-level subjects previously completed, formal in-house training programmes that have been assessed and approved by UTS and other evidenced capabilities of the participant. The recognized learning may comprise up to 12 credit points for the graduate certificate, up to 30 credit points for the graduate diploma and up to 48 credit points for the masters.

Additional work may take the form of existing formal subjects, usually at UTS, as determined by the individual proposal. It may also be in the form of Advanced Performance Improvement Activities (APIAs). These APIAs are work-based projects that have been negotiated with the work supervisor as part of the performance contract. They are specific business or information technology learning activities that have measurable outcomes for the participant's employer, as evaluated both by UTS (academic standards) and their company manager (performance management). Such APIAs may attract anything from three to 48 credit points, depending on the scope of the activity and the award level.

Implementation of the pilot

Following the signing of the memorandum of understanding with the client, the initial working group established the first, pilot intake of employees. Initially, 11 participants put themselves forward for the first proposal and portfolio workshops. A second cohort of similar size followed. They included participants who were targeting sub-degree and postgraduate business qualifications. However, progress for the early cohorts was slow; at the conclusion of 1998, only one participant had completed the initial proposal and portfolio. Early in 1999, a further cohort of 20 participants commenced. In addition, a second large organization (Company Y) has negotiated a similar memorandum of understanding with UTS, and the faculty has approved accreditation of one of the organization's in-house professional development programmes. At the time of writing, there is every indication that work-based learning will become an ongoing arm of the faculty's accredited academic programme.

Impediment issues

While the above account presents a fairly sterilized description of the facts as may be recorded (for example, on committee minutes), there are hints, even in those accounts, of several highly contested issues, none of which has yet been fully resolved. It is worth reflecting on some of those issues – which are discussed below – as they have been played out within the implementation process. They may suggest lessons for the future redesign of the work-based learning implementation and accreditation process.

Contested control between work-based learning partners

The first issue concerns consultation and controls of the process, and ultimately of work-based learning itself. The publicity surrounding the implementation specifically used the discourse of partnership involving a triumvirate of interests: the employer as corporate client, the university as service provider and the employee as student. Thus, for instance, a media release stated:

> A major agreement which redefines the way academic and business communities work together in education and employee development will be signed today between the University of Technology, Sydney (UTS) and [Company Z]. The three-year agreement . . . is a dynamic new alternative to traditional forms of learning offered in Australia. The partnership will also revolutionize employee development and best practice performance management . . . an essential feature of the scheme was

that each participant's program was determined on a case-by-case basis through negotiation between UTS, [Company Z] and the employee.

(UTS 1998)

Inevitably there were occasions when the interests of each partner were perceived to be compromised by the other. At that point, the relative priorities of each are drawn in sharp contrast, with pressure on each to conform. Some of this has been played out in terms of the various time frames involved. The client was, in its terms, purchasing a service, and wished to ensure a guaranteed delivery date. As early as April 1997, 'response time' was identified as an issue for Company Z. Those Faculty of Business members of the working group who were negotiating directly with the client experienced considerable pressure from the client for a rapid turnaround. For instance, the client expected a quick approval from UTS for the course accreditation document. It was unsympathetic to the university requirements of an extensive approval process which went from Board of Studies back to work-based learning Programmes Committee, then to Faculty Board, back to Board of Studies and finally to Academic Board. What should in the client's eyes have taken two or three weeks in fact took approximately two months (and that was fast-tracked compared to conventional course approvals). The pressure on the working group created considerable frustration and stress on individual academics, sometimes expressed in strong statements referring to the legal contract and contractual obligations to the client. Such statements, while perhaps understandable within a market discourse, generated anxiety and friction in an academic environment where freedom and autonomy are highly prized. From a university perspective, and given the collegiate process of review, it was essential that approvals be carefully considered and involve the academic community, in part to ensure adequate quality assurance control.

Contested control within UTS

Another issue of control concerned internal processes. IIC, as the commercial arm of UTS, does not have a government operating grant, and is required to generate a profit, much of which is returned to UTS. Among other things, this means that IIC staff feel the market imperative much more keenly than is the case for UTS academics. Again, the slowness of the process of implementation generated considerable tension.

UTS itself is not a uniform corporate entity. The Faculty of Business saw itself as a prime mover in the development of work-based learning, in partnership with the much smaller Faculty of Mathematical and Computer Sciences, who were none the less equal partners in the inter-faculty working group. Staff from the latter faculty expressed some frustration in dealing with the Faculty of Business. The Faculty of Business itself was dependent on the expertise and assistance of other units and faculties, notably the Centre for Learning and Teaching and the then School of Adult Education for specific expertise in developing the proposal and portfolio and overseeing staff development. While this input was useful, some academics within business felt that these pedagogical experts did not understand the language or needs of industry. Other faculties, notably engineering, proffered their own work-based learning initiatives, using quite different models, but maintaining their prerogative to create work-based learning awards designed to meet their own needs.

Meanwhile, Company Z and other potential clients urged UTS to present a single unified corporate profile. In an attempt to generate such an image, while creating overall corporate control of work-based learning, the central administration created several core bodies, each with some authority in relation to work-based learning, but with little overlapping membership. In fact, by mid-1998, it was clear that decisions about work-based learning were being made at six or seven different points within UTS. Communication between relevant staff of these bodies was not always effective. Even within the Faculty of Business, decisions relating to pricing and costing were being made separately from the work-based learning Programmes Committee even though the costings directly impinged on pedagogical issues (e.g. how many hours of individual academic advising were possible?). At the central level, two members of the vice chancellor's working group, neither of whom were on the work-based learning Board of Studies, constructed generic 'quality assurance guidelines' for award course approval and accreditation for work-based learning. However, these failed to recognize the unique requirements of work-based learning course implementation. There appeared to be little consultation between the members of the faculty working group (who were designing a generic process), the members of the Vice Chancellor's working party (who designed the quality assurance guidelines) or the work-based learning Board of Studies (who were meant to use the guidelines in approving the Faculty proposals). The Vice Chancellor had made available strategic initiative funds for the development of work-based learning. However, no one appeared to know where those funds were located, or how they could be accessed. In the meantime, much of the developmental work of the Faculty of Business was continuing on a self-funded basis in anticipation that development funds from the client would be forthcoming.

In an attempt to clarify some of these issues, the chair of the Faculty of Business work-based learning Programmes Committee sought answers from the UTS working group to a series of questions concerning work-based learning. One question was 'what is the role of the working group in overseeing project management of work-based learning programmes?' In response, the working group noted:

> It was agreed that individual faculties have the responsibility for project management of work-based learning. The working Group has a strategic role for the development of work-based learning at UTS, and can provide advice to faculties on a range of issues.
>
> (Author's notes of meeting held on 11 June 1998)

A challenge to learning

Another major issue concerns the nature of learning itself. Kolb (1984: 38) defines learning as 'the process whereby knowledge is created through the transformation of experience'. While experience is an essential component of learning, it is not the experience itself that is crucial, but the transformation of that experience by the learners' reflection of the experience within a socio-cultural context (Kolb 1984; Miller and Boud 1996). Within the initial development of the proposal and portfolio, there is considerable emphasis given to the 'enabling objective' designed to assist the applicant to develop skills of self-reflection in the process of compiling their own learning agenda. However, the emphasis on this enabling objective has itself generated considerable debate within the faculty and across the university. There is a continuing move within the faculty to downgrade the importance of developing 'learning how to learn' skills. Some participants have been left largely to their own devices in identifying and articulating their learning needs and current capabilities, with little support from the workplace supervisor, and little prior experience in self-directed learning. The time and amount of learning required for an employee/learner to develop an adequate proposal and portfolio have been seriously underestimated.

While this issue is implicit in much of the contested decision-making, it is perhaps most explicitly played out in the formal recognition of courses external to the university. As part of the proposal and portfolio process, participants seek recognition of current capabilities. This recognition may include learning achieved through standard employer in-house training courses. It is in the client employer's interest to negotiate recognition of some of these training courses up-front. This requires the university to assess the value of the learning achieved in these training courses, the evidence of such learning and the equivalent university credit points that will be accredited on the basis of this evidence. A recent example of this assessment/accreditation of client training packages involved Company Y. This client sought accreditation of existing personal development training to the value of the equivalent of a graduate diploma.

In an attempt to grapple with this issue, the Faculty of Business work-based learning Programmes Committee developed a simplified model of the intended outcomes of learning, in terms of three main components:

1. Content learning.
2. Embedded in practice application of knowledge.
3. Critical reflection/theoretical understanding.

In general, universities have privileged the third outcome, while the workplace emphasizes the second. Both are probably equally concerned with the first, though again, this knowledge is evidenced differently by the employer and the university. In moving to work-based learning partnerships, the university is acknowledging the validity of knowledge embedded in practice. What remains to be seen is whether the employer is prepared to acknowledge the validity of and importance of critical reflection, or whether the pressure will be to remove such considerations. As noted by Garrick and Kirkpatrick (1998: 177) 'Universities are faced with new challenges as they attempt to develop workplace-based courses that retain a critical dimension'. They argue that the presumption that industry needs and demands override educational goals is embedded in the discourse of workplace-based learning. Certainly the discourse of outcome-focused competency-based learning appears to emphasize competency at the expense of critical reflection. Equally, it is true that no in-house training thus far assessed has a strong theoretical or reflective component. The suggestion is clear that, to some extent at least, the employer is looking for short-term productivity gains. Equally clear is that if we simply accept the role of credentialling existing competency-based training, then the university is not adding value to work-based learning (Barnett 1994). Any short-term advantage in terms of credentialling will rapidly diminish in the credibility stakes.

In the particular case cited above, Company Y sought recognition and accreditation for a set of six in-house modules. After detailed assessment of the modules by two committee members, the work-based learning Programmes Committee recommended approval of the modules. However, the committee determined that in order to achieve the relevant level of credit, written evidence of some critical reflection was required. In doing so the committee arrived at a 'bottom line' establishing three criteria in relation to critical/theoretical learning:

1. Some part of the assessment must be written (not necessarily the major part).
2. Participants must be required to engage with the literature on which the module is based (i.e. evidence of readings and the application of those readings to practice).
3. Participants must be able to reflect critically on their own learning (evidence of critical thinking in relationship to the readings, the theoretical frameworks presented and analysis of the applicability of these frameworks.

The client was given the option of either taking responsibility for the inclusion of such a framework within the existing modules, together with various quality assurance mechanisms, or allowing the additional assessment within the framework of the proposal and portfolio, in which case responsibility would rest with the UTS advisers. In the event, the client accepted the additional requirements in principle, and chose to take responsibility for the additional assessment. In effect, it agreed to upgrade the training programme to meet essential minimum university standards. This decision probably augurs well for future negotiations.

Cost

The fourth issue deals with matters of cost. Cost is a concern in itself. However, it is also one which impinges on issues of control and of pedagogy.

The initial enthusiasm for work-based learning was driven, at least partly, by the need to generate new revenue streams for the university, and a more effective use of human resource development costs for the employer. The Faculty of Business receives approximately one-third of its revenue from full-fee paying students, and with reduced government operating grants, there is a strong imperative to identify alternative revenue streams. For work-based learning, the imperative is to provide a service that is attractive to the client while none the less providing new revenue streams for the faculty. While some of the early publicity flagged the work-based learning awards as cheaper than conventional degrees (because so much is done in the workplace), it has now become clear that the university-delivered components of work-based learning are labour-intensive and expensive.

There are several components of the higher cost, including the element imposed by the central administration of the university, the additional administrative infrastructure required within the faculty and the individualized supervision of the proposal and portfolio and APIAs. There are also the considerable, but largely invisible, costs of staff development.

The Faculty of Business has grappled with a cost structure that is reasonably attractive to the employer, but provides break-even for the faculty. To achieve this, the faculty has had to impose a minimum cohort size of ten, and more standardized (less customized) activities for the achievement of the proposal and portfolio subject. A maximum number of three hours of individual consultation can be given to each participant (above the 12 hours group seminar) in the preparation of their proposal and portfolio. Similar limits on individual academic supervision will apply to the individual APIAs. While such limits will ensure greater financial viability for the faculty, they also shift some of the real costs of learning back to the workplace. The roles of the workplace supervisor and those of the student will become more central. Thus far, the work supervisor has received little or no training for the role. While the academic supervisor remains responsible for academic outcomes, most of the actual supervision of the process rests with the work supervisor. There will be little opportunity for continued academic guidance in that process. While this reorientation of learning process may provide equally high quality learning outcomes, it is not at all clear that this will necessarily follow.

Other administration matters ultimately impact on cost. Chief among these are the mechanisms designed to track the academic progress of each participant's unique programme, and to achieve rapid response times, particularly the approval mechanism for proposed client in-house training courses. New mechanisms may be required to allow a single point of contact within the university for all new work-based learning contracts, particularly where several faculties are involved. On the other hand inappropriate people negotiating industry contracts on behalf of other faculties will not help the situation.

The role of the academic

Perhaps the most fundamental issue concerns the role of the academic. Within the pilot programme, academics are being asked to play several roles. For the new intake of participants, they take the roles of adviser and learning facilitator. Working with individuals and small groups, the adviser guides the way through the process of developing the proposal and portfolio. To some extent this is an administrative task, although it requires academic judgement in terms of what counts as achievement at each academic level. It was also the intent of the design that the adviser takes participants through the preparatory 'enabling objective'. This was designed to enhance the participant's capacity to become an autonomous, independent learner. In practice, this task has been carried out partly by specialist academics with adult education background.

The other major role that academics take in the initial process is that of assessor. Each proposal and portfolio must be assessed for coherence and appropriate level of award sought. Apart from the individual assessment of each proposal, various in-house and external training programmes need to be assessed for potential accreditation by the university.

Finally, in the case of each APIA, academics will have a role as supervisor in guiding the student through the work-based project. However, in this, they share the task of supervision with the workplace supervisor, who will necessarily carry the bulk of the carriage of the project design, supervision and initial assessment.

In all this, the academics have lost much of their traditional role. The academic input is important, but at several steps removed from the actual learning process. The curriculum is ultimately located within the workplace, and is individually renegotiated with each participant. Actual teaching is seldom required. It is replaced by two important but somewhat problematic new roles: that of the assessor (with pressures to accredit the client's courses) and that of manager of the learning process. As assessor, the academic is required to evaluate learning in the workplace and determine its academic merit and worth on its own terms. As manager of the participants' learning, it is their responsibility to establish the necessary conditions for learning. Levy (1995) identifies that good practice in work-based learning includes structuring of learning opportunities in the workplace, providing appropriate on-the-job learning opportunities, and identifying and providing relevant off-the-job learning opportunities. The role of academic manager is about identifying, structuring, providing opportunities, assessing, but not teaching or lecturing.

It is perhaps understandable that the introduction of work-based learning has generated considerable resistance by many academics within the Faculty of Business. Their new roles in work-based learning are unclear. The loss of traditional academic authority may be seen as a threat to professional standards. The discourse of the market place may be offensive to the academic values of autonomy and collegiate decision-making. There are additional, more practical reasons for resisting the new development: academics with already overloaded schedules have little time to contemplate the new demands, particularly when no time allowance or funds are available for the required additional staff development training. On the face of it there are inadequate rewards, recompense, recognition or support for the radical reorientation of roles being demanded. However, not to embrace the new work-based learning roles is to risk yielding this work, and future core business of the university, to outside, commercially based interests.

Conclusions

This account of the implementation of work-based learning within the Faculty of Business at UTS has highlighted the complexities that have surrounded the introduction of this innovation. It has been suggested that the various stakeholders involved in work-based learning have different interests and conceptual frameworks. The result is necessarily a set of highly contested issues which has meant that implementation of work based learning has been complex and, at times, messy.

The successful implementation of work-based learning requires considerable skill and courage on the part of all involved within the partnership organizations and within the university. The lessons that can be learnt from our experience suggest that we have not recognized the importance of adequate staff development of both university academics and workplace supervisors. We need joint briefing sessions that describe the multiple roles that are involved in work-based supervision. We also need better mechanisms within the university to ensure transparency of process, and better collaboration between administration units and faculties. We need to find more effective ways of helping student participants to move to a self-reflective, critical, self-directed learning paradigm.

However, work-based learning is an important development in higher education. If the university 'gets it right', then we will have advanced the understanding of learning and the role of the university within the modern economic context. If the university 'gets it wrong' then the university risks being marginalized as an educational leader of society. The willingness to engage with the issues and to work through them with industry partners is a good sign that this will not happen. The faculty is prepared to embrace change and the new opportunities that these bring. At the same time, it must stress the need for thoughtful and principled reflection, both within the university and in the partnership organizations.

Acknowledgements

In writing this chapter I have benefited from the useful comments and advice of Bob Robertson, Peter Booth, Nicholas Shipley, Guy Callender, John Garrick, Nicky Solomon and David Boud.

References

Barnett, R. (1994) *The Limits of Competence: Knowledge, Higher Education and Society.* Buckingham: SRHE/Open University Press.

Garrick, J. and Kirkpatrick, D. (1998) Workplace-based learning degrees: a new business venture, or a new critical business? *Higher Education Research and Development,* 17(2): 171–82.

Kolb, D. (1984) *Experiential Learning: Experience as the Source of Learning and Development.* Englewood Cliffs, NJ: Prentice Hall.

Levy, M. (1995) Work-based learning and outcomes, in J. Burke (ed.) *Outcomes, Learning and the Curriculum: Implications for NVQs, GNVQs and Other Qualifications.* London: Falmer Press.

Miller, N. and Boud, D. (1996) Animating learning from experience, in D. Boud and N. Miller (eds) *Working with Experience.* London: Routledge.

Onyx, J. (1992) Designing a course for adult learners: a question of access, in *Quality of Teaching Matters at UTS.* Sydney: Centre for Learning and Teaching, UTS.

Sheather, G., Martin, R. and Harris, D. (1993) Partners in excellence: a new model for cooperative education. *Educational and Training Technology International,* 30(1): 5–31.

UTS (1998) Media release, University of Technology, Sydney, 12 February.

11

Smart Work: What Industry Needs from Partnerships

Nicholas Shipley

Of central importance to the emergence of work-based approaches to learning is an understanding of the issues driving organizational learning agendas that aim to overcome the perceived shortcomings of traditional, 'university-based' approaches. This chapter identifies some of the gaps that new, work-based partnerships between industry and tertiary institutions attempt to overcome. More importantly it identifies some of the changing demands that informed organizations are placing on their involvements with tertiary institutions. It considers the challenges for human resources management in making learning strategic within their organizations.

Among other matters, this chapter considers the context in which work-based learning has emerged at the University of Technology, Sydney. It then considers the performance drivers that may motivate organizations to engage in a work-based learning partnership. Finally, it explores issues that arise for human resources management in attempting to unify organizational and individual development through the management of performance, learning and knowledge. In relation to this, some of the 'desirables' and 'undesirables' that may shape the approach to a learning partnership and its methodology are identified.

The following pages are derived from the experiences I have had in designing, developing and implementing collaborative educational programmes with a variety of large Australian organizations. These experiences are presented anecdotally, and have unfolded through a series of involvements in education as general manager of a private commercial college and most recently as the Manager of Work-based Learning Programmes for Insearch and the Faculty of Business at the University of Technology, Sydney (UTS).

The genesis of work-based learning at UTS

The publication of the Karpin Report (ITFLMS 1995) on management education stimulated a significant review of the ways in which providers of educational services might more adequately satisfy the needs of Australian business. A number of concerns were identified, including the need for tertiary institutions to close the divide between their courses and the requirements of industry. This meant producing more relevant learning.

Of the many possible conclusions one might have drawn from Karpin's recommendations, one may have correctly surmised that a significant latent demand existed for the provision of more appropriate and workplace-relevant management education. This conclusion presented an irresistible challenge to educators in a search for positional advantage in an increasingly competitive market place.

During 1996, the Programme in Applied Business was established in partnerships between Insearch Institute of Commerce (UTS's commercial provider of vocational qualifications) and a number of leading organizations. This initial programme opened broader dialogue with organizational decision-makers that highlighted more clearly the nature of organizational learning agendas.

The Programme in Applied Business features an accredited curriculum and incorporates a process of negotiation that involves liaison between the institute's instructors, workplace mentors and company-sponsored participants. This tripartite relationship enables learners to negotiate, under the supervision of their employer, a relevant and work-based pathway that demonstrates learning outcomes prescribed in the course curriculum.

While the approach offered by the Programme in Applied Business was appropriate to some organizations, it became increasingly evident that other partnership approaches were needed. Significantly, partner organizations favoured relationships with tertiary institutions that offered them the opportunity to 'own' the curriculum, and provided an articulated framework of vocational and higher education qualifications. These two requirements highlighted the limitations within the Programme in Applied Business.

But the need for new partnership approaches was also underscored by a number of other factors. Among these was ensuring a meaningful and demonstrable intersection between the individual course participant's job, their learning and the goals of the organization.

The issue of organizational 'ownership' of the curriculum, perceived instrumentality and employer control of learning presented a wide range of issues and challenges to determining an appropriate response to partnership opportunities from UTS. Towards the end of 1996 an exploratory relationship was established between one of Australia's largest corporations and UTS with the aim of clarifying the scope of ongoing collaboration. The work undertaken led to the formalization of a work-based learning partnership with the company early in 1998. This partnership has been critical in shaping the university's understanding of organizational learning agendas and in developing and implementing its response.

Avoiding the curriculum tail wagging the organizational dog

Early discussions with managers in the organizational development unit of the company highlighted some of the tensions that existed in the minds of key players in the organization, in adopting a university curriculum as a basis for developing their own organizational learning and capability. For the university's partner, the primary benefit of establishing a partnership with a tertiary institution was achieving improvement to organizational performance, not simply satisfying the university's course assessment criteria and issuing credentials to employees. It was made clear that the intent of the partnership was to focus on enhancing organizational capability through individual learning, and that it must not be driven by the demands of an externally set curriculum and the attainment of qualifications. Strategy and business plans, job specifications, performance agreements and organizational capability frameworks would provide the basis of an individual learner's curriculum and ensure that the 'tail' (being the university curriculum) would not 'wag the dog' (the development of organizational capability through individual learning).

Addressing these issues required a shift in the university's perspective away from the achievement of predetermined course aims as the focal point of learning. Instead, its role became one of assisting participants in identifying, developing and recognizing individual learning in the context of their current jobs and future professional development. It is this overarching requirement that sets the stage for identifying and clarifying the dimensions and indicators of a successful work-based learning partnership. It provides a basis upon which to identify the key drivers and motivations for potential partners of the university, the desirables and undesirables and tension points that help understanding of why an organization may wish to engage with a work-based approach to learning.

Competitive advantage through learning

One assumption that should be made explicit in relation to the relevance of learning to the capability of an organization is that corporate strategies generally seek to optimize sustainable competitive advantage in the markets. Markets, of course, are dynamic and require organizations constantly to re-evaluate their competitive position, strengths and weaknesses, and the capabilities that are required to succeed.

The players in any market may seek to gain advantage from a number of competitive bases (Aaker 1992). For example, advantage may be sought through product differentiation, cost or pricing leadership, quality, innovation, customer service or a variety of other means. The bases on which an organization chooses to compete will determine the capabilities critical in informing its success. For example, a strategy emphasizing leadership in product development would suggest the need to develop the organization's ability to encourage and stimulate innovation. An alternative strategy may aim to achieve sustainable advantage through competitive pricing. Achieving such positioning may require an organization to focus its attention on harnessing technology and production methods that will continually keep production costs lower than its competitors', and enable it to offer its products at a lower market price.

Whatever the selected competitive base, we can accept that survival and the achievement of sustainable market advantage are among the primary goals of most organizations. Achieving this goal requires organizations to be more capable in certain critical areas than their competitors. This establishes a need for an inexorable link established between an organization's performance, capabilities and the contribution of individual's learning and development.

The notion that the learning of individuals has an impact on organizational performance is becoming more broadly accepted (Stevenson 1999). In order for an organization to be the 'provider of choice' and to achieve premier positioning in the minds of buyers, it also needs to be the 'employer of choice'. That means its employment practices must serve to attract, retain and develop the best talent.

A key challenge for organizations is therefore to forge a symbiotic relationship between the goals of competitive advantage and optimizing capability. Developing a framework for the acquisition and development of new talent and motivating existing employees to learn, develop and contribute to organizations' goals through their learning is of paramount importance.

Organizational performance and individual learning

Achievement of organizational goals and competitive advantage provides a plausible enough argument for employers to consider encouraging and sponsoring work-based learning in the workplace. What motivations exist for the employee and how can employers induce staff to participate in such learning?

It does not, of course, naturally follow that a strategy decision made in the boardroom will automatically stimulate employees to engage proactively in performance-enhancing learning. To varying degrees (which will be influenced significantly by organizational culture), employees' engagement in organizationally oriented learning and development will be determined by the incentives and rewards associated with improving their performance.

Clearly, if the link between organizational performance, capability and individual learning is accepted, the challenge for management is to create an environment in which employees engage willingly in performance-focused learning. Attention needs to be paid to creating systems and incentives that encourage learning and ensure that it is translated into performance improvement at the level of individual job responsibility. This in turn provides organizations with the incentive to invest in staff development.

A performance management process that systematically cascades and links organizational goals to individual job responsibilities and personal and professional development needs is one paradigm with which organizations may wish to engage in formalizing work-related learning. Other organizational paradigms for engaging in work-based learning approaches are discussed below.

A clearly articulated linkage of one form or another should aim to provide a framework for ensuring the relevance of learning to the organization and for providing measures of its value. The importance of evaluating the contribution of learning to the business, and, in particular, assessing the return on investment in learning is essential if a cogent case for the organization's involvement in learning is to be made.

Learning inducements

A strictly Taylorist view of human motivation may lead us to believe that individuals are unlikely to put in the extra effort without good reason. The extent to which an individual's involvement in learning is generated by a sense of compliance or a genuine desire to realize the aims of the organization and/or professional development is likely to be context- and culture-specific. For example, there is scant evidence to suggest that employees can be compelled to learn. Conversely, organizations are less willing to provide motivating rewards for learning unless there is a demonstrable adding of value to the business.

Organizations signalling institutional support for engaging in work-based learning need to identify the means by which employees will be supported and rewarded. Simply stating that increased learning effort 'is now a part of your job', particularly if perceived to add further layers of responsibility and workload, is not likely to be met with enthusiasm. A wide variety of positive inducements may be considered, which may broadly be divided into three categories.

1. *Remuneration.* Organizations may see the provision of pecuniary incentive as important in engaging employees in making the extra effort. Some may achieve this systematically by adopting performance-based pay or offering bonus rewards based on achievement of specific performance- or project-based outcomes that require individuals to engage and demonstrate personal 'stretch'. Some executives will see this as an unnecessary and additional expense to the business, particularly during times of change, or where business pressures put extraordinary strain on the allocation of resources. Pecuniary incentive, however, is likely to be the most universally appealing and obvious alternative for engaging employees in structured learning.
2. *Career Progression.* Enhancing career prospects may be seen as an alternative, if less universally attractive, inducement to engage employees in

capability development. While this approach raises the question of tensions between recognizing and differentiating job performance and academic attainment, it underlines a critical problem for organizations in sponsoring university learning. Anecdotal evidence suggests that a significant proportion of individuals attaining, for example, an MBA will leave the sponsoring organization within a year of completing their award in search of promotion and opportunities to apply their newly acquired learning. Some executives reject the notion of academic qualifications as a reliable predictor of performance. However, if learning is linked to the job, new opportunities emerge for systematically linking it to career progression and succession planning.

3. *Recognition.* The notion that employment with an organization is for life is also increasingly being queried (McKenzie and Wurzburg 1998). The industrial relations arena, through enterprise agreements and other means, is progressively focused on 'employability', or enabling employees to attain skills which are recognized and portable beyond today's job.

Again, some concerns arise for organizations and a circular problem presents itself. First, the perceived value and hence portability of certified learning will be influenced significantly by the reputation and accreditation status of the conferring body. Second, for many conferring bodies, in both the vocational and higher education arenas, the certification of learning is predicated on the validated attainment of predetermined and accredited learning outcomes. These outcomes are usually inflexible and non-negotiable.

The dilemma presented for employer organizations is that sponsoring certified learning may require the adoption of curriculum outcomes which are not seen as being central to its own priorities, or consistent with organizational capability development needs. With the exception of circumstances where compliance to industry licensing or legislated standards drives the development agenda, an organization must satisfy itself as to how the certified learning promotes organizational capability. In the minds of senior executives this is more likely to be achieved by encouraging the acquisition of capability that differentiates their organization from others, rather than simply conforming to externally mandated benchmarks.

Recognition, for some employees, is clearly an important incentive for engaging in job-focused learning and performance improvement. It is also one of the principal ways in which a tertiary institution can contribute to learning, and in turn organizational development. As already discussed, the central issue for the organization seeking to establish a link between learning and performance is establishing a process and reward system which can drive its own curriculum.

Models of organizational adoption

So far we have identified some of the organizational and individual motivations for engaging in work-based learning. We have underlined the importance of synthesizing the contrasting but interrelated motivations of the employer and employee, and of addressing the systemic support of learning.

It is proposed that the 'why', or drivers, of work-based learning partnerships require clear articulation by the organization. Before we examine the 'what' of work-based learning and characterizing the desirables and undesirables of the product or solution, it is worth considering some of the differing organizational drivers that are emerging.

Proposing a set of definitive, neatly categorized drivers as to why an organization might engage in work-based learning would be naive at best. The reality is that for organizations and individuals alike, the range of drivers may be equivalent in diversity and number to those participating. As work-based learning emerges as an important new approach, so our knowledge and understanding of the reasons for engagement improves. While not exhaustive, the following broad categories or drivers – six in all – may help to summarize some of the principal influences identified to date that are informing the adoption of work-based approaches.

The performance management driver

The principal driver outlined above suggests that organizations seek to enhance organizational performance by systematically linking the business goals to individual performance. Learning becomes a tool for ensuring that employees are capable of undertaking the performance of their job while addressing the development that will enable them to advance their career. This approach is particularly useful if the employer is seeking to provide a learning approach that is accessible to the whole organization.

The logic of developing such a systematic link is clear. It aims to make learning an integral part of the individual's job, and not a supplement to it. It presents a clearly articulated argument for supporting and encouraging learning directly related to the job at hand, by making performance agreements the effective curriculum of learning.

Notwithstanding these benefits, effectively leveraging performance management systems to make learning an accepted way of organizational life presents significant challenges to human resources management. It requires consistent management of performance, involvement of line personnel and real outcomes relating to reward and recognition. In such conditions, the success of a work-based approach to learning is more likely to succeed. The absence of these conditions may require an organization to identify other ways of engendering ownership of learning.

The strategic plan driver

Another performance-related approach to work-based learning is recognizing business imperatives as a basis for individual capability development.

The business plan generally identifies the key drivers of an organization at any given point. In the absence of a performance management process which can reliably provide an organization-wide framework for devising individual learning and development plans, an organization may organize projects teams to focus their learning on the achievement of specific business objectives.

For example, senior management may identify the need to attain more effective return on the employment of capital assets, implement new work methods or systems requiring organizational change, or enter new markets. Such strategic initiatives could be used to form the basis of a learning curriculum for individuals or teams involved in the promotion of organizational goals.

The compliance driver

Some organizations will, to differing degrees, be motivated to employ work-based learning approaches through a need to comply with licensing, accreditation or legislated standards. Clearly the need here is to engage in a systematic means of ensuring that staff meet certain minimum requirements. In such a case the curriculum will be informed by mandated standards and generic industry competencies.

Many examples can be found in contemporary business. One that is of significance in the Australian financial services sector at the present time is the introduction of draft legislation that provides a stronger framework for regulation of the sector. In conjunction with this draft legislation, the industry's regulatory body, the Australian Securities and Investment Commission has issued an interim statement that more rigorously defines the learning requirements for the industry from a compliance viewpoint. While the sector is still trying to interpret the implications of this regulation, it is widely considered that significant additional focus on means of engaging employees in work-related learning will be required.

Succession planning driver

Of central importance to long-term organizational health is ensuring that the capability base which has guaranteed survival and growth is resident in the organization beyond the employment term of a set of individual employees. Understanding and defining critical organizational capabilities, appraising the shelf life of the organization's current 'stock' of ability and planning to replenish its inventory of capability becomes the goal of succession planning. The need to identify and develop employees with the greatest potential to step into the shoes of present leaders may be the catalyst for adopting a work-based learning approach.

In some instances, development of staff into key roles will be foregrounded by an analysis and definition of the ideal capability sets through an organizational capability framework. Assessment centres may be used to 'take stock', identify individual capabilities against this framework, pinpoint gaps and single out individuals for specific development initiatives. As such the organization's capability framework becomes the curriculum, and a work-based learning programme is designed to close the gaps.

The industrial relations driver

Examples of work-based learning being used to enhance employability can be seen where industries forecast significant downsizing and shedding of staff. Trade unions will try to negotiate strategies that will protect their members, either through financial payments or by enabling them to augment and strengthen their skills and secure future employment. In such a case the acquisition of portable qualifications may be seen as a safeguard against unemployment.

Similarly, employment agreements that recognize the need to attain minimum levels of competence may provide a catalyst for adopting work-related approaches to learning. In a similar fashion to compliance-driven initiatives, the aim is to achieve benchmark standards of ability, though the driver is more likely to be driven by negative motivations. Here a problem avoidance solution is sought through work-based learning more than a positive human resources developmental agenda.

The encouragement of an innovation driver

Each of the scenarios above suggests a systemic, instrumental rationale for the adoption of work-based learning approaches. Learning becomes a tool for the achievement of organizational objectives, and individual involvement is predicated by reasonably defined sets of delimiting 'rules' which guarantee support and funding of the employer.

In some instances, organizations may take a more informal approach to engaging in work-based learning. This is not to say that organizations adopting a more liberal and less constricting framework for enabling employees will not have equally high expectations of the outcome and return. They are simply more prepared, or encouraging, for the ends to be more self-defining. Essentially, these organizations would accept that innovation is derived from freedom rather than adherence to a formulaic approach to development.

A number of questions arise in relation to this approach. Is measurement of contribution purely anecdotal? Does it really add value over and above what may be ordinarily expected of employees? Is the programme really going to be driven by personal interest and acquisition of qualifications rather than a clear notion of organizational strategy?

Each of the above drivers raises myriad questions about the right, or most appropriate, paradigm for adoption. The question facing organizations is more likely to be one of 'fitness for the purpose' – a quality assurance concept. Can work-based approaches be adapted to encompass and satisfy an almost limitless variety of organizational and individual motivations? If so, what are the features that characterize the products or solutions that tertiary institutions offer to prospective partners?

Work-based learning partnerships: desirables and undesirables

Identifying the organizational *raison d'être* for moving to work-based approaches to learning and establishing a clear basis for the involvement of staff are necessary determinants of the successful implementation of a value-adding learning partnership.

In this section, consideration is given to the attributes and benefits that the design of an educational solution must cater to if it is to succeed in meeting the needs of the world of work. Some of the attendant tensions related to these attributes are also discussed. Producing a definitive list of critical product attributes is not the aim, which is to present, based on accumulated experiences, some of the desirables and undesirables that have been identified by organizations in relation to their partnerships with tertiary institutions.

A *value-adding approach*

A problem faced by many organizations is that of placing a value on learning. While it is broadly accepted that learning is an essential capability for organizations, it is often among the first areas of activity to fall victim to the accountant's profit and loss scalpel in times of difficulty. Many would suggest that this is because it is difficult to demonstrate a cause and effect link between the dollar expenditure on training and improvement in business performance. Return on investment in the field of learning is much debated. While it is not the purpose of this chapter to explore this issue in detail, it may be beneficial to introduce discussion of the changing view of business performance measurement and the importance of this to determining the value adding of learning.

Traditional approaches to business performance measurement have focused chiefly on financial performance. While it would be foolish to suggest that these are less important in contemporary business, Kaplan and Norton (1996) propose that financial measures are more commonly used as lag indicators. Broadly, a lag indicator is one that is reflective of historical performance rather than a predictor of future performance. Other measurement perspectives are more likely to provide lead indicators capable of predicting business outcomes by focusing on the antecedents of healthy financial performance. They propose that measures of customer perspectives, internal business perspectives, learning and growth perspectives are essential if financial outcomes are to be met.

Emerging practices and the adoption of broader measures of performance, including learning as a lead indicator, are setting the stage for more informed linkages between work-based learning and organizational performance. Such measurement approaches provide management with frameworks for supporting a sustainable and demonstrably value-adding place for learning. The product offering of the tertiary institution must be able to complement these frameworks.

Cost-effectiveness

Even organizations that are committed to the developmental learning of staff will question the value for money of their dollar investment in learning. Managers are clearly accountable for making decisions about which approach will derive the greatest cost benefit to their organization. The emergence of work-based learning presents new ways of evaluating cost benefit. The question of comparative value extends from simple contrast between the anticipated outcomes of similar products (e.g. the cost of one course against another), to consideration of the benefit derived from transferring learning to the workplace; hence the shift in focus from comparative cost of alternative deliveries, to the value of the outcome received.

No simple formulaic answers will satisfy all organizations. However, the measure of a successful partnership can be more effective by establishing clear guidelines of the desired benefits at the outset, and specifying the performance indicators that will be used to determine success.

Stakeholder ownership

In most circumstances, the human resources or training manager who develops policy and provides support in developing work-based learning approaches is not the ultimate stakeholder. Line managers, as internal stakeholders of a work-based learning approach, will ultimately be the buyers of the product. In order that their ownership is engendered, it is essential that a robust methodology be constructed for evaluating and communicating the benefit. Ownership and involvement of internal stakeholders is an essential underpinning of a sustainable partnership.

A lever of cultural change

An organization's ability to adapt to the increasing pace of change is critical. More often, managers view the seeming lack of organizational readiness to respond to change as reflective of their employees' poor understanding of the need to embrace change. Thus the need to create a supportive environment through learning and a shared vision which underscores the transitions required for change. Moving towards achieving such an environment may be seen to help to negate attitudinal inhibitors of organizational development.

Needless to say, cultural change is a long-term process that relies significantly on the ability to shift attitudes and values. Reflective, work-based learning in association with a planned and rigorous programme of professional development can be harnessed as a tool through which leverage of change can be achieved.

A cross-sectoral approach

Change and development do not begin and end at the top of an organization. While university education traditionally aligns with learning at more senior levels of organizations, provision for the support of learning and development for all employees is important. The intersection between the domains of vocational and higher education is often unclear terrain. In particular, tensions which at times polarize the philosophical perspectives of the two sectors gives rise to questions that may cloud what some see as non-negotiable boundaries between the two. These tensions, which are of significance to players in the educational arena, are often seen as unnecessary 'turf wars' by partner organizations. Industry will view favourably a provider who is able to establish a seamless transition from vocational to higher education, and a single point of entry.

Many of the attendant issues of providing seamlessness remain unresolved from an educator's perspective, particularly where from the client's point of view this seamlessness translates into the requirement for articulation and credit transfer. None the less, the ability to offer qualifications that span both vocational and higher education is an important attribute of a work-based learning partnership.

Quality learning: a just-in-time approach

The ability to cater for individual learners in line with the contingencies of work emphasizes the need for learning opportunities that are driven by the demands of work. A tension sometimes exists in catering to this requirement on the part of providers of education and training, whose services are commonly limited by constraints of geography and economics.

Similarly, issues are presented in expanding and contracting the provision of tailored, demand-driven training and maintaining consistent quality. Quality problems are characterized by the perishability of supply of training service, the inseparability of quality from availability of limited skilled personnel and the intangibility of the service that makes quality control problematic.

Providers of work-based programmes must seek to overcome problems of synchronizing demand with the provision of supply and timely access to learning opportunities.

Mass production versus customization

A central argument for the provision of work-based learning is that of meeting the unique needs of individual learners, and the contingencies of work. Clearly, customization of the educational 'product' and services requires more than a simple window dressing exercise, which may amount to little more than a modification of the standard courses with contextual case studies and company logos attached.

How realistic is it, though, for client organizations to expect a tailored Savile Row suit for the same price as an off-the-rack suit at the local department store? Accepting that customization in a work-based programme is critical, the price sensitivity and notion of cost benefit in the market place will be an instrumental factor in determining the ability of a university to sustain the provision of such a service.

Some concluding remarks

What can organizational partners hope to gain from a university that they cannot provide for themselves? In many cases, industry-based organizations are better resourced and have internal structures that better lend themselves mobilizing resources to meet the demands of being a commercial provider. Indeed, a significant trend in the USA is towards the establishment of corporate universities, whose sole aim is to serve its internal learning needs (see Ritzer 1998, especially Chapter 11).

In Australia, while large organizations often have training budgets that are the envy of universities, legislative and social barriers to the development of corporate universities are more substantial. However, as the university monopoly on the conferral of degree-bearing qualifications begins to crumble, and pressure on funding presents concerns about the quality of university education, some of the existing points of resistance may dissipate. In such circumstances, why will organizations need to form partnerships in work-based learning with a university and how can such arrangements continue to add value?

These questions are of course polemical ones. Organizations may respond by questioning the business they are really in. How will they really benefit by trying to replicate the learning, research and intellectual capital resources of a university? Will they simply succeed in reinventing and reliving the problems that universities have learned to manage? While some of the cultural and philosophical values of universities mean that corporations cannot exert the same degree of control as they may with a commercial training provider, a sustainable and plausible case for work-based partnerships exists.

The key to such partnerships has to be embodied in recognition that universities' capabilities are not simply limited to the role of purveyor of established bodies of knowledge or issuing credentials. Similarly, legitimate knowledge can no longer be seen as the sole domain of the academy. The obvious synergies to be drawn from work-based learning partnerships lie in the ability of the university and organization to combine resources and identify benefits that flow back to both in terms of improved performance in their contrasting but complementary domains.

Acknowledgements

In preparing this chapter I would like thank the following people for their insightful comments: Anne Stewart, Wayne Deeth, Peter Stone, Gerhard Smid and Nicky Solomon.

References

Aaker, A. (1992) *Strategic Market Management.* New York: Wiley.
Industry Task Force on Leadership and Management Skills (ITFLMS) (1995) *Enterprising Nation – Renewing Australia's Managers to Meet the Challenges of the Asia-Pacific Century* (Karpin Report). Canberra: Australian Government Publishing Services.
Kaplan, S. and Norton, P. (1996) *The Balanced Scorecard: Translating Strategy into Action.* Boston, MA: Harvard Business School Press.
McKenzie, P. and Wurzburg, G. (1998) Lifelong learning and employability. *OECD Observer,* 209: 13–17.
Ritzer, G. (1998) *The McDonaldization Thesis: Eplorations and Extensions.* London: Sage.
Stevenson, J. (1999) *Corporate Capability: Implications for the Style and Direction of Work-based Learning.* London: International Centre for Learner Managed Learning, Middlesex University.

12

A Challenge to Assessment and Quality Assurance in Higher Education

Richard Winter

The widespread debate about quality in higher education seems at first to be a debate about institutional management. It arises from a sense that higher education (HE) institutions are undergoing a process of rapid change, and that steps need to be taken to 'manage' change. This means that the various innovations associated with this change are implemented in such a way that important educational values are preserved. But a concern for management does not always sit comfortably within educational institutions (Barnett 1992). The parameters of quality management (quality assessment control/assurance/audit) in educational institutions often start by admitting that parameters are not at home in an educational context. They belong elsewhere, in commerce and industry. However, I hope to show that these apparently alien terms help to shine light on some assumptions at the heart of current higher education practices, as well as, in particular, on appropriate quality assurance procedures for work-based learning.

'Fitness for purpose' and 'meeting customer expectations'

Foremost among the imported terms is that of 'fitness for purpose'. From its origin in manufacturing industry, 'fitness for purpose' was introduced into recent discussions of quality management in higher education. The introduction was rather tentative in spirit, rather in the manner that an uncouth stranger on official business might enter a genteel gathering of friends (see FEU 1991: 2; De Wit 1992: 4; Pring 1992: 10; Wicks 1992: 58). Pring, for example, ends his argument by showing the stranger to the door. 'Fitness for purpose', he says, refers to 'specific job-related requirements', and is 'a narrowly conceived understanding' inadequate to the needs of 'a broader educational vision' including the 'dominant academic tradition', whose 'standards' are 'more often than not unspoken' and do not 'entail

. . . explicit formulation' (Pring 1992: 12, 16, 21–2). For other writers, how-ever, fitness for purpose can play a central role in higher education. For example, De Wit (1992) initially presents five 'key themes' in the analysis of quality assurance for universities, three of which clearly concern imple-mentation ('a strategic approach', 'interconnected processes' and 'continuous improvement'). This leaves only 'fitness for purpose' and 'meeting customer expectations' as the two themes concerned with what the concept of quality might mean. The reference to meeting customer expectations as a resource for defining educational quality is particularly significant, as indicated in the Further Education Unit (FEU) document *Quality Matters*: 'A Total Quality Management (TQM) culture is predicated upon a commitment to customers' interests, needs, requirements, and expectations' (FEU 1991: 5).

While sympathizing with Pring's reservations concerning this intrusion into higher education of managerial concepts, I think we need to beware of dismissing the stranger with undue haste: perhaps they bring a potentially fruitful challenge, from which academics may derive some useful lessons. In this exploratory but critical spirit, then, let us consider the notions of 'fitness of purpose' and 'customer expectations'. What they seem to require above all is that providers of higher education opportunities should define as clearly as possible the purposes that such opportunities are supposed to realize, so that:

1. The outcomes of higher education may be carefully monitored (to estab-lish whether or not these purposes are in fact being realized).
2. The educational processes and procedures of higher education may be analysed (in order to judge their appropriateness in the light of the defined purposes).
3. It can be established whether or not these purposes and processes are acceptable to students.

Let us, then, provisionally adopt this general approach to the 'quality' de-bate, and see what its implications are for curricula involving work-based learning in particular and for higher education in general.

Work-based learning: specifying purposes and outcomes

The quality assurance problems of work-based learning are only too appar-ent. How can the intellectual qualities of workplace practice be identified, evidenced and assessed? How can levels, standards and progression for such work be formulated and calibrated against the familiar formats of existing courses (essays, practical examinations, dissertations etc.)? One important approach to these issues has been through the detailed specification of required learning outcomes (or competencies) by deriving them analytically from institutional purposes (Jessup 1991). The problem here, however, is that there are two institutions involved – the university and the workplace – and in many ways their purposes do not coincide: the workplace tending to emphasize productivity, for example, and the university critical analysis (Barnett 1997). However, at least the description of educational processes in terms of outcomes means that institutional expectations are made explicit, so that the *meaning* of education can be properly discussed *between* institutions. Moreover, when expectations are made explicit, students can compare them from the outset with their own, and judge in advance the probable relevance of the course on which they are proposing to embark. Similarly, if purposes are made explicit, the adequacy or otherwise of the enabling procedures may be evaluated against them.

Although this emphasis on prespecified outcomes can lead to a crudely reductionist approach to curricula, this is not inevitable, since an educational outcome may be described in complex terms (Winter 1992), and it does at least have the merit of making the parameters of the quality assurance issues more visible. Let us, therefore, first of all review some of the difficulties in specifying the purposes, outcomes and processes of curricula derived from work-based learning.

To begin with, statements of specific required competencies need to be exhaustively checked, to ensure that they are both realistic (rather than mere evocations of an ideal) and general (rather than a contingent feature of a particular context), and that they embody the requirements of good practice (rather than just actual practice). This involves negotiating between practitioners, their managers, professional bodies and 'academic' professional theory. My own recent experience with a practice-based honours degree programme suggests that even after such negotiations have apparently been carried out successfully, further adjustments need to be made, even (for example) concerning the amount of credit to be allocated to a set of learning outcomes. Quality assurance procedures will therefore need to include arrangements for continuous scrutiny and rapid revalidation of amendments.

But creating an agreed form of words is only the starting point, since the statements of learning outcomes need to be fairly open-ended in order to match the personal, problem-solving, interpretive characteristics of the higher education process. This means that staff involved in assessments must be continuously involved in sharing and negotiating the interpretation of the learning outcome statements. Double-marking and moderating thus become particularly crucial, and so too – judging, again, by my own recent experience – do staff seminars devoted to the comparison of tutors' responses to students' files of evidence. The point is that when explicit statements of required outcomes are made publicly available, as the basis for assessment decisions, much more effort needs to go into creating the staff consensus on which the justice of those decisions depends. This is required, though, if the assessment process is to survive its exposure to public scrutiny by students and their employers, as well as by quality auditors.

Equally important is the emerging problem of specifying educational 'levels' or 'stages', which is also beginning to suggest the limitations of evidence of learning generated entirely in the workplace. The National Council for Vocational Qualifications (NCVQ) has come to accept that workplace evidence needs to be complemented by evidence of 'knowledge and understanding' (Black and Wolf 1990), but also admits that to specify a competence required in employment is not necessarily to specify an educational level (Oates 1994: 23). However, if guaranteeing the quality of an educational award means specifying its purpose (so that its process can be evaluated), this must entail identifying the educational outcomes which are characteristic of that award, and hence its level or stage. Such clarification is required to facilitate progression from one educational stage to the next (for example, from an honours degree to a higher degree). Unfortunately, the basis for this progression is not easily specified, largely because most assessment seems to focus on criteria that are common to several educational stages (see Winter 1994).

How, then, might we try to ensure the 'level' of work-based learning, i.e. its appropriateness for a given educational stage? The most apparently straightforward method involves relating each work-based learning outcome to a description of its underpinning academic theory, taken from a traditional taught course. This is the approach adopted in the Ford ASSET Programme at Anglia Polytechnic University (UK), which developed a work-based honours degree in engineering (see Winter and Maisch 1996: 75–9). However, it is likely that in the end this approach will bring us back to the problem that the allocation of academic knowledge to educational stages is itself highly problematic. For example, the same topic may be placed at a different stage in different programmes, and assessment criteria do not differentiate between stages, as noted above.

Another possible method has three components, as follows:

1. Most of the programme can be defined by pathway regulations concerning prerequisite and co-requisite units of learning.
2. The coherence of an individual student's selection of units (within a given stage) may be explicitly argued by the student in a retrospective 'integrative unit'.
3. Each award needs to include a 'project' specifically designed to enable students to demonstrate the general learning outcomes characteristic of a given educational stage. (In an HE context, for a 'professional' award, this will entail an analytical commentary as well as practice-derived documentation.) In this way one can minimize what would otherwise be the immense and intractable problem of assigning all units of learning to an educational stage for assessment purposes (see Winter 1994).

A more elaborate method of specifying work-based learning appropriate to a particular educational stage was adopted by the Social Work ASSET Programme (also at Anglia), which developed a work-based honours degree in social work. This approach involves developing a set of overall assessment criteria, applicable to every unit of learning, based on an analysis of the general intellectual and professional requirements implicit in the work from which the learning is being derived (see Winter and Maisch 1996). These general criteria resemble 'core transferable skills', but they are not separate from the rest of the programme. Instead, in the ASSET model, these core criteria (see Appendix 12.1) constitute the basis for assessing every unit of learning with the programme. The effect is complex, since the assessment is always in two dimensions, combining the demonstration of one of the specific practice competencies and fulfillment of one of the core criteria. For example, one of the competence statements in the ASSET Programme is: 'Consult other professionals in order to make and justify decisions arising from conflicting views as to priorities of risk.'

The assessment problem here is how to ensure that the term 'consult' is approached in a way that provides an appropriate degree of analytical elaboration. Without the use of the core assessment criteria a candidate might simply include correspondence showing that they had asked advice, which does not in itself constitute evidence of any sort of educational achievement. In contrast, the core assessment criteria require candidates to present evidence (in response to the competence statement) which demonstrates specific educational and professional values. For example, they may choose to demonstrate their commitment to the 'non-oppressive' quality of their consultation with a *junior* colleague, or their respect for clients expressed in the sensitive discussion of alternative risks, and the management of value conflicts during the negotiation (core criterion no. 1). Alternatively, the candidate might present evidence to show how they learned from the consultation process (core criterion no. 2). And so on (for more details see Appendix 12.1).

Quality assurance and the nature of assessments

A particular problem for the management of quality (and one that applies to higher education in general) arises where the work-based learning curriculum is part of a classified honours degree programme. This means that it involves an assessment process including grading, rather than the assessment format proposed originally by the NCVQ: 'pass' or 'insufficient evidence as yet'. The problem with grading, from a quality assurance perspective, is that the number of learning outcomes requiring specification needs to be multiplied by the number of grades being awarded. In other words, in order to be even minimally explicit (recognizing the inevitable ambiguities of language), each set of grades should be a positive statement of a distinct outcome, rather than a series of evaluative adjectives ('good', 'outstanding', 'poor') in relation to a single outcome, since in the latter case the assessment decision will rely on the evaluative adjective, which is, by its nature, undefined. The ultimate scope of the difficulty may be indicated as follows:

If every assessment decision needs to be justifiable in terms of the evidence, in relation to a specification, on which it is based, then numerical assessments (marks out of 20 or percentages) will need to show an actual number of items present or absent in the piece of work being assessed.

This would spell the end of such time-honoured practices as awarding percentage marks for essays, since it would entail specifying a hundred separate criteria.

From a quality assurance ('fitness for purpose') perspective, the simplest arrangement for awards would be a pass/not-yet-pass decision in relation to specified outcomes. This would be the easiest form of decision to justify to quality auditors, for the reasons set out at the end of the previous section, i.e. that they may be made (relatively) explicit and thus form the basis for a securely inferred evaluation. This format would be particularly appropriate for work-based assessments, where, by definition, students' contexts for learning are highly varied and difficult for the university to control. Unfortunately, this form of assessment is highly unusual in higher education institutions, where, on the contrary, the preference is for forms of assessment that are extremely difficult to justify in the terms we are considering. Instead of assessments which are criterion-referenced and provisional (pass/not-yet-pass), higher education uses, especially in the honours degree, assessment decisions which are norm-referenced (i.e. comparative) and permanent.

Let us, then, consider, from a quality assurance perspective, assessments that are permanent and negative. That is, they take the form: 'this person cannot do X' (as opposed to 'this person has not yet demonstrated the ability to do X'). This would be difficult to justify because permanent assessments make an implied claim to judge students' fixed capacities (rather than their learned capabilities) and thereby make a prediction of future performance for which, by definition, no evidence could be produced. Similarly, it would be difficult to justify (by providing evidence in relation to a specification) the time-honoured practice of ensuring that grades are distributed according to a normal curve (few 'firsts' or 'A' grades, rather more 'upper seconds' or 'B' grades, a majority of 'lower seconds' etc.). Since each individual assessment decision within this framework is based on an implicit comparison of one individual's work against an indefinite number of others, full and convincing evidence for each individual decision could never be produced.

These are not just esoteric epistemological matters, for they involve very real practical problems. For example, the conventional norm-referenced academic assessment structure makes it almost impossible for universities to demonstrate a rise in quality, since any improvements in 'results' may equally be presented as a fall in the 'average standard', to which all results are implicitly compared. The fundamental evasiveness of academic assessments are also especially problematic when higher education processes are conceptualized from the perspective of 'customers' with the 'rights' enjoyed by other consumers. If students, students' employers and even society in general adopt this perspective they may begin to require of higher education that its judgements be made more transparent, and could test their rights in this respect through litigation.

Higher education and 'customer expectations'

So let us, finally, consider quality management in terms of the role of 'customer expectations'. I cited above the emphasis placed in the FEU document *Quality Matters* on the importance of the customer in defining quality specifications: a total quality management (TQM) culture is predicated upon a commitment to customers' interests, needs, requirements and expectations (FEU 1991: 5). In other words, it seems as though the fitness for purpose of higher education arrangements will need to be demonstrated not only to the satisfaction of visiting academic quality assessors, but also to the satisfaction of the 'customers' of higher education. It is important to recognize that the term 'customer' is conceptually much broader than 'student', and the implications of this will be considered later.

But let us start by considering the student as a customer. The plausibility of this approach receives reinforcement from the encouragement given by the UK government (from the late 1980s onwards) to the publication of 'charters'. These, in general, outline the rights of the 'users of services' to the specification of explicit standards and also to the right to effective complaints procedures. Although it is all too easy to ridicule the hypocrisy underlying much of this, it must be granted a surface plausibility. The right of complaint, in relation to information concerning publicly specified criteria, is an important counterweight to the self-promotional claims of competing profit-oriented institutions whose rhetoric is otherwise quite consciously persuasive rather than informative. It was therefore quite predictable and appropriate that the National Union of Students should have seized an obvious political opportunity and put forward a draft 'students' charter' that includes the right to make appeals against academic judgements. The practical problem, then, is that the introduction of quality assurance procedures into higher education may necessitate allowing students to acquire the right of appeal against academic decisions. And if students do acquire this right, as the principles of quality assurance suggest they should, we will find that some of the decisions which are most characteristic of our current award format are not susceptible of justification, as indicated above, within the type of quality assurance framework being proposed.

When we turn to consider the employer or even 'society in general' as a 'customer' of higher education (or, to use the current term, a 'stakeholder'), we again find that higher educational institutions have significant problems. Academics have been used to seeing themselves as the arbiters of intellectual and cultural standards. But the notion of customers with rights or 'players with stakes' means that higher education will need to see itself as a point of intersection for powerful external economic and political forces, as a site of competition between alternative definitions of what academic staff previously thought of as 'their' concerns. And work-based learning courses can be expected to exemplify these processes in a particularly precise and urgent fashion. Considering the students' perspective first:

1. They will have a degree of self-confidence, in pursuit of their rights as 'customers', born of their relative autonomy in their role as practitioners.
2. They will expect the quality assurance procedures operating in their university course to be comparable with similar procedures which they are used to operating in their own profession.
3. They will be aware that the educational issue, in the vocational context, is their own adequacy in relation to a required level of professionalism, rather than their superiority or inferiority to other practitioners.

From the perspective of employers and of the wider society, work-based learning raises the question of the 'relevance' of educational courses in a way that cannot be evaded. If learning is 'based' in professional practice then educational outcomes must be couched in terms that can be justified as a contribution to the workplace. This, of course, creates an interesting dilemma. Are all workplaces sites of learning, as the apologists for so-called 'learning organizations' would have us believe? If so, then employers have a vested interest in the education of their staff, and their role as customers of higher education is clear and constructive. But what if the learning organization is merely an unrealistic ideal or a cynical rhetorical ploy, to be contrasted with a reality where workplaces are so highly pressured by increasingly unfettered competitive forces that already overstressed staff have barely time to think, let alone learn? Who should or can decide whether any given employer is a 'genuine' stakeholder in education, or (alternatively) a cheat who should rightly be excluded from the game, or (as is frequently the case) yet another victim caught between the pressures of budgetary control and the ideal of education? In the ASSET Programme, for example, we found that students who were led by the statements of competence and the core assessment criteria to be quite critical of aspects of their working environment sometimes worked towards changing it (Winter and Maisch 1996: 138). And the main process to support learning in the workplace was not (as we had anticipated) supervision of junior staff by managers but 'peer groups' meeting on 'neutral' territory (sometimes in the university). They felt 'safer' there to discuss critically the practice implications of the specified outcomes and criteria (Winter and Maisch 1996: 141).

There is another dimension to the expectations and rights of students, namely the provision of an adequate learning environment (libraries, study space, and the like), and here it must be admitted that work-based learning students have a problem over and above those of 'traditional' students. Where students engaged in a course of study continue to be employed, usually on a full-time basis, the problem of providing such an environment also entails negotiating with employers a guaranteed remission of other professional duties. This is needed in order to make available the time to attend tutorials and to undertake the compilation of evidence, writing of commentaries and so on. Such negotiations with employers are difficult because it is often not clear who controls the budgetary resources necessary to guarantee a specific amount of study time for workers in a variety of departments and at various levels in an organization. But unless these resources are made available and very clearly implemented, students will feel under intolerable pressure to meet the operational demands of their professional role, rather than the demands of the educational process, and thereby suffer significant loss of morale (see Winter and Maisch 1996). The format of the contract required between the employer, the student and the university in order to achieve guaranteed resourcing and effective study time is a further dimension of the quality of educational provision which will need to be open to scrutiny. In this and other ways, then, work-based learning may be the point at which higher education institutions may be able to exert some form of 'leverage' to render workplaces more conducive to learning. Indeed, unless this occurs, the educational effect of work-based learning risks being undermined by the pressures of the workplace.

Conclusions

It might be thought that a discussion of quality assurance procedures for work-based learning curricula would largely involve questioning what needs to be done to ensure that such learning can enjoy the same level of quality assurance as currently characterizes 'traditional' methods of tuition. In fact, the issue seems almost to be the other way round. Although we must accept that to evaluate higher education courses by ascertaining fitness for purpose against specified outcomes is not a sufficient basis for the assessment of HE 'quality', we must also, surely, accept that it is a reasonable suggestion, perhaps even a necessary starting point. It is certainly not just an uncouth intrusion into higher education from an alien realm. In other words, quality assurance procedures in higher education need to be based (in part) on the public specification of educational outcomes, so that the effectiveness of educational processes may be evaluated against these specifications. However, it can then be argued that the curricula and assessment criteria of work-based learning courses, precisely because they do not and cannot rely on any pre-existing implicit consensus, conform much more closely to quality assurance requirements than the traditional courses whose 'quality' is frequently taken to be a yardstick for higher education as a whole.

The undoubted difficulty of trying to be explicit and precise about what has been learned by students in work contexts certainly creates the impression that work-based learning, like quality assurance itself, is highly problematic, but it is not clear where the problem lies. It may even be the case, as I have suggested in this chapter, that if and when educational institutions are forced to make their judgements more open to scrutiny, the real quality assurance problems will appear to reside (in some respects at least) as much with the traditional format of higher education courses as with arrangements for work-based learning. Indeed, one might even suggest that from a quality assurance perspective the distinctions between work-based and university-based study are gradually becoming unimportant. Many of the issues raised in this chapter – the obscurity of HE assessment procedures, for example, and the importance of negotiating course arrangements with students and their employers – are already seen as highly relevant for the management of academic courses. Ideas formerly seen as alien intrusions are becoming accepted as inevitable and, if not comfortable, at least, in the end, beneficial.

Appendix 12.1: The 'ASSET' Programme: core assessment criteria

Note: *All* criteria must be *implicitly* demonstrated in the evidence for each *element* in each module; the evidence for each element must be *explicitly* related to *one or more* of the criteria.

Criterion no. 1: 'Commitment to professional values'

Demonstrates understanding of and commitment to professional values in practice, through the implementation of anti-discriminatory/anti-oppressive/anti-racist principles. This involves demonstrating:

1. Awareness of the need to counteract one's own tendency (both as a person and as a professional worker endowed with specific powers) to behave oppressively.
2. Respect for dignity, diversity, privacy, autonomy.

Criterion no. 2: 'Continuous professional learning'

Demonstrates commitment to and capacity for reflection on practice, leading to progressive deepening of professional understanding. This involves demonstrating:

1. Willingness and capacity to learn from others, including clients, supervisees, colleagues.
2. Recognition that professional judgements are always open to question.
3. Ability to engage in self-evaluation, recognizing and analysing one's strengths and limitations.

Criterion no. 3: 'Affective awareness'

Demonstrates sensitivity to and understanding of the emotional complexity of particular situations. This involves combining sensitivity with effective management of emotional responses in the course of professional relationships.

Criterion no. 4: 'Effective communication'

Demonstrates ability to communicate effectively in complex professional contexts. This involves communicating in a form and manner which is clear, sensitive and appropriately varied in style and medium according to particular audiences and purposes.

Criterion no. 5: 'Executive effectiveness'

Demonstrates ability to pursue the stages of a chosen approach in relation to a clearly established purpose. This involves demonstrating decisiveness combined with sensitivity in making difficult judgements in response to complex situations.

Criterion no. 6: 'Effective grasp of a wide range of professional knowledge'

Demonstrates an understanding of the relationship between various types of professional knowledge, and an ability to apply this understanding effectively through practice. This involves demonstrating:

1. Comprehensive knowledge and critical evaluation of professional methods, policy, procedures, general theory, research findings, legislation.
2. Ability to relate specific details to other contexts and to general principles.

Criterion no. 7: 'Intellectual flexibility'

Demonstrates an open-minded awareness of alternatives. This involves demonstrating the ability to analyse issues in terms of dilemmas and/or to analyse situations in terms of continuous change.

References

Barnett, R. (1992) *Improving Higher Education.* Buckingham: SRHE/Open University Press.
Barnett, R. (1997) *Higher Education: A Critical Business.* Buckingham: SRHE/Open University Press.
Black, H. and Wolf, A. (1990) *Knowledge and Competence.* London: HMSO/Careers and Occupational Information Centre

De Wit, P. (1992) *Quality Assurance in University Continuing Vocational Education.* Birmingham: University of Birmingham, HMSO and Department of Employment.

FEU (1991) *Quality Matters.* London: Further Education Unit.

Jessup, G. (1991) *Outcomes.* London: Falmer Press.

Oates, T. (1994) Taking care to look where you're going: caution and credit framework developments, in M. F. D. Young, P. Wilson, T. Oates and A. Hodgson (eds) *Building a Credit Framework: Opportunities and Problems.* London: Post-16 Centre, University of London Institute of Education.

Pring, R. (1992) Standards and quality in education. *British Journal of Educational Studies*, 40(1): 4–22.

Wicks, S. (1992) Peer review and quality control in higher education. *British Journal of Educational Studies*, 40(1): 57–68.

Winter, R. (1992) 'Quality management' or 'The educative workplace': alternative versions of competence-based education. *Journal of Further and Higher Education*, 16(3): 100–15.

Winter, R. (1994) The problem of educational levels, part 2. *Journal of Further and Higher Education*, 18(1): 92–106.

Winter, R. and Maisch, M. (1996) *Professional Competence and Higher Education: The ASSET Programme.* London: Falmer Press.

13

Setting the Standards: Judging Levels of Achievement

Frank Lyons and Mike Bement

Since 1991 the University of Portsmouth has been offering a degree programme involving a three-way alliance between employers, employees and the university. It provides study opportunities for people in employment. It is founded on the twin ideals of recognizing relevant prior learning from any source and the student-centred approach to study by learning contract. Students on the programme can include credits for both prior and current formal learning and learning in the workplace towards their awards. To justify the mix of each individual degree, students are required to relate their proposed study to their own professional and career aspirations and to their pre-existing learning. Employees from more than 100 companies have now put together their own bespoke degrees through this scheme. Because each study programme is tailored to meet the learning needs of the employee-student, to deliver work-related learning valued by the employer and to satisfy the award standards required by the university, it is called the Partnership Programme. These needs are reflected in the learning contract, which is agreed between the parties and sets out the details of each learning programme.

Although most people will readily accept that we all learn through work, it is understandable that the quality of learning realized through work-based learning degrees such as the Partnership Programme is questioned. For the immediate stakeholders, the questions asked of the work-based learning elements vary. The employee-student asks:

- What will I be taught in my course?
- What will I learn through work-based learning?
- How will it enhance my career and contribute to my award?

In asking about value for money, the employer-sponsor asks:

- How will my employees be developed?
- How will this meet the learning needs of the company?
- What are the time and money costs of work-based learning?

The tutors in the university making the award ask:

• How can work-based learning realize the same aims as campus-based learning?
• How will we know it is the student's own work?
• How will we answer the questions posed by the quality auditors?

For each of the stakeholders involved, work-based learning raises questions which are variations on the themes of purpose, value and quality.

Purpose

In the UK, as elsewhere, policy initiatives relating to research, consultancy and curriculum developments have drawn higher education institutions and industry ever closer (Howells *et al.* 1998). Universities are assisting with the process of maintaining the competitiveness of a knowledge-based economy in the global market, while responding to the needs and aspirations of employers and employees. Work-based learning degrees are part of this trend to relate higher education to work. This theme is explored in a more concerted way in other parts of this volume, as well as its companion (Symes and McIntyre 2000).

The purpose of work-based learning degrees is to supply lifelong learning opportunities for the employed by providing job-relevant education, upskilling, career development opportunities and the transfer of new technologies and best practice to work. The work-based element serves to maximize the learning opportunities found in the workplace to the benefit of both the learner and the company in its strategic and commercial development. Entry to the programme, which includes the accreditation of prior learning (APL), including experiential learning (APEL), provides an equality of access opportunity to a wider client group. Writing an APL portfolio also serves to introduce students to the practice of reflecting on their own professional and career achievements and development needs. The learning contract element to these degrees enables truly student-centred learning. Typically degree programmes are not bound to a single discipline, nor need they be mapped on to existing requirements about multidisciplinary study, such as those found in business studies or computer studies.

Value

In the context of conventional degree frameworks, questions about the quality of the learning opportunities and the credit worth of the learning outcomes have rightly been questioned. The first of these concerns is real enough, particularly where the employee-learner comes from a company where the technology and business practice is relatively stable. Such traditional enterprises are clearly ready for learning about new technologies and best practice. A work-based project with such a focus can provide an ideal learning opportunity for employees and turns the company into a learning company. The difficult process here is to work with company representatives to persuade them of the potential learning opportunities. The partnership definition of work-based learning is relevant here: achieving 'planned learning outcomes using workplace resources, based on a given task or function' (Lyons 1998a).

In practice this means learning from one or more of the following:

- commercial development projects;
- review of company procedures;
- introduction of new quality standards;
- attendance at in-company and manufacturer's training courses;
- job shadowing;
- secondment to another job role or department;
- reading and research;
- online learning;
- being mentored.

Concerns about the credit worth of such work-based learning translate into the way it is valued both as a process and in terms of the volume and level of learning achieved. It must be remembered that for the employed student this learning is not about 'experiencing the world of work', or putting theory into practice, but about learning to develop career and professional standing and how to put practice into a theoretical context.

For the Partnership Programme the challenge was to demonstrate that both prior experiential learning and new work-based learning were of equal value to normal university studies, even though they might be justifiable in relation to practices and values external to those in the academy. The traditional appeals to 'academic excellence', 'understanding the canon' and 'grasp of the discipline' proved difficult to apply to programmes developed through learning contracts which involved work-based learning and different cognitive processes. Industrial and commercial traditions revealed a very different set of norms, where, for example, 'on time and in budget' delivery, competency and practical professionalism were as important criteria when appraising quality as were those of the academic. This point was clearly illustrated at an examination board debate early in the history of the Partnership Programme. One work-based project involved the adaptation of an existing military satellite navigation system. It resulted in a valuable civilian product that was judged in different ways by the academic and the industrialist. For the tutor it was graded as an average piece of redesign using conventional engineering ideas and involving little innovation. The company mentor viewed it as a first class commercial development.

Quality

Prior learning portfolio

Students are admitted to the programme by demonstrating their ability to benefit. All students are asked to review their existing educational perform-ance and identify their learning requirements by drafting a learning port-folio. This draft is also used to identify any prior learning that can be accredited whether it is experiential or academic.

Partnership programme practice in APL has changed greatly over the nine years of the programme's existence. Originally, a series of workshops, supported by counselling sessions with advisers, helped students to assemble their prior learning portfolios. Both students and staff found that this was time-consuming and impractical, and a distance-learning approach using a guide developed by Lyons (1998a) soon replaced it. This APL guide was based firmly on the student establishing the authenticity, relevance and sufficiency of the learning presented in the portfolio. In further revisions of this guide, the opportunity has been taken to translate our original, rather academic, statements of principle into more accessible language illustrated with an exemplar of good practice. The format is essentially a curriculum vitae expanded to include details of: the experiences that have led to learn-ing; proven learning outcomes quantified as levels and volumes of learning; and initial thoughts on proposed learning. Often students are able to pro-duce good quality first drafts that need no further revision.

Developing a learning contract

From a review and accreditation of their past learning experiences partner-ship students go on to negotiate their individual learning contracts. During the development and subsequent delivery of these contracts students are faced with a number of real quality management tasks:

> A student must show that the work planned forms a unified and achiev-able package, that the work-based learning and University courses are complementary, and that they provide sufficient opportunities for the assessment of progress and achievement.
>
> (Bement 1993)

To function as a management tool, a learning contract must be approved in the way it articulates:

- the work-based and other study components that the partnership student proposes;
- the planned learning outcomes of the contracted programme;
- the thinking and justification behind the programme;
- the time within which the programme is to be achieved;

- the resources necessary to achieve success;
- the type of evidence that will be presented to demonstrate the work-based learning;
- the volume and level of the credit that the work-based learning is worth;
- the criteria by which the work-based learning outcomes will be graded.

The contract must justify the total study programme, the relationship between the parts and the connectedness to APL. Here the students must express their professional career or academic aims and purposes. It is here that questions about different knowledge, cultural values and standards are addressed. These issues, where relevant, will have been explored through negotiation with university tutors, company representatives and professional bodies. Contracts are only accepted when all parties have reviewed and accepted the proposed programme and sign up to the contract. For the university the only limitation is that the contract only covers areas of learning in which the university has the expertise that would enable it to contribute meaningfully to its assessment. In quality terms the partnership approach means the acceptance of learning contracts that are justified and outline a coherent programme with integrity and balance.

Test of coherence

From the perspective of a particular discipline, contract study could be criticized as 'pick and mix'. This critique assumes that the crossing of discipline and discourse boundaries and the use of diverse methodologies will produce incoherence. From the work-based learner's perspective, coherence relates to how the parts of the contract hold together. In relation to the study elements chosen from the university's portfolio of units, the student is asked to consider how this relates to their learning needs. This involves more than a restatement of the unit learning outcomes published by the university. Similarly, the value of the work-based learning outcomes must be justified. It is the work of the student that provides this rationale. For example, a partnership student who put together a contract involving an in-house magazine development used company market research and research into company quality procedures. The project also called upon university units in software engineering, marketing and human relations management. This contract fitted his needs as the public relations manager for a computer manufacturer.

The integrity question

Decisions on integrity draw on a number of considerations. These include how the individual's learning programme involves the most recent research, develops best practice (in more than just the student's company), facilitates progression towards the intended and stated purpose of the degree, adds up to sufficient learning to realize the volume and level of credits claimed and is sufficiently resourced. In tune with the partnership emphasis on reflective practice, students are required to present a realistic review of all the resources they will need for the completion of their learning. The qualities of the workplace and its potential as a learning environment are critical considerations, but are far from the only resource issues that must be addressed. Tuition fees must be costed, and provided by either the employer or the learner. The employer must agree to provide leave of absence from work, and must approve of the work-based projects proposed. As significant are the consultations proposed with fellow professionals and in-company trainers. There must be provision for the funding of travel to and from the university, and for textbooks and other study materials, including, where appropriate, access to a computer at home in most cases. Students must have access to campus facilities such as libraries and laboratories, and to web-based information. They must be able to meet university staff, including their personal tutors, in the same way as campus-based peers. Students must have reasonable access to and support from their workplace mentors. Finally, as mature learners often with family responsibilities, partnership students must negotiate personal support, study time and study space – and must often renegotiate them as their learning programmes develop and personal circumstances change.

Balance in the learning contract

Contracts are reviewed in a number of ways. These include evaluating them in terms of:

- the balance of practice and underpinning knowledge;
- the proposals to learn about how to apply theory and concepts to complex, specialist and new situations;
- the intentions to work in multidimensional situations that require the sophisticated use of methods;
- the depth and breadth of learning.

The student is expected to be able to:

- draw together necessary and often disparate skills and forms of knowledge;
- work within different fields;
- transfer learning across disciplines and discourses.

At the higher standards of graduateness, the meta-cognitive ability that comes from breadth of study can reveal those depths of understanding associated with an ability to achieve an epistemological mix and even the creation of new knowledge through the use of a professional method.

Award titles and transcripts

Coherence, integrity and balance all relate to the purpose of the study, which, when achieved, will be reflected in the title of the awards made. These titles are deliberately generic, as in the following examples: engineering and management studies; applied computing; business. Although these titles signify the fields to which the awards relate, they do not claim that the fields are fully covered. Hence a business degree need not cover the full range of disciplines (economics, quantitative methods, accountancy, business law, information technology) covered in a conventional business studies course. The requirement is only that sufficient volume and level of credits, related to the area of study, are included. The content of the study programme is fully and clearly presented in the award documentation in the form of an award transcript which records all the learning outcomes achieved and their level and volume. The overall integrity of the award is then visible to all interested parties. Awards are available at all higher education levels, including certificate, diploma, bachelor and master's degrees.

The volume, level and assessment of credit

For the partnership student to be able to design work-based learning that meets the quality challenge, reliable measures of the volume and level of work-based learning are required. And once the learning has been delivered, there have to be suitable standards for its assessment. In order to plan, manage and measure learning from experience, work-based projects or any other source, three sets of tools are required. These are:

1. Means by which volumes of credit can be standardized.
2. Means for establishing appropriate levels for the learning outcomes.
3. Criteria by which work-based learning may be judged and graded.

Thus the tools for learning management and measurement may be seen as a three-legged stool (a work-based 'tripod' as it were), having the necessary and sufficient conditions for stability. The removal of any one of the supports renders the stool unstable and it will collapse.

Standardized volumes of credit

Three measures are used to estimate the volume of credit that a proposed component of work-based learning could command. We begin with the conventional hours of study measure in which 100 study hours are the equivalent of ten credits. We also compare the learning involved in work-based learning with that existing in other university modules of study. Finally, we have devised a set of 'tariff' statements of what a ten-credit module might imply for a given volume of learning. The following is an extract from the partnership work-based learning credit tariff (by level of study) included in the Partnership Programme guide (Lyons 1998b):

- research, design, assemble and test a personal computer interfacing system within an office environment (20 credits at level 1);
- understand the theory of two or three analytic methods and be able to apply them in simple model situations (10 credits at level 1);
- attend, critically report on and then apply the principles and techniques of a three-day workshop/course (10 credits at the level of application);
- understand a theoretical area and the associated practical principles, and know how to apply them in two real situations (20 credits at level 2 or 3);
- understand the theory of five or six analytic methods and be able to apply them in real situations (20 credits at level 2 or 3);
- develop the understanding enabling the production of an extended business plan (20 credits at level 2 or 3);
- develop the understanding enabling the production of a feasibility study, marketing review and company strategy relating to a future product (30 credits at level 3 or M);
- develop the understanding enabling the production of fully developed quality procedures (30 credits at level 3 or M);
- produce an extended policy document (health and safety, anti-discrimination, bonus payment scheme etc.) (20 credits at level 3 or M);
- produce an evaluative piece of research on a project with recommendations regarding development (30 credits at level 3 or M);
- understand project planning and project management such that a plan can be drafted and operated (20 credits at the level of application).

All these approaches have problems. Hours spent on a work-based learning project can include routine work activities that do not result in new learning. Comparisons with the learning from university modules, although seductive for tutors who like to view work-based learning as equivalent to final year projects or dissertations, do not compare like with like. The credit tariff method has proven the most effective, particularly where those sensitive to its approach use it as a guide when aggregating the various learning outcomes to flow from projects. It is hoped that as these professional judgements about credit worth are made, their recording will result in an expert system whose legitimacy is accepted by all.

Credit levels

To establish credit levels we use generic statements on the level of credit for learning outcomes found in our two matrices: 'cognitive attainment' and 'study, transferable and professional skills' (see Appendix 13.1). In developing these models, we were influenced by the work of Bryan and Assiter (1994). We were also influenced by our experience in teaching mechanical engineering and sociology at all levels in the university and struck by the similarity of our expectations of students in their attainments in these contrasting disciplines. The matrices have been used either to determine where to locate learning that has already been done, or to set appropriate learning outcomes for a curriculum element during its design, thus defining learning that will be achieved in the workplace in the future. Students are introduced to the use of the matrices while drafting their APL claims, and develop familiarity with them when drafting successive learning contracts.

In practice we have found that the students' use of the matrices is a reasonable indicator of their general level of understanding. Level 1 students make limited use of the matrices, recognize the way they work (supervised, appraised by others) and are able to describe what they do and know. The other subtleties of level 1 indicators are rarely appreciated. By level 3 or M students recognize and can break down the complexity of their work and learning, can reflect on the techniques and tools they use in work, can recognize and analyse their competencies and can express their learning outcomes in a language that relates to their proposed level of achievement, as in the example of a level 3 work-based project below:

Title: The topside redesign of *HMS Illustrious*, with particular responsibility for electromagnetic (EMC) and mutual interference (MI) considerations of all the resited or new transmitting and receiving equipment.

Aims: To evaluate existing and redesign the topside arrangements on *HMS Illustrious*, with regard to the siting of new equipment fits and existing aerials.

Outline: Within the team working on the project my areas of responsibility include:

- planning, organizing and assisting in the topside redesign of *HMS Illustrious* with regard to EMC and MI;
- comparing the siting and parameters of the equipment fitted before and after the study;
- data measurement and collection on weapons parameters, on-site ship surveys, modelling;
- writing comprehensive reports and helping to produce CAD drawings on all aspects of the above findings;
- conducting a feasibility study on the benefits of using modern photographic and computer enhanced techniques.

Learning outcomes

On completion, I will have learned at a professional level:

(a) how to plan a project of this magnitude from inception to conclusion;
(b) how to calculate all parameters, i.e. frequencies, blind arcs, wooding etc. of all emitters and receptors to be fitted in addition to

---

those remaining, while keeping electromagnetic and mutual interference problems to a minimum;
(c) the transferability of research findings for future ship's applications;
(d) the cost-effectiveness of methods used;
(e) the advantages of using photographic and computer techniques
over existing methods;
(f) the understanding of EMC and MI theory and measurement
methods;
(g) CAD applications and computer modelling.

Assessment criteria and the grading of achieved learning

Within the learning contract the learner details the proposed learning intentions as outcomes that can be measured and audited. In turn this means that
evidence submitted for assessment must demonstrate the outcomes realized.
Technical and theoretical knowledge is proven through reports for work,
learning diaries and logbooks. Skills and competencies are demonstrated in
the production of artefacts, or the submission of testimonials by senior
professionals. For the *HMS Illustrious* project the evidence presented was:

• interim and final reports (including designs);
• a self-evaluation report highlighting the key learning achieved in the project.

The latter reflective assessment is to demonstrate ancillary learning not
proven by the submission of the report or other artefacts delivered to the
participant company.

To assist in the grading of work-based learning outcomes sets of standardized generic grading tools form part of the guidance information supplied
to all partnership mentors, students and tutors (Lyons 1998a, b, c, 1999).
Although frequently revised, these were the first of the tools to be devised.
The intention was that students and their supervisors would use generic
statements as the starting point for negotiating criteria directly relevant to
the work-based learning undertaken. The following criteria show the learning
achievements that must be demonstrated in learning of a first class level 3
standard. First class achievement is indicated by:

• thorough understanding and assimilation of key concepts (both practical
and theoretical), trends and interactions within the learning outcomes
specified in the learning contract;
• overview of the field of study used as a basis for creativity, synthesis,
innovative thinking, predictive judgement and diagnosis;
• awareness of the significance of the field of study within the wider context
of work and society, and a demonstrated ability to move across boundaries;
• evidence of a thoroughly professional attainment in terms of the coherent presentation of the work;

- evidence of a process of continuous evaluation and reflection integrated with technical aspects of the work, together with evidence of critical self-evaluation;
- reference to, and thorough assimilation of, the latest published material in the field of study.

Working from this generic model, students are required to modify the criteria to suit their particular work-based learning outcomes, in negotiation with their mentors and tutors. The criteria for assessment developed by the student with the *HMS Illustrious* project in electromagnetism and mutual interference were as follows:

- understanding of EMC and MI such that I can confidently apply the principles to the redesign of the topside of *HMS Illustrious*;
- appreciation of how difficult it is to redesign a capital warship's super-structure, with EMC and MI constraints applied by the proximity of fundamental frequencies and radiation paths;
- clear and comprehensive report writing techniques at a professional standard;
- appreciation of CAD production and use of new techniques and bespoke software to manage the task;
- appreciation of timescales required for a design and evaluation study of this type.

Taking the levels debate forward

With project funding from the Department for Education and Employment, level matrices, derived from the Portsmouth model, have now been developed and adopted by the South East England Consortium for Credit Accumulation and Transfer (SEEC), which has a membership of 40 universities and colleges (SEEC 1997). The aim was to secure agreement among the members, and as far as possible nationally, on guidelines for credit definitions and levels, and issues relating to the articulation between academic and other awards. These matrices have already been used in work-based learning schemes developed in many UK universities, including Liverpool John Moores, Glamorgan and East London.

The guidance produced in the project has been taken up by government funding bodies and provides a useful means of comparative assessment of academic practice among awarding bodies. The debate is now about their use within a benchmarking process within UK universities, to be employed in the setting of degree standards. Benchmarking would result in broad statements about outcome levels within discipline areas. Recent benchmarking trials (QAA 1999) in the fields of history, law and chemistry have confirmed our feelings that our initial levels indicators confuse what are, in effect, threshold levels of attainment with the achievements of the normal graduate and the first class honours candidate.

We now have extensive experience of using our matrices and increased clarity about the professional competencies expected by industry and commerce. However, we believe that there are areas where our practice has perhaps not moved forward as fast as it should. In particular, we recognize that there is likely to be too much educational jargon and higher education valuation and background built into the models we propose to students. It may be that this is natural, since we were not (or at least did not realize we were) reinventing either the university or The University.

Competency models are now firmly established outside the academy as a tool for the definition of good management practice. In the commercial world they add valued educational outcomes to the important dimensions of business-related values and customer and community awareness. Competencies provide definitions of good management practice, as well as embracing technical specializations of all kinds. Many organizations, such as Glaxo-Wellcome, Ford, Shell, Motorola, UK government departments and agencies including the Inland Revenue, have developed their own competency frameworks.

The British Defence Evaluation and Research Agency (DERA) employs a competency model (DERA 1999) typical of the excellent material now being produced by commercial organizations. The agency uses it as a means of measuring staff attributes already in place, but, perhaps more importantly, puts it to work in determining competencies yet to be attained. For us in the Partnership Programme office, it has been very instructive to review the DERA level indicators and how they correlate to those we have been using in our matrices. It is pleasing to note that such correlations occur, especially in the more advanced levels.

We have lately been working on competence statements for professional doctorate degrees, which are to be of the level of the PhD but which are to indicate attainment in the generation and communication of professional knowledge, as opposed to research knowledge. In effect this development takes the level indicators for work-based learning to the highest levels. The level of learning that would be required is:

Knowledge – the learner's grasp of facts, theories, concepts, methods and principles.

Whereas the master attains mastery of knowledge in a complex and specialized area predicated on certainty about the conventionally accepted knowledge base, a doctorate additionally attains command of the latest internationally available knowledge in complex, often multidisciplinary and professionally uncharted areas.

Beyond the master, the holder of a professional doctorate is able to:

- demonstrate meta-cognitive abilities in relating and transferring new professional, theoretical and research understanding into new areas of practice;
- apply the latest knowledge with the self-awareness of where an epistemologically sound and useful contribution can be made;

- provide authoritative solutions on a regular basis when faced with practical, ethical and research problems.

Skills – the learner's operational ability to manage research and work, communicate ideas, and reflect on own and others' practice.

Beyond the ability of the master, the professional doctor is able to:

- manage resources and make professional use of others in overtly stated research projects and professional developments;
- command the attention of others in providing professional and intellectual leadership, inspiration and motivation;
- routinely evaluate and report on own and others' work with fully justified argument and recommendation for improved practice;
- give presentations and deliver reports and 'papers' to critical communities and professional peers for developmental purposes;
- accept responsibility for the achievement of individual and group outcomes;
- manage and contribute to the professional development of others;
- show awareness of the political, ethical and business implications of the knowledge and professional practice being developed.

Learning at work: some conclusions

The learning contracts of partnership students are now graded, the mark contributing to the credits they are awarded for their learning management module. To gain these credits among other learning outcomes, they must demonstrate skill in negotiating their contracts. The best contracts are professionally negotiated and show clear aims and justifications for their learning. To achieve this they need to be accurate in their use of the concepts that inform the language of credit-based learning. Such students can write true learning outcome statements, can self-assess their work against appropriately drafted assessment criteria and know the level at which they are learning and working. Unfortunately, not all the tutors and mentors have achieved a similar grasp of levels and the other concepts used in contract managed work-based learning. Perhaps this demonstrates the size of the staff development project necessary to make levels part of our everyday language in the university and the world of work. What it certainly demonstrates is that in implementing the concept of work-based learning students make the transition from theory to practice, and vice versa.

Appendix 13.1

These tables present the normal levels of understanding and performance expected of average students at each study level from year (level 1) undergraduate studies through master's degree (level M).

Cognitive attainment by level of study

	Level 1	Level 2	Level 3	Level M
Knowledge The learner's descriptions of facts; theories; concepts; principles; data; classifications; the nature of work.	Emphasis is placed on factual knowledge, grasp of terminology, the nature of the field of study and own work situation.	Achieves broader appreciation of the scope of the field of study and work and the variety of ideas and approaches that may be applied.	Demonstrates confident familiarity and detailed knowledge of the field of study and work including selected specialisms.	Focuses on complex and specialist areas, predicated on certainty about the conventionally-accepted knowledge base.
Interpretation The learner's understanding of knowledge (facts, work processes, criteria, ethical implications etc.).	New knowledge is understood, but without being integrated into existing knowledge. Ethical issues in field of study and work practice viewed from a personal viewpoint.	Beginnings of a 'mapping' of knowledge into an overview of the field of knowledge and nature of the company. Appreciation of related general social and environmental implications of study.	Confident in the relationships between areas of principle and fact. Aware of the provisional nature of the state of knowledge and professional ethical responsibilities.	Ability to deal with complexity, lacunae and/or contradictions in the knowledge base. Ability to diagnose while exercising professional and ethical judgements despite incomplete or confused information.
Application The learner's use of knowledge (facts, criteria etc.) in real work situations.	Work is directed with rote application of principles and standard techniques. Reliance on guidance by tutor, mentor and manager.	Understanding of the need to select principles and facts appropriate to the problem in hand. Manages to apply principles under guidance.	Confident and accurate selection and application of principles used in the identification and solution of a range of real problems.	Accurate isolation and identification of problems and areas of investigation. Confident, autonomous and self-reflective application of appropriate problem-specific principles and best practice.

Analysis The learner's ability to break down knowledge into its constituent parts in a variety of ways for various purposes.	Acceptance of the principles and classifications presented by mentor and tutor. Ability to analyse with guidance.	Ability to recognize familiar ideas or principles in real work situations or texts and analyse accordingly.	Identifies and classifies principles and ideas from new data at work or texts. Uses appropriate analytic techniques in a wide range of situations.	Ability to edit complex documents. Ability to classify facts, principles and theory for a variety of ends. Ability to work from a brief.
Synthesis and creativity The learner's ability to bring together different elements of knowledge in a new way or within a new framework; producing new ideas or solutions.	Able to collect and collate information in standard formats. Creativity is absent or imitative.	Understands the need for the marshalling of facts and ideas in an argued case. Can produce new ideas or designs in closely defined situations.	Ability to bring together principles and facts in support of an argument. Ability to design novel solutions with minimum guidance.	Ability to define, elaborate and defend a thesis. Confident ability to synthesize novel design solutions.
Evaluation The learner's ability to assess what is known, quality of work, validity of conclusions against a variety of criteria.	Heavy reliance on tutor's/mentor's assessment of work. Can use standard evaluative techniques but unclear about the need for criteria.	Understanding of the need for known and agreed criteria. Able to select appropriate evaluative tools and assess significance of data in straightforward situations.	Accurate assessment of both technical and own levels of performance. Accurate predictions of outcome from courses of action selected.	Ability accurately to assess and report on own and others' work, with justifications. Can accept others' evaluations and act appropriately on them.

Study, transferable and professional skills by level of study

Level 1	Level 2	Level 3	Level M
Beginning self-reflection on strengths and weaknesses; developing consciousness of own levels of competence and future learning needs.	Awareness of the scope of tasks. Use of tools of self-reflection and of self and appraisal of others with guidance.	Ability to reflect on strengths and weaknesses and to assess own work with acceptable accuracy against published criteria. Similar ability to appraise the work of others.	Habitual reflection and appraisal. Evaluation leads to action. Ability to articulate plans to remedy shortfalls. Can give critical advice and accept others' evaluations of self and act on them.
Developing new approaches to work and study, including: teamwork; independent enquiry; ability to justify, reason and argue about work and study area.	Some guidance from tutor and mentor still needed in management of learning, and from manager at work, but responsibility taken for most decisions. Used to group working, independent research, justifying work decisions.	Ability to manage own work, research and learning with minimal guidance, both in independent and group situations. Clear understanding of group processes. Ability to justify current and future personal career academic and professional goals.	Autonomous. Diverse in research skills. Professional use of others in support of self-directed work and learning. Instinctive awareness of importance of group processes and confident understanding of group dynamics.
Developing awareness of the need for a flexible approach to problem-solving, design tasks, evaluation and views of the world.	Able to question the value of new approaches. Viewpoint can oscillate between enthusiastic adoption of new methods and a pervading emphasis on their drawbacks.	Confident knowledge of appropriate general and technical subject-specific skills. Ability to articulate own viewpoint and use as a basis for questioning, discussion and debate.	Confident selection of tools for the job. Ability to develop new approaches in new situations. Quick to perceive merits or demerits of new ideas, techniques or technologies.
Recognition of the necessity for study skills appropriate to the subject (library, laboratory, computer literacy, articulate and accurate written and oral presentation). Development of a questioning attitude.	Exploration of an expanding range of skills and techniques. Valuing of study and transferable skills, both in the group and as an individual. Beginning to apply professional standards in practice.	Confident and flexible application of subject-specific skills in evaluation, problem-solving, design and analysis of real-world issues. Valuing professional standards.	Creative use of techniques and skills. Skilful and confident planning and successful execution of programmes of work 'on time and within budget'. Works effectively and professionally as a team member or leader.

References

Bement, J. M. (1993) Learning in the workplace: the Portsmouth partnership experience, in Proceedings of the Second Congress on Engineering Education, Lodz, Poland.

Bryan, C. and Assiter, A. (1994) *ALE Project User Pack: Giving Credit for Cognitive Skills Acquired in Work*. London: University of North London.

DERA (1999) *DERA Competency Framework*. Bath: Defence Evaluation and Research Agency.

Howells, J., Nedeva, M. and Georhiou, L. (1998) *Industry and Academic Links in the UK*. HEFCE Report 98/70 PREST. Manchester: University of Manchester.

Lyons, F. S. (1998a) *Application for the Assessment of Prior Learning: Student Guide*. Portsmouth: Partnership Office, University of Portsmouth.

Lyons, F. S. (1998b) *Drafting your Learning Contract: Student Guide*. Portsmouth: Partnership Office, University of Portsmouth.

Lyons, F. S. (1998c) *Mentoring*. Portsmouth: Partnership Office, University of Portsmouth.

Lyons, F. S. (1999) *Tutoring on the Partnership Programme*. Portsmouth: Partnership Office, University of Portsmouth.

QAA (1999) Quality Assurance Agency for Higher Education, http://www.qaa.ac.uk/public.htm

SEEC (1997) *Guidelines for Credit and Consortium General Credit Rating*. London: South East England Consortium for Credit Accumulation and Transfer.

Symes, C. and McIntyre, J. (2000) *Working Knowledge: The New Vocationalism and Higher Education*. Buckingham: SRHE/Open University Press.

14

Earning Academic Credit for Part-time Work

Iain S. Marshall and Lynn S. M. Cooper

The practice of introducing work experience into academic programmes has a long tradition. In Britain, the so-called 'sandwich placement' was one such programme. The notion of 'sandwich' evoked the image of a slice of work experience, inserted between two layers of academic input. In North America and elsewhere, 'cooperative education' and 'intern programmes' were used to describe academic arrangements in which students experienced the world of work. The practice of work placement has been unevenly distributed across the higher education sector in Britain. Those universities from the polytechnic sector that took on university status during the 1980s have been more active in offering programmes with an integrated work element than older universities (Foster and Stephenson 1998).

In the 1980s, two emerging ideas helped to revolutionize the further education and higher education sectors in Britain. These related to the way academic learning was credited and structured. First, subject inputs were broken up into a series of discrete blocks, bounded by time, called 'modules'; second, each module was allocated a number of credit points. A degree consisted of 120 credits at each of three levels, the credit total to be made up from a number of 'modules', each having a standard credit rating such as 10, 15 or 20 credits. The spread of these two ideas throughout the higher education sector – especially the former polytechnic group of new universities – contributed to a paradigm shift. Whereas traditionally a degree had been obtained by spending three or four years studying a combination of subjects at a university, the experience now involved assembling credits. Once the 'unit of credit' was acknowledged by academics, it became possible for students to group modules together creatively in order to gain qualifications through credit accumulation.

There were significant effects of these changes that led to the inclusion of work-based learning in modular degrees. One was that credit tariffs allocated to work-based learning became equivalent to those achieved in any other 'subject' modules. As a result, academic institutions were able to allocate appropriate resources to support the quantity of credit generated by these modules. This second change was particularly important in helping to address situations where students enrolled in work-based learning modules were given inadequate staff support.

One would have expected that these developments would lead to an expansion of the number of work-related courses. In fact the opposite happened. The number of integrated sandwich placements in university programmes fell during the 1990s, as did the number of full-time undergraduate students involved in work experience. This was unexpected because it was a period during which the Department of Employment encouraged work-based learning recognition.

One reason for this reduction in work-related programmes relates to the decline in employment in the manufacturing industry in the UK. This has resulted in leaner companies with flatter administrative structures. These made it more difficult to find placements in industry for the increasing numbers of students in higher education. Another possible reason is the requirement for existing academic staff to manage with decreasing resources, increasing staff/student ratios, more administration and the pressure to attract and undertake funded research. Further, the fixed nature of the university calendar and academic timetables restricted the possibilities for work-related courses.

Other possible reasons related to the mismatch between the recruitment needs of companies and the skills and knowledge of graduates. The perception of this mismatch resulted in the Dearing review (NCIHE 1997) of university programmes. He, along with employers, had made pronouncements to the effect that higher education should better prepare students for the world of work. To offset these concerns, Dearing made several recommendations in relation to higher education and employers. One was that they should 'collaborate to develop more sponsorship and work experience opportunities which provide real benefit to both students and employers' (NCIHE 1997: 6). Another was that they should 'aim for a less-pronounced distinction between academic and vocational subjects', and that 'individual students . . . plan and map' their way through courses in which the key skills of employment are embedded (NCIHE 1997: 38–41).

In 1993 Napier University reported on a project funded by the UK Department of Employment (Marshall 1993). This was a record of a successful pilot scheme to award academic credit to students for learning achieved during their sandwich placements. The report was widely circulated to universities and polytechnics in the UK. The model reported involved student-driven and negotiated learning outcomes, which had been developed between student, employer and academics. The model was created to shift the attention away from providing the student with 'work experience' towards the recognition of 'learning achieved'.

The context in which an innovation can take place is of key importance. The experience that Napier University had gained in awarding academic credit for sandwich placements had meant that the work project was easier to pilot than might otherwise have been the case.

Development of a work-based learning module

A working party was set up at Napier University in late 1997 to identify new models that might improve the benefits to be gained from work-based learning. We set about examining trends in the provision of work-based learning, looking at examples of currently available courses, and exploring possibilities for increasing and expanding their availability. One possible response available to us in the light of the Dearing recommendations cited above was to consider reviving and expanding the sandwich placement module. This would have entailed allocating resources to fund, manage and support student placements with companies. Another possibility was to acknowledge that many full-time students were already in part-time employment, and undertaking a range of tasks, albeit with limited areas of responsibility.

The recognition within the working group, which included a student representative from the Napier Student Association, that large numbers of students were engaged in part-time employment encouraged support for the development of a module specifically designed for part-time students. If it was acknowledged that students, through their employment, are being exposed to value systems and practices from which they might learn, there was a possibility that part-time work experience might be utilized as the basis of more formal learning.

We devised a module that contained a number of learning outcomes capable of being achieved by students employed in a range of part-time jobs, and which our academic colleagues, we hoped, would acknowledge as worthy of academic credit. Such an acknowledgement with regard to students' part-time work, we hoped, would help to counter the negative attitudes held by many academic staff towards 'full-time' students doing 'menial' jobs (Harvey *et al.* 1998: 53–4). Yet it is through no fault of their own that many students are increasingly forced to support themselves financially. They need money, yet the time they spend earning is not deemed worthwhile in terms of their academic commitments and often competes with them. As a result, students can be negative or ambivalent about their part-time jobs and feel depressed and guilty about the time they devote to them when they ought to be studying or attending lectures.

The proposed work-based learning module was discussed with members of the working party and a proposal was submitted to University Quality Assurance Committee in January 1998. It was approved and offered to students for the second semester in 1998.

There are three existing categories of module at Napier: core, optional and elective. Core modules are a compulsory part of courses that follow a named route (e.g. BSc biological science), and students are required to pass them. Optional modules are selected from a list approved for a named route qualification. Elective modules offer more free choice for students, who at Napier are required to pass two electives as part of most degree programmes. These electives can be at level 1, 2, 3 or 4, and experience shows that in electives, students often select at level 1.

Since our intention from the outset was to have a work-based learning module accessible to as wide a range of students as possible, we decided to offer it as an elective module at level 1, with Napier standard 15 credit value. In this way, we were acknowledging officially that many students have part-time jobs, and using this awareness, together with the university's modular course structure, to provide a more flexible timetable. By introducing the module at level 1, students from their first year are able to gain recognition for their paid work experiences. Thus we have begun to explore ways of using a work-based learning model to provide an alternative to conventional university courses, which will enable student work to gain academic recognition and credit.

From our conversations with sandwich placement students, we already knew that students gained more knowledge than the required learning outcomes as result of a work placement. In developing the new module, we hypothesized that students with part-time jobs would be in a better position to utilize the concepts, ideas and theories to which they were exposed in their undergraduate programme. This, coupled with their natural curiosity, would pay rich educational dividends. This reflects the view expressed by Boud and Feletti (1997) with regard to problem-based learning. They suggest using 'an approach to structuring the curriculum which involves confronting students with problems from practice which provide a stimulus for learning'. The difference in our module would be that the students rather than lecturers would be asked to identify the problems to be addressed. If undergraduates were indeed learning from their experiences, the challenge for the university was to devise a system of structures and assessment procedures capable of recognizing relevant learning.

Our aim was that students would learn to identify problems at work and to explore possible solutions to them through fruitful collaborations with the workplace and the university. In this way they would gain a heightened awareness of their own behaviour and that of others in organizations, derived from the self-monitoring that occurred during the process. The students' tasks would involve applying theories acquired at university to work-based problems.

The module was designed in such way as to be student-centred and learner-driven. One of its attractions was its flexibility, which would allow students to join at any time during the semester and to be assessed when they chose to submit a report. This report would describe how they had achieved each of the agreed learning outcomes.

Napier, as a former polytechnic, has a wide variety of vocational degrees. This meant that the undergraduates who took part were drawn from a wide range of courses, including civil engineering, social science, marketing and management and biomedical science. We had aimed to recruit an initial group of 20–30 students. In the event, we finally enrolled 43.

As the students enrolled, we asked them to attend a meeting where the module tutor described the process, and explained the underlying 'learner-driven' assumption. The learning outcomes were explained and questions invited, and the learning pack was distributed.

At about the same time, in early 1998, we received an unexpected publicity boost from a freelance journalist picking up news of the innovation from conversations with a member of the Napier Student Association. The story was reported immediately in the national press, local TV and radio, which presented the course in two ways. First, there were cynical reports of honours students obtaining academic credit for 'pub work'. Second, there was a more insightful article about the university's attempts to link practice with theory and give recognition to learning achieved outside the lecture theatre and the tutorial room.

Learning objectives

We had in view when designing the work-based learning module a number of outcomes for our students. These fell naturally into three general groups: practical, objective and subjective. In retrospect, given that this was a new venture, some of our outcomes were ambitious, though many students achieved them, and we have learnt much about the reasons why some found it difficult to achieve them.

We set out to give students an opportunity to be self-directed and self-motivated, to take responsibility for designing an appropriate practical project by identifying a 'real' problem or issue at work which it was within their grasp to address. In order to complete a successful project a student would have to collaborate with their employer or colleagues and also make appropriate use of academic staff for the purposes of guidance and information.

Alongside these relatively practical learning objectives, it was our intention that students would learn to step back and take a more objective and process-oriented view of the project. This would mean that the learning they achieved might lead ultimately into long-term, transferable outcomes. In order to do this, it was important that students understood the idea of transferring skills from one domain to another, and to identify some that were transferable from university to their work. Along similar lines, we intended that students should become aware through their experiences of the relationships between theory and practice, and of the ways in which academic course content and work practice might complement one other.

Our final group of learning outcomes (see Appendix 14.1) concerned the generation of a more autonomous, self-reflective attitude to work. According to Hughes (1998: 217), this involved employees being more able to learn from their 'work through cycles of action and reflection'. Through encouraging students to reflect on their own learning processes, it was hoped that there would be a change in attitude to part-time work in relation to academic study and an accompanying shift in their overall self-concept.

Supervisory inputs

University and academic input

At the outset a set of materials was provided to students with basic information: a copy of the module descriptor, listing the seven learning outcomes, a synopsis of the history and aims of the module, a 'to do' list and the framework of the learning contract. Our main support for student activity in the workplace was the module learning outcomes that were expanded and explained in a learning pack. This pack restates the aims and intended outcomes of the programme. Added to this, students were given the opportunity to discuss the aims, process and intended outcomes at the initial meetings with their module tutor. The initial session was an introduction to the aims of the module and involved a detailed discussion of each of the learning outcomes.

A time and location for weekly drop-in meetings was set and students taking the module were expected to attend as many as they could. These were intended as 'drop-in' sessions for students to ask questions, obtain information, get feedback, discuss difficulties and meet other students. Students were invited to contact the module tutor by phone or email whenever the need arose.

Students were strongly encouraged to form learning sets of up to six students, and to share information and give support and reassurance to one another. Sets might be 'actual', with students meeting at prearranged times, or 'virtual' through exchange of email. It was also suggested that students keep a journal of their thoughts and activities and that they should refer to this when compiling their reports. Neither the journal nor the group contact were compulsory requirements of the course but were suggested as supports for students' learning activities.

Fifteen students attended the first meeting and, subsequently, weekly meetings provided a regular starting point for new students. Here they could make contact with the module tutor, discuss the aims and learning outcomes and collect a learning pack. It was also an opportunity for them to meet other students in the programme who were using the time as a 'drop-in' opportunity to ask questions or provide a progress report. Work by Hughes (1998) suggests that the approach and intentions of the teacher are an important factor in influencing work-related learning. As the module progressed we became more aware of the nature and extent of the support needed by students in order for them to achieve what we expected of them.

Role of the employer

A key requirement was that students discuss their module and its aims with someone in authority in their place of employment and, at the very least, gain their approval to undertake the tasks needed to achieve the learning outcomes. Students could not proceed without this approval. Any activity connected with the module that did not form part of a student's work contract would be completed outside work hours.

Some employers suggested issues or problems they wanted a student to address, and asked for and expected a report containing a description of the work and its outcomes.

Contacting and liaising with an employer or manager was entirely the responsibility of students. As part of the evaluative exercise, the module organizers contacted employers only after the reports had been submitted and marked. At this point we asked employers for feedback on their views of the module and in particular their perceptions of the students involved.

Assessment

The module was assessed in three stages. Evidence of an initial draft proposal was required by the third week, work in progress was examined by the tenth week and the final brief report was submitted in the fifteenth.

Value was placed on examples of student initiative, persistence in the face of difficulty and the student's reflections on their experience. The production and presentation of a report at the end of the module gave students a chance to demonstrate evidence of outcomes achieved. Marks were allocated according to the learning outcomes specified.

As the students started at different points during the semester, they submitted work at different times. At the time of writing, 31 students of the initial 43 have completed the course and submitted a report describing how they have addressed each of the seven learning outcomes. Reports that did not demonstrate sufficient evidence to achieve a pass were returned to students at a review meeting, for further work and resubmission.

Evaluation

In evaluating our pilot module we have drawn on the work of Martin (1996), which deals with the effectiveness of different models of work-related university education. She examines the link between the academic practices of work placement and students' perceptions of their own development of generic skills and general satisfaction with the placement. We have attempted to adapt certain aspects of her work to our more varied student-centred module, and to examine both staff and student perceptions.

In our evaluation of the module, we focused our interest on the three main areas of enquiry included in the learning outcomes. These included what we intended that students should learn from the module, the means by which we expected them to learn it and the specific part played by their experiences in a workplace environment in enabling them to achieve these goals. We were particularly interested in students' perceptions of their own learning and the extent to which their understanding of their learning goals and achievements matches our own.

If we examine the means by which students learn from the workplace we become aware that there exists a range of issues, problems and questions potentially of interest to full-time undergraduates. These are perceived by students as 'real', as distinct from class 'case studies' or questions raised by university tutors. In addition, students can learn from their peers and from work colleagues, including managers and supervisors. They gain experience of being managed and, possibly, of managing others. Most importantly, they are provided with easily accessible opportunities to observe human behaviour at work. As a result, some students became aware that in undertaking the module, they frequently attract positive attention from their employers.

We expected to see such evidence in the students' journals and in their final reports. These provided us with the basis for a tool to measure the extent to which student experiences coincided with the expectations of the module team in terms of:

- range of issues, problems and questions of interest to full-time under-graduates;
- contact with peers with more/less experience of work, from whom they can learn;
- opportunities to observe, read and analyse behaviour in a work context.

We expected that students would learn from the module a number of basic pedagogic outcomes. First, they would be able to name the transfer-able skills they wanted to develop and identify opportunities for acquiring them in the context of their workplace. Second, they would be able to choose and carry out a suitable project, managing their time appropriately, collaborating with employers, work colleagues and academic staff during the period of the project's completion. Third, they would be able to engage in reflective practice on their learning processes.

Transferable skills

The skills of listening, questioning, observation and giving feedback are transferable to the context of work. Higher education is expected to provide graduates with transferable skills or capabilities of a general nature. Knowledge alongside skill will ensure capability . . . it is compet-ence and not subject knowledge that employers require of their staff.

(McGill and Beaty 1992)

Most of the students enrolled in the module had a narrow interpretation of 'transferable skills'. They took them to mean useful skills acquired from their job experience that might benefit them in future employment. There was relatively little evidence of students recognizing or reporting on trans-fer of learning from academic courses to the world of work in the form of either content or procedure. Few students identified specific aspects of their university work that were useful in their job. The projects gave them confidence, however, and appeared to foster interpersonal skills. Identifying links between the different environments and the individual skills appears to have been more difficult.

Student responses to the learning outcome about transferable skills were varied and illustrated a variety of interpretations both of the notion of 'transferability' and of 'skills'. Only one student referred specifically to subject matter learnt in her university course: 'The motivation levels of staff can be improved by acknowledging Hertzberg's theory in conjunction with my recommendations.' Many students referred to the skills learnt on the job and their source. They pointed out that the direction of the transfer varied from student to student, although in general it seemed to be from work to university rather than the other way around:

> The task gave me an insight into referencing and pure desk research which is something that is of great relevance to the course I am studying.

> Next year I will have a lot more self-directed study so this project should hold me in good stead for my future career at university.

> Contact skills learnt at the project will remain with me. Good experience of communication. I learnt how to manage my time. I improved my interpersonal skills.

Many of the comments from students were vague as to the nature of the skills they were acquiring:

> I am able to continue my learning process and transfer my skills to other workers.

> I will be able to build on the experience to help with the way I approach projects and assessments in the future.

Only one student actually named the skills he had learnt, which were: 'timetabling, researching a topic, compiling a report, editing my own work, conducting interviews, assessing if targets have been met.' Some students gained insights that, while not specifically in the area of transferable skills, were not unrelated: 'I have noticed differences between the operation of the practical organization and the written word of the textbook.'

It seems that the notion of transferable skills is more difficult for students to grasp than was at first imagined. What seems to be apparent is that students find it hard to connect the work skills to the content of their university study. One student summed it up: 'I realized that no matter what we learn in class, the real values can only be learned in a real life experience.'

Projects

Students were asked to identify an area of interest in their workplace and to discuss it with their manager. The objective was to design a do-able project that would result in a report to their employer. The report would also be submitted for academic assessment. It was suggested to students at the outset that, having planned their projects, they discuss it with their tutor before proceeding. In the event not all students complied with this requirement. None the less, the projects which were chosen were in the main achievable and realistic. The outcomes were useful in the working environment. This is because of the advice and involvement of managers on site, some of whom made suggestions regarding useful topics.

The projects (see Appendix 14.2) chosen by the students were varied and on the whole dealt with issues relevant to their employers. They tended to take the form of either the collection of information or suggesting improvements to existing workplace procedures and practices. Some of the projects were quite innovative. Students commented that the projects brought them into closer contact with management than had previously been the case and in some instances made their presence more obvious and gained them respect from their employers and colleagues. All the students involved appreciated the opportunity to use their time commitment at work as academic credit.

Some of the projects were complex and their outcomes were of practical benefit to the participating companies. Although most students compiled acceptable reports, the identification of any links between learning in the work environment and learning in the university proved more difficult for them. In fact the biggest handicap to the successful completion of a project and its description lay in difficulties experienced in clearly identifying the transferable skills involved. Only one student made direct use of her knowledge of theory (in this case, motivation) in the project work. None of the project accounts made reference to literature or drew in any overt way on experiences other than their own.

Engaging in reflective practice

Boud and Walker (1993) have identified three factors as being essential to reflection on experience. First is the learner's ability to recall and describe the experience; second is the attention to feelings associated with the experience; and third is the re-evaluation of the experience, integrating past and present learning, leading to its validation. They conclude that learning from experience is 'far more indirect than we often pretend it to be' and that naming the process and admitting that there is an event, which is unresolved', can help it.

On examining the project reports we discovered that although some of the students had attempted to respond to the learning outcome requiring them to reflect on their experiences during the project, very few were able to do this successfully and many simply ignored it altogether. We cite below a selection of extracts from students' reports where they believe themselves to be reflecting on their experiences.

Where students genuinely attempted to reflect, they included comments such as:

> The project gave me the opportunity to explore my part in a large overwhelming company.

> Information about the company was useful. I was astounded by the huge profits made by the company. I felt that everybody who works in the store ... means more than they think they do.

One of the things that distinguishes these comments from some of those made by other students is the use of connotative words such as 'overwhelming' and 'astounded'. Yet there are no reflections about why their work experiences generated such responses.

Other students made more general comments about learning and work, about the conditions of work and about being a worker:

> I put theory I had previously learned into practice. I acquired a new perspective ... saw things I had been doing in a new light ... taking the initiative to do things without being told.

> My relationship with the manager improved.

> Skills I have learnt from this module are around communication ... I had to liaise continually with my colleagues ... this increased my confidence. The manager has become more aware of me.

> It made me realize how difficult it is to preserve harmony in a big company.

> The need to work is vital to most students ... I found that having a slightly different focus for part of my working week was a tremendous boost.

The positive comments implicit in these observations are not accounted for in terms of attempting to understand the drives or motivations that underlie being a learner and a worker.

Student perceptions

Towards the end of the second semester in 1998, students were sent a questionnaire that provided us with some initial data for analysis. Of the 31 students surveyed we received replies from 18. Their answers provided us with more information about the student experience of the module.

Most students had consulted with their employers and had received constructive help from them, although some employers had voiced some concerns about confidentiality in the work being presented. About two-thirds of the respondents had approved learning contracts and a similar number had joined learning groups and attended tutorials. Most of the students found the learning pack useful, but only just over half agreed that it provided them with sufficient information to carry out the project.

Only 11 of the 18 respondents kept a journal of their work in progress. When asked what they liked about the module, students agreed that self-direction and flexibility were very important, as was the opportunity to combine study with work. The main criticism made was that the learning outcomes were unclear and that insufficient guidance had been provided.

The students enrolled in the programme are currently providing us with further information about work-based learning. Our aim is to find out from them which part of what they learned they most valued. We also need to learn how to provide more appropriate support for current and future students undertaking the level 1 module; and we hope to go on from here to develop appropriate level 2 modules which build on the learning achieved.

Students who had completed the pilot module were contacted and invited either to meet a researcher for an interview or to answer three questions and send email responses. The questions they were asked were as follows:

1. What were your experiences of the module and what is its value to you?
2. How do you believe that you and others taking the module have benefited?
3. How do you think the module might be improved?

The responses reflected students' appreciation of the opportunity to take initiatives connected with their part-time jobs. They felt validated by the recognition of this aspect of their experience through earning academic credit. Their reservations were concerned with the lack of clarity and detail in some of the learning outcomes and the perceived lack of flexibility in the tutorial times and accessibility of staff.

Feedback from employers

When we spoke to employers after the submission of the projects, in general their comments were favourable. Employers felt that the module had helped them to learn more about the students. They were impressed by the projects and expressed surprise in some cases at the capabilities of the students. They were positive about the emphasis on student autonomy in the module, with students retaining control over their own project design, and saw no need for the university to be more closely involved. We are aware of the need to find appropriate ways of liaising with employers that does not compromise the independence of students. This is something we are exploring as part of the next stage of the module's development.

Conclusions

One of the issues arising from piloting the work-based learning module is the question of what and how much we need to impart as academics. Some of what we assumed as understood by the students needs, in fact, to be imparted. It is important that students understand the relevance of their projects in terms of theory. Martin (1996) makes the suggestion that some of this can be achieved through detailed comments on their assignments. She also recommends that 'aims and objectives need to include the development and evaluation of specific graduate attributes'.

There is a need, for example, to identify the particular skills that are marked out for transfer and to help students to understand what transfer means. We also need to teach students skills for self-reflection since they are not automatic (Stephenson 1998). However, we believe that in giving students the opportunity to solve real problems at work, which are of their own choosing, is vital. In this view we are joined by others in the area who have recognized the importance of giving students the 'opportunity to engage in relevant and significant problems as a professional would' (Martin 1998).

It is our experience that students enrolled in vocational courses are capable of generating ideas and taking responsibility for their work in a way that many academics might find surprising. Finding a path between student autonomy on the one hand and academic responsibility on the other is difficult. We do have a responsibility to provide structure that will allow students to become autonomous. Yet we have to guard against undermining the student-driven quality of our modules. It may be that by not insisting on a student joining a peer learning group and by not making journals compulsory we have missed opportunities to provide greater support and assistance. We are currently reconsidering and reflecting on the whole issue of required input from the students, including timetabling and attendance at tutorials.

We are in the process of learning about the tremendous potential that these modules have for the academic and personal growth of the student. The future development of our work-based learning module will be assisted by more evaluations of our findings, which have already provided us with some notable insights. These, we hope, will allow us further to integrate academic input and student exploration in areas such as course content and practical application at work.

Appendix 14.1: module descriptor

Napier University Undergraduate Module Descriptor

Module no.:   PS12009
Module title: GENERAL WORK-BASED LEARNING
Module leader: Mr I. Marshall
Department: PSYCHOLOGY AND SOCIOLOGY
Approval date:

Indicative student workload (in notionally efficient student hours (NESH)):

Contact flexible weighting of assessment components

Lectures	2	
Tutorials/seminars	10	Continuous 100%
Practical		
Supervised assessment	0	
Student-centred-learning	138	
Other (specify)		
Total workload	150	0

Indicative assessment catalogue:

Assignment deadline:	Week	3
	Week	10
	Week	15

Timetable details:

Prerequisite(s)

Any student who meets the university conditions to register for level 1 modules will be eligible to take this module, subject to the conditions listed below. There are no excluded combinations. The basis for this module is learning in the workplace through the student undertaking a structured project. Each project is based on practical development of transferable skills that can be derived from a structured work-based project.

The module is open to any student who can fulfil the following conditions:

1. Evidence can be provided as to the suitability of the student for this course of study, which by its nature would be suitable to those students who are able to work independently, and towards self-directed study.
2. The student is required to attend a meeting with a module tutor in order to discuss their objectives for this module.
3. The student is required to negotiate with the employer organization that is supporting the project, and gain agreement to carry out the project.

Learning outcomes:

By the end of the module all students will be able to:

1. Present and analyse a situation to a given brief using appropriate methods.
2. Solve pertinent structured problems both individually and, if appropriate, in a group.
3. Report on learning achieved on the project, in an appropriate reporting style.
4. Make recommendations and/or suggest guidelines for change based on project findings.
5. Reflect on experience and/or practice.
6. Collect relevant information independently.
7. Plan and implement personal transferable skill objectives.

Description of module content:

Students will be applying their cognitive and intellectual skills and in some cases the bodies of knowledge they have already acquired to carry out a project within the workplace. Within this context they will undertake the following:

1. The practical application of skills development in the workplace, e.g. communication skills, time management skills, literacy and numeracy skills, interpersonal skills.
2. The negotiation of a structured placement report, formalizing the agreement between the employer and tutor.
3. Report writing and presentation skills, analysis of specific workplace scenario, gathering company information, evaluation of information relevant to a work-based learning module

Appendix 14.2: student project topics

- Awareness of company structure, store structure, job structure.
- Formulating a presentation for a company to get a new contract.
- How merchandising techniques increase sales.
- Communication problems within a store.
- Survey of customer service standards.
- Propose, plan and execute a photo-shoot.
- Broadening knowledge of stock control system.
- Analysis of competition between two companies.
- Research into detached youth work.
- Understanding staff attitudes to change in a bar.
- Evaluation of a staff development programme (× 2).
- Staff welfare and customer service incentives.
- Results of introducing computer system into small business.
- Compiling a database of PR contacts for a company.
- Evaluate a management programme at retail outlet.
- Description of a doctor's call-handling service.
- Setting up administrative support for a section of a pharmaceutical company.
- Identifying problems in a grocery store.
- Analysing activities and procedures in a chemist's store.
- Find out about the corporate image of a major foodstore.
- Evaluation of a customer service scheme (× 2).
- Description of staff training in a sports shop.
- Factors contributing to job satisfaction in a wine company.
- Producing a customer-relevant cocktail menu for a pub.
- Report on internship at CBS news in Washington, DC.
- Problems of staff strategies in a health care company.
- Account of job at an insurance company.
- Report on connections between displays and shoplifting in a newsagent.
- Report on brewery's approach to staff management.
- Does seasonal staff training in major chain store prepare them for Christmas rush?
- Employee motivation in a wine store.

- Evaluation of problems in a DIY store.
- Report on customer satisfaction in a kilt-hire company.

References

Boud, D. and Feletti, G. (1997) *The Challenge of Problem Based Learning*. London: Kogan Page.

Boud, D. and Walker, D. (1993) Barriers to reflection on experience, in D. Boud, R. Cohen and D. Walker (eds) *Using Experience for Learning*. Buckingham: SRHE/Open University Press.

Foster, E. and Stephenson, J. (1998) Work-based learning and universities in the UK. *Higher Education Research and Development*, 17(2): 155–70.

Harvey, L., Geall, V. and Moon, S. (1998) *Work Experience: Expanding Opportunities for Undergraduates*, Centre for Research and Quality, University of Central England.

Hughes, C. (1998) Practicum learning. *Higher Education Research and Development*, 17(2): 207–27.

McGill, I. and Beaty, L. (1992) *Action Learning in Higher Education*. London: Kogan Page.

Martin, E. (1996) *The Effectiveness of Different Models of Work-based University Education*. Report No. 19. Evaluations and Investigations Program, Department of Employment, Education, Training and Youth Affairs. Canberra: Australian Government Publishing Service.

Martin, E. (1998) Conception of workplace university education. *Higher Education Research and Development*, 17(2): 191–205.

Marshall, I. (1993) *Contract Learning in Sandwich Placement*. Edinburgh: Napier University.

NCIHE (1997) *Higher Education in the Learning Society* (Dearing Report), Report of the National Committee of Inquiry into Higher Education. London: HMSO.

Stephenson, J. (1998) Supporting student autonomy in learning, in J. Stephenson and M. Yorke (eds) *Capability and Quality in Higher Education*. London: Kogan Page.

Part 3

Past, Present and Future

15

Capital Degrees: Another Episode in the History of Work and Learning

Colin Symes

Universities are no strangers to change. The recent upheavals to the way they are administered and funded are typical of this change. Much less subject to analysis and commentary has been the slow revolution that has been occurring in their pedagogic practices. The advent of the virtual university and the application of information technology in the classroom is one aspect of this revolution, as is the subject of this book, work-based learning. Although such learning has been rehearsed elsewhere in the education system, particularly in the technical and further education sector in the UK and Australia, the particular form of work-based learning that has emerged in the university in the past decade is new. However, it is not unexpected given the policy climate and the press to make higher education institutions more accountable. For unlike some other sectors of the education system, universities have not been places that have embraced the concerns of work; quite the opposite, they have often been hostile to their incorporation. Despite sandwich placements and cooperative education – the natural antecedents of work-based learning – most academics have been resistant to the instrumental mentality underscoring current policy prescription. Indeed, what emerges from the 'thick descriptions' of work-based learning contained within the case studies in earlier chapters is the degree to which the advocates of work-based learning have been able to exploit the policy climate to create a more propitious climate for such learning. At the same time, universities have been able to use the other important element of recent public policy on higher education – that of equity and access – and to demonstrate that the logic of such policy leads naturally to work-based learning. Thus it is the contention of this chapter that the processes of normalizing work-based learning were advanced through a web of documentation, and that much of the regulatory machinery that has been deployed to ensure that it attains academic respectability is also textual. Indeed, this very book, which also contains many guidelines on the implementation of work-based learning, is also a contribution to this textual environment.

Excursus on learning and work

In reality, as the apologists of work-based learning seemed to have forgotten, learning and work have always been linked, albeit in more indirect ways than is the case at present. The education sector, through its various 'dividing practices' (Foucault 1979), has always sought to measure up the population against the demands of the labour market. The recent desire, on the part of governments, to produce more able populations runs counter to the trend through most of the twentieth century, which was for the education system to screen the whole of the school population and to separate according to mental type. The resultant patterns of education reflected the broad divisions inherent in the labour force: those who were more likely to work with their heads were given a superior and more extensive education than those who were likely to work with their hands. That the social representation in each category of education correlated with class patterns, not to mention those of ethnicity, race and gender, abrogated the meritocracy such a system of education was supposed to create. Part of this had to do with the 'cultural capital' that lay at the heart of the education system, and that was not evenly distributed throughout the population. Children with a middle-class background were more likely to have more of this capital than their working-class peers, and therefore were in a better position to make the most of their educational opportunities. Hence education systems could only mitigate the effects of a natural lottery to a limited degree. As Young (1993) has pointed out, the long-term consequences of this were the creation of low-ability societies, which recent policy intervention has begun to redress.

At same time, education systems were also charged with instilling the various facets of the work ethic and ensuring that students understood the values of industriousness and punctuality, of being deferent and respectful – and generally accepting that the principle of working for a living was a noble one. Much of this was done in secret, through the aegis of the hidden curriculum, through complex systems of reward and punishment. Girls were taught that it was a noble calling to be a housewife and mother, and that they should suspend any career aspirations. Even the ethos of schools contributed to the formation of labour (Bowles and Gintis 1976; Willis 1979). Working-class schools, for example, have tended to be more authoritarian than their middle-class counterparts, whose students are encouraged to be independent and exercise the types of initiative characteristic of professional work. Thus the link between education and work is far from a new one, and is reflected in the subtle processes of education at all levels of its expression.

Policy impetus

The emergence of work-based learning in the setting of the university provides a glimpse into the processes of innovation that occur in an institutionalized culture. It has occurred in an institution that is not renowned for its capacity for innovation, and that, like the church, is hidebound with traditions. Universities, for the most part, are conservative institutions that have taken their role as the curators of knowledge seriously. The underlying assumption is that its curatorship should only be entrusted to a small group of individuals, who have gone through rigorous processes of selection and proven themselves smart enough to engage in teaching and scholarship. The resultant institution was one which, until very recently, was a bastion of privilege, accessible only to those at the very apex of the meritocracy. It was also tied to a narrow conspectus of knowledge drawing on the arts and the sciences, and associated with an avowed distrust of instrumental concerns.

The recent changes to higher education, arguably as dramatic as any that have occurred in the whole history of the university, have led to a repositioning of higher education in society. Much of this repositioning has been policy driven, with governments in the Western world, particularly in the UK and Australia, demanding that higher education modernize itself and align itself to the economic needs of the contemporary nation state. Roderick West in Australia, and before him John Dawkins, and Lord Dearing in the UK, produced reports on higher education that articulated the need for more work-oriented universities.

This thrust towards a human capital vision of higher education was based on the assumption that good though higher education was, its students were inadequately prepared for the workplace and were unable to put into practice what they had learnt at university. As part of the policy rhetoric to support this, employers and their representatives such as the Confederation of British Industry (CBI) were named and cited as wishing that graduates were more familiar with the nature of workplaces and their demands (Saunders 1995). But the same thrust had also come from global policy-making bodies such as the OECD, which recognized the need for their membership states to invest in human capital if they were to take advantage of the knowledge-based economies which were beginning to emerge in the 1980s. In the current globalized economy, the alternative route, at least for Australia, was to cut its labour costs and to compete with developing nations in South-East Asia, an unrealistic option and one fraught with dangers (Marceau 2000). Higher education was to be used as a part of a nation-building strategy for cleverness, as a device to maintain position in a globalized economy. Policy thus gave its blessing to 'smartening' the population, but in economically useful ways that linked into the growth occupations of the labour market. These were in information technology, financial services and the leisure industries – sport, tourism, media, culture – and required the skills of symbolic/numerical analysis (Reich 1992) at which university graduates normally excel.

Policy at the national and international level thus provided a textual space wherein the discourses of work-linked learning could be situated and given a rationale. It has led to universities in which the instrumental has come to be favoured over the liberal, and in which 'working knowledge' is dominant. This has meant that the spatio-temporal frameworks of the knowledge involved tend to be local and immediate – and are of economic rather than cultural value, and designed to enrich business, not the individual. Thus even quintessentially liberal disciplines such as philosophy and English have been 'made over' into more instrumental ones, relevant to present preoccupations.

Among other outcomes this policy has led to dramatic changes to the demographics of universities, and to substantial increases in the number of young people participating in some form of higher education. The meritocratic university was predicated on the assumption that the pool of natural talent was not an extensive one, but was normally distributed in such a way as to be restricted to the upper percentiles of the population. The new times university has been a more egalitarian institution, and assumes that the pool of talent is more like a lake than a pool, and that the nation that fails to acknowledge this risks squandering its intellectual resources. As many of these resources were contained in the strata of the socially disadvantaged, attention was given by policy-makers to making university more accessible to the disadvantaged through more open admission routes. Work-based learners have been able to take advantage of these routes and their generous definitions of access. At the same time, the public provision of higher education in terms of the money allotted to it has not been commensurate with increasing the equity of universities and led to a situation in which they, like many other organizations in the public sector, have been fiscally challenged. In order to compensate for the pecuniary deprivations visited upon them universities have become more market-oriented and sought other ways to underwrite their operations.

One way in which universities have done this is to exploit the receptivity that business and industry has for knowledge and learning, and which they have recognized as being an important ingredient in the chase for economic advantage and competitiveness. The newly constituted culture of information, ushered in by the desktop computer and the Internet, has magnified the importance of epistemological activity in the new times economy. The ascendancy in that economy of applied forms of knowledge and transdisciplinarity (Gibbons *et al.* 1994) has given prominence to the university as a place where knowledge and its producers are created. But it has also produced a context in which knowledge production is no longer the preserve of the university. The recognition that knowledge and information have become tradable commodities has seen the establishment of companies with a knowledge industry focus – the think inc. sector. The range of these companies includes consultancies, research and development organizations and, most recently, companies which specialize in 'mining' information from the data quarries that have grown up around IT, and processing it into useful, value-added knowledge.

One further element of the think inc. is the rise of the 'learning organization' (see Senge 1992). This is the company that invests in the learning of its employees in the belief that it will pay dividends in terms of long-term productivity and efficiency gains. But this also extends beyond creating a culture in which learning is encouraged and recognized. One leading Australian company has an incentive scheme, designed to encourage its employees to purchase personal computers – for use at home. It anticipates that many of its employees will immerse themselves in the technology, and eventually put back into the company the results of such immersion. In the same spirit of recognizing the value of an intelligent workforce, many leading law firms in Australia now scour the law faculties for their best and brightest, after the end of the first year, offering them employment (I am grateful to Bob Lingard for this observation).

Hence, governments have an interest in obtaining better value for money from their higher education institutions and ensuring that students obtain a form of education that equips them with the skills on which the prosperity of a knowledge economy rest. But they have also been associated with policies that have encouraged universities to forge closer alliances with industry and business. Policies on research, for example, have consistently advocated funding being allotted to areas of economic growth or areas that result in palpable benefits to industry and business. 'Academic capitalism', as it has been called, has taken root in the university and looks like being a growth area, at least in the immediate future (Slaughter and Leslie 1997). Interestingly, one or two of the contributors to this book have argued that work-based learning provides a useful entree for universities to gain a foothold into business and industry, where they might conduct more formal research.

Such a climate, then, is a propitious one for demonstrating the links that now exist between work and education. One can see this in the symbolic economy associated with the new times university, in the advertising and the promotional emblems that are features of this economy. The idea that academy study has use value and leads to employment is common. Universities now boast that they are parts of the real world and that their graduates are in demand, and that employers value their credentials. University graduates are portrayed as intellectual capital incarnate. It was not always so, of course (Symes 1999). Universities and work were once regarded as the mortal enemies of one another, and universities were to be places that closeted their students from the exigencies of the professions, let alone other more mundane areas of employment. And of course there are still many academics opposed to the directions of the contemporary university and its espousal of mercantile and pragmatic goals (Coady 2000), and who see the 'new times' university as threatening the emblematic features of the traditional university.

But if the university has become a place, notwithstanding this group of apostates, where the cult of relevance has gathered a new congregation of worshippers, it needs to be pointed out that the advocacy of work as the curriculum is by no means new. The family tree of its advocacy can be traced back to John Locke and Jean-Jacques Rousseau, and its most recent exponents were the American pragmatist John Dewey and socialist pedagogue A. S. Makarenko. Unease about the separation of powers implied in the dichotomy between mental forms of knowing and manual forms of doing, which the existence of the university epitomized, prompted their belief that the most comprehensive education was one that embraced thinking and action. Bringing work into the classroom or making the classroom a workplace represented a more adequate philosophy of education than that expressed in most educational environments, where mental knowledge was the dominant currency of cognition. Much of the moral impetus of work-based learning flows from the desire to rescue the epistemology of practice from margins of education and to give it the intellectual respect it deserves. But it also stems from a certain scepticism towards consequences of the institutionalized learning that is encapsulated in the deschooling thesis. This held that institutions disable individuals, suppressing their capacity to learn for themselves. It was Illich's (1971) contention that learning should be returned to its origins, and that individuals should learn from the world, and not, as occurs in schools and universities, about the world. Work-based learning emphasizes 'from the world' learning.

In the past few years the nature of practice has been better understood as a result of the competency movement. The need to analyse the practices of work and to chart the nature of the competencies associated with them has uncovered the complexity of work and the degree to which skill is a multilayered phenomenon involving many mental and manual attributes. There is no work, be it of either the professional or the manual kind, which is 'thoughtless' or which does not involve 'handiwork'. Any division between mental and manual work is groundless. And it is better to regard the division as one that is seamless and to see work as a product of embodiment (Beckett 2000), as involving a synergy of anatomical processes: brain, hand, taste, ears, eyes, smell and so on.

From policy to actuality

Work-based learning does just not emerge from discourses that have attempted to valorize work practices and give them the intellectual recognition to which they are entitled. As has been suggested, the idea that work should be an integral element of the educational experience is neither new nor revolutionary. Its recent acceptance in the context of the university has more to do with the zeitgeist than a road to Damascus experience. The prevailing tide of policy, which has sought use-value for higher education, has contributed to this acceptance, as has the regulatory machinery that is internal to higher education.

Universities have always been places where intellectual quality control has been a dominant feature of academic life, and one to which the complex committee structure of the university has given exemplification. This is one aspect of university democracy in action, which encourages the academic community to have its say in determining policy, be it to do with academic or administrative matters. Work-based learning has no more been able to escape passage through these legitimation rites than any other aspect of academic policy and practice. For despite the rhetoric of deregulation that has accompanied neo-liberalism, that ideology now governing public sector administration and subvention, the incorporation of the university has been accompanied by more regulation, not less. The watchdog culture of university administration is such that much practice in the academy is subject to more accountability and systems of audit (Power 1997) – much of it conducted under of the rubric of quality assurance. As Winter and Stephenson suggest in their chapters, the fact that universities have adopted quality assurance rhetoric means that they have a common language with business and industry. This has helped the cause of work-based learning, whose underlying principles are close to quality assurance concerns such as 'fitness for purpose' and 'meeting customer expectations'.

Thus it might be expected that in a context where academic freedom is treasured the regulatory machine of quality assurance would in fact asphyxiate innovation. Yet the contrary is true. As in the case of the arts (Elster 1983), constraint can sometimes be conducive to innovation and invention, particularly when it is combined with the forces of marketization. It seems counter-intuitive but regulation, particularly when it encompasses so many aspects of administration, has actually created more scope for manoeuvre, offering more, not fewer, opportunities for inventiveness. As a number of contemporary social theorists have reminded us, regulation is not always disabling; it can actually be enabling. The arithmetic of this new organizational culture is simple:

Regulation + market = invention

This is certainly true of the university. The regulatory panoply governing the 'new times' university has been a force for change and not the opposite. As is clear from many of the case studies in Part 2, the advocates of work-based learning have exploited the regulatory machinery of the university and the plethora of reporting procedures that have grown up in the wake of its corporatization. The many regulatory bodies that now surround higher education – exemplified in bodies such as QAA and NCVQ – are an integral part of the culture, particularly in the UK, in which work-based learning has germinated. Its success in the UK compared with Australia, where work-based learning has not gained such wide acceptance, is perhaps owing to the more stringent control of higher education qualifications that prevails there.

Thus work-based learning has emerged within the interstices of policy and accountability guidelines, which govern most aspects of university practice these days. Its advocates have been able to use to their advantage the elasticity of the policy envelope that access and flexibility guidelines have provided. As has been argued elsewhere (Boud and Symes 2000), access draws on the discourses of equity, and was intended to improve the social representation scorecard of the university. But it can also be used to give its imprimatur to making university provision more accessible by recognizing that learning can occur in other sites than on campus, such as workplaces.

Such an option was attractive for companies such as Bovis Construction (the subject of the one of the case studies), which had already espoused learning organization rhetoric and was keen to have its in-house training courses given academic credentials. The trouble was that universities at the time, at least in the UK, were not structured in such a way as to accommodate short courses as a legitimate part of a degree. As Norman Evans points out, the breakthrough that enabled work-based learning to gain a foothold in the university was the introduction of credits for academic courses. Not in itself a revolutionary change, it was one that enabled courses to be modularized and allowed greater mix 'n' match of units across the university. It also meant that relatively short courses of a week in duration – of the sort offered by companies in their in-house training – could be given appropriate recognition and counted towards a degree. An incremental change in the policy environment thus provided another access point for the acceptance of work-based learning – moreover, it was one that had national blessing through NCVQ.

Another such incremental change was the principle that prior learning – and that had been widely used in the USA – could be recognized. This was initially introduced as an access provision that would enable more of the population to be admitted into the higher education system. But its consequences were such that it gave academic legitimacy to workplace experiences and made them equivalent to more conventional forms of study and learning. The fact that of prior learning non-scholastic experiences, particularly those gained at work, could be recognized as equivalent to university ones, and could even earn academic credit, meant that work experiences could be counted towards a degree. If this was the case then the reverse could be made to hold: that ongoing, not just prior, work could become a constituent element of a degree programme. As has been demonstrated at Napier, even the part-time work that many students use to support themselves through university could be brought into the circle of educational acceptability and given academic recognition.

The micro-culture of work-based learning

The emergence of work-based learning as a viable pedagogy in the university has been associated with its own brand of regulatory machinery – much of it of a textual kind. One symptom of this machinery is the number of hoops through which the advocates of work-based learning have had to jump in order to mount such learning. One of the reasons for this, as several contributors to the book suggest, is that work-based learning lies on the cusp of illegitimacy as far as many academics are concerned. The flirtation with non-academic organizations that work-based learning has entailed is seen by many academics as a threat to the university, which could undo its standards and its academic standing. In this respect, work-based learning has had to prove its mettle far more than more orthodox forms of university learning and demonstrate that what is happening under its banner is worthy of being within the preserve of the university. Hence, work-based learning seems to have been more subject to interrogation and surveillance than is ordinarily the case with university courses. This is particularly the case with ensuring that the learning outcomes of a work-based course match those of any other university course of study and that academic standards are no less rigorous off-campus than they are on. Much of it, though, is also prudential, ensuring that work-based learners are not exploited by their employers and that they have the same access to the same facilities, both human and material, as their on-campus counterparts.

One symptom of the control to which work-based learning has been subject is the web of documentation that surrounds it: portfolios, learning agreements, contracts, memoranda of understanding, assessment inventories, reports and so on. The universe of inscription associated with work-based learning is a complex and diverse one and is, presumably, designed to keep track of its participants and activities. In some respects, as Stephenson and Winter note in their chapters, such documentation makes the learning processes involved more transparent, more susceptible to be challenged and renegotiated, much more so than is possible with ordinary courses.

But it also has the effect of standardizing the practices of work-based learning within and across universities. In Latour's (1990) terms, the inscription environment associated with work-based learning, as in other communities of practice, produces a measure of educational 'consistency' among those associated with work-based learning. The documentation itself helps to render work-based learning more visible and more accessible. It also serves to generate the micro-culture that is associated with work-based learning. One of the notable observations that can be drawn from the case studies, for example, is the degree to which various organizations were conduits for the promotion of work-based learning. Among these were the Policy Studies Institute, the Learning through Experience Trust and the Council for National Academic Awards, through which the rationale for work-based learning was consolidated and promulgated. It is of note, for example, that prominent players in the work-based learning movement were participants in the various study tours to the USA organized by Norman Evans's Learning through Experience Trust. And Derek Portwood was brought to UTS (Australia) to advise its Faculty of Business on establishing a work-based programme. Such episodes as these, and the many like them not recorded in the case studies, were crucial in generating the epistemology of work-based learning and the protocols of its practice, and spreading these through a global network of publications and communications. This also ensured that the practices associated with work-based learning remained consistent, and that practices done in its name that were wildly inconsistent with these were not acknowledged or ratified.

It is possible to see this in the student 'end' of work-based learning. Already, the pedagogy associated with this learning displays a number of common features: the appointment of a supervisor in the workplace and at the university, the preparation of a learning contract, the writing of various reports, the keeping of a journal and the preparation of a portfolio. It is of note that most of these features are textual, and are designed to demonstrate that the students involved in work-based learning have acquired an understanding equivalent to that of their peers elsewhere in the university. One poignant aspect of this reportage is that students are expected to demonstrate that they are capable of the kind of reflective and critical thinking held to be the quintessence of university study (Barnett 1997).

In fact, one of the abiding tensions inherent in work-based learning is the degree to which the university should compromise its standards for the sake of earning a place in the business and industrial sun. Onyx and Shipley have alluded to this in their chapters, and the fact that businesses demand more alacrity than universities are capable of, with their tardy and painstaking administrative procedures. The 'fast capitalism' of the corporate world is incompatible with the administrative procedures of the university, where decisions are debated before they are taken.

This incompatibility also applies to the curriculum: business wants palpable results and is often opposed to the more reflective approach to learning associated with the university. There is a danger then of academic values being subsumed to commercial values, of making learning pay whatever the cost. Critical perspectives, the essential element of university education, could easily be obscured in the rush to make learning more productive. Thus it is pertinent to point out that much of the initiative for work-based learning has emerged from the least 'academic' quarters of the university – those closest to the ethos of business, which are expected to be self-funding and profit making. Most universities these days have a private arm, which acts as a broker between the university and the worlds of industry and commerce. These are the organizational manifestations of the aforementioned academic capitalism. The Cambridge Programme for Industry and Insearch at UTS are but two examples of these semi-private operations which have involved work-based learning. It is no accident too that work-based learning has emerged in the more pragmatic and mercantile faculties such as business, which are more receptive to applied ends.

Conclusions

The amplitude of policy thus now has sufficient breadth that there is not too much to which it would not give its stamp of approval. Indeed, it is somewhat ironic that it is the disciplinary regime of the traditional university that has had most to fear from the pragmatic and entrepreneurial thrust of the new times university. Hence the aforementioned hue and cry from the representatives of the traditional university who have an interest in maintaining the university as is, and deprecating those changes to which managerialist philosophy has given its imprimatur.

Work-based learning has come of age during a period when governments are enamoured with the idea of encouraging universities to forge alliances with industry and business. But its emergence has also been in conjunction with the diversification of higher education, to which government policy has given its blessing, and which has been associated with the 'customization of provision' (Garnett *et al.* in this book). In fact, this 'tailorization' of higher education that many see as threatening the integrity of the traditional university is entirely consistent with the meaning of the university, which as its etymology testifies confers unity on diversity. The traditional university through its disciplinary diversity provided a forum in which representatives from different disciplinary backgrounds could achieve some unity of purpose. The new times university has extended that diversity not only to its constituency, which is now more diverse than ever, but also to the ways of doing a degree: the so-called regime of flexibility. There remains the medieval way that occurs in the lecture theatre and the tutorial room; there is also the open way, utilizing virtual technologies such as television and now the Internet, which enables study to occur off-campus – virtually anywhere. Work-based learning is only another pathway for obtaining a university degree. Those who take this pathway and those who escort them along it have helped to increase the accessibility of the university. As such they deserve more than passing interest.

References

Barnett, R. (1997) *Higher Education: A Critical Business.* Buckingham: SRHE/Open University Press.

Beckett, D. (2000) Eros and the virtual: enframing working knowledge through technology, in C. Symes and J. McIntyre (eds) *Working Knowledge: The New Vocationalism and Higher Education.* Buckingham: SRHE/Open University Press.

Boud, D. and Symes, C. (2000) Learning for real: the vocationalisation of the university, in C. Symes and J. McIntyre (eds) *Working Knowledge: The New Vocationalism and Higher Education.* Buckingham: SRHE/Open University Press.

Bowles, S. and Gintis, H. (1976) *Schooling and Capitalist America.* London: Routledge and Kegan Paul.

Burton-Jones, A. (1999) *Knowledge Capitalism: Business, Work, and Learning in the New Economy.* Oxford: Oxford University Press.

Coady, T. (2000) Universities and the ideals of inquiry, in T. Coady (ed.) *Why Universities Matter: A Conversation about Values, Means and Directions.* Sydney: Allen & Unwin.

Elster, J. (1983) *Sour Grapes: Studies in the Subversion of Rationality.* Cambridge: Cambridge University Press.

Foucault, M. (1979) *Discipline and Punish: The Birth of the Prison.* Harmondsworth: Penguin.

Gibbons, M., Limoges, C., Notwotny, H. *et al.* (1994) *The New Production of Knowledge: The Dynamics of Science and Research in Contemporary Society.* London: Sage.

Illich, I. (1971) *Deschooling Society.* Harmondsworth: Penguin.

Latour, B. (1990) Drawing things together, in M. Lynch and S. Woolgar (eds) *Representation in Scientific Practice.* Cambridge, MA: MIT Press.

Marceau, J. (2000) Australian universities: a contestable future, in T. Coady (ed.) *Why Universities Matter: A Conversation about Values, Means and Directions.* Sydney: Allen & Unwin.

Power, M. (1997) *The Audit Society: Rituals of Verification.* Oxford: Oxford University Press.

Reich, R. (1992) *The Work of Nations.* New York: Vintage Books.

Robins, K. and Webster, F. (1999) *Times of the Techno-culture: From the Information Society to the Virtual Life.* London: Routledge.

Saunders, M. (1995) The integrative principle: higher education and work-based learning in the UK. *European Journal of Education,* 30(2): 203–16.

Senge, P. (1992) *The Fifth Discipline.* Sydney: Random House.

Slaughter, S. and Leslie, L. L. (1997) *Academic Capitalism: Politics, Policies and the Entrepreneurial University.* Baltimore: Johns Hopkins University Press.

Symes, C. (1999) 'Working for your future': the rise of the vocationalised university. *Australian Journal of Education,* 43(3): 243–58.

Willis, P. (1979) *Learning to Labour: How Working Class Kids Get Jobs.* Farnborough: Saxon House.

Young, M. (1993) A curriculum for the 21st century? Towards a new basis for overcoming the vocational/academic divide. *British Journal of Educational Studies,* 41(3): 205–13.

16

Future Directions for Work-based Learning: Reconfiguring Higher Education

David Boud and Nicky Solomon

In Parts 1 and 2 of the book we have shown how work-based learning is being implemented in higher education and have identified some of the issues that have been, and continue to be, faced by work-based educators. Work-based learning is still in its infancy and there are many different directions in which it might develop. The aim of this final chapter is to identify the salient features of work-based learning in the light of how they might be explored further and to speculate on future directions. It is clear that although work-based learning represents a substantial and provocative innovation, it has not been the subject of much research. If it is to develop further, this must be redressed. Thus, in the final sections of the chapter we identify some possible directions for research.

We start by outlining some key issues within the existing models that must be addressed in the short term if work-based learning is to develop and then move on to discuss broader issues that will need to underpin the development of work-based learning in the mid term.

As suggested throughout this book, work-based learning confronts many of the challenges that are being faced by universities as they enter the twenty-first century. There is increasingly widespread recognition that universities cannot continue in their present state, but little certainty about the directions they might take. Of course, there are a number of issues they must confront. Globalization, the commodification of learning, the competition from virtual learning providers and the fierce competition for students in a marketized system of higher education are but some of these issues. They must also confront the particular challenges flowing from the decline in public funding, which has created a space for institutions to seek new streams of revenue, and the desire on the part of the state to exert new forms of control over higher education. In the climate of fiscal deregulation and administrative reregulation, the identity of the university, like many other institutions in the public sector, is at risk. Work-based learning provides an interesting *mise-en-scène* on which the dramatization of these various challenges and issues is staged.

In the first chapter we identified some of the key features characterizing the current model of work-based learning. Collectively, these features represent a conceptual shift in contemporary higher education practices. It is a shift that focuses our attention on the way a transdisciplinary initiative that involves numerous partners and individualized learning programmes can be incorporated into a disciplinary university. This cannot of course be done in a straightforward and uncontroversial way. It involves a clash of cultures, between worlds of the academy and business, and a considerable rethinking of what constitutes legitimate knowledge and academic learning. For work-based learning involves, it has been suggested throughout this book, new sets of educational practices. These construct new kinds of identities for academics and learners, not to mention the university itself.

It is important to locate these immediate challenges within an approach that acknowledges how universities are already finding ways of addressing analogous issues. These include the development of an increasing number of cross-disciplinary programmes, the increasing involvement of professional bodies in the design of courses, the increasing customization of learning provision to be found in flexible learning and the recognition of prior learning.

Immediate challenges

The immediate challenges confronted by work-based learning fall into five distinct areas. All need attention if the practice of work-based learning is to flourish, although the degree of attention required will vary according to the existing structures and practices inherent in particular universities.

Economic issues

It might appear incongruous to start with the economic issues, but unless these issues are resolved there will be an immediate barrier on all further development. One of the key questions to be faced is: what is the economic costing model on which work-based learning is based?

Work-based learning cannot be costed using the same principles as conventional courses because it deploys staff in quite different ways. Students do not meet their teachers in tutorials and lectures at preset times. The amount of contact time varies widely according to the nature of the programme that has been negotiated. The nearest analogy to work-based learning in matters of costing is the research degree. Yet this analogy is not an entirely fair one because students are gaining substantial support from their workplace and are not normally engaged in research that uses university facilities and that leads to the relatively high costs of such study. Another consideration is that employers are normally resistant to paying significantly more than the cost of conventional tuition when they are making substantial inputs into the programme.

A major factor in work-based learning is the amount of one-to-one contact that occurs between university staff and students. The stages at which this occurs can be easily identified. They are the following:

- initial advice on the learning portfolio;
- learning plan negotiation;
- renegotiation of learning plan;
- academic advising during programme implementation;
- advice on assessment products.

This is in addition to the group-based activities in which students are oriented to work-based learning, develop their portfolio and learning plan and are equipped with work-based learning and monitoring strategies. There are also assessment activities that do not require contact: assessment of the learning portfolio and assessment of the learning outcomes.

Until an institution has gained experience in the actual demands of learners from particular organizations, it is particularly difficult to cost work-based learning. Assumptions have to be made about the amount of the high-cost element – one-to-one interaction – and limits may have to be placed on this. The amount of staff input and, therefore, cost is a function of the amount of support an individual learner needs. There will be wide variation, even among a group of learners with similar educational attainment, but this can increase sharply when students who have poor academic skills are 'classed' with high achievers.

There is a financial incentive to minimize the number of students with such poor skills and it may be necessary to guide them into other programmes to ensure that their skills are sufficient before embarking on the more rigorous demands of work-based learning.

Institutional issues

Where should work-based learning be located? How does it link to the other activities of the institution? Most institutions start their involvement with work-based learning through a special project located within a newly established unit in order to develop processes and procedures which can subsequently be mainstreamed into existing parts of the institution. As numbers increase, decisions have to be made about how work-based learning is to be sustained as part of normal business. The most common approaches to date have been to locate it as part of a programme structure within existing schools or faculties, as at Anglia Polytechnic University, or within its own faculty structure, as has occurred at Middlesex University. There are advantages and disadvantages in both. The former allows for closer integration with academic staff within existing structures and may lead to closer ownership of programmes throughout the institution. The disadvantage of this is that work-based learning programmes could be forced to the margins of academic activity within their own special unit and that the necessarily transdisciplinary features of work-based learning are minimized. The latter has the advantage of bringing together a critical mass of staff devoted to the development of a new practice, thus permitting research and development to occur more readily. The disadvantage is that by containing work-based learning in special units, the important challenge it provides to other aspects of university work is lessened and ownership throughout the institution is restricted.

While different approaches will be found within different universities according to their own traditions and structural arrangements, at least two points need to be considered. First, how can the organization of staffing be arranged in such a way that normal academics are involved in work-based learning programmes? Partner organizations want a relationship with a university, not with a contract-labour supplier. They want full-time academics involved, not sessional staff hired for the purpose. If existing academics are not used, then the impact of work-based learning on the other practices of the institution is minimized and the resultant learning is not used, as it should be, to improve other programmes within the institution.

Second, how can universities ensure that the substantial time and effort involved in developing partnerships is used for more than the provision of new niche courses? In particular, how can these partnerships be used to assist the university more widely? The obvious area is that of research. Unless work-based learning partnerships are used to leverage into research partnerships, then they will not find a comfortable home in research-oriented universities. The day-to-day contact which academic advisers have with an organization means that they are ideally placed to identify cooperative research projects and suggest to the partner new forms of collaboration. Research partnerships will only be fostered if research-active academics are closely involved in work-based learning programmes. While it would be unrealistic, and unnecessary, for all the teaching staff involved to be research-active, strategies for consciously deploying researchers to appropriately located students is one of the best ways to ensure leverage occurs.

Prudential issues

The credibility of work-based learning programmes is not solely a function of the contribution of the university. Partner organizations have a crucial and necessary role to play, complementary to the educational institution. If work is the curriculum, then the work in which learners are engaged must be of a nature that offers the potentiality of providing a vehicle for a university education.

Learning is not only supported and resourced by the employer. For it to be appropriate and effective, excellent working relationships need also to be formed between educational institution and employing organization. It is difficult in practice for new partnerships between two organizations to come into operation for each student. An investment in a joint infrastructure is needed. Mostly this is an infrastructure of procedures and opportunities rather than of a physical kind, but it requires time and commitment none the less. There are massive diseconomies of scale when small numbers of staff are involved. Good working relationships are needed between university staff and those fostering learning within the organization.

Questions need to be asked of potential partners in order to ensure that an appropriate environment for learning can be established. These include:

- Does the organization have an explicit corporate commitment to learning and the development of its employees (e.g. frameworks of corporate capabilities)? Is this valued and articulated by the CEO and other executives, including those in operational areas? Is this widely known and accepted by employees?
- Is the organization prepared to commit resources to employee development beyond those needed for them to conduct their current work responsibilities?
- Does the organization have a track record in collaborating with other organizations (public and private) for purposes of employee development?
- Is the organization willing to invest in developing the support structures for employee learning, including the development of supervisors and managers in their learning roles?
- Are there well established career paths within the organization that mean that opportunities for promotion are available in all areas?
- Are ideas from employees for the development of the organization encouraged and celebrated?
- Does the organization have the capacity to negotiate a learning partnership with an educational institution and carry all parts of the organization involved with it?
- Is the work of the organization of the type that can be susceptible to reflection and critical problem-solving that is typical of undergraduate and graduate studies?

Unless it is possible to answer most of these questions positively, there is a strong likelihood that the conditions for establishing work-based learning do not exist. However, a commitment by the organization does not necessarily translate into commitment by particular divisions or departments or by workplace supervisors. A positive organization-to-organization relationship needs to be translated into a similar department-to-department one as well.

Quality issues

Much effort has already gone into the development of frameworks for levels and standards as a prerequisite for offering work-based learning programmes.

These frameworks provide a critical site for responding to questions from both academics and their 'business' partners. Such questions focus on the 'quality' of the entry and exit requirements and of the allocation of academic credit points for learning outside conventional higher educational frames. A framework, therefore, needs to be able to justify as well as inform the practices around:

- entry requirements into a work-based learning award;
- the assessment of recognition of prior learning claims;
- the specification of learning outcomes of a work-based learning programme;
- the recognition and accreditation of learning and training programmes that are developed within organizations;
- the assessment of recognition of prior learning claims.

However, it is still common for such frameworks to be used only for work-based and negotiated learning and not for other mainstream teaching and learning provision. When this is the case it leaves the institution open to the criticism that while these frameworks are suitable for work-based learning, they are not good enough for everything else.

Such considerations have prompted a search for 'graduateness' in the UK, and for 'generic attributes' in many Australian universities. Nothing has been agreed system-wide and the search for a framework that all universities can or should adopt may well be fruitless and undesirable. However, the presence of such a framework for a given university or network of similarly accredited institutions across all their teaching and learning provision is becoming increasingly necessary. Not unexpectedly, there is resistance to transdisciplinarity in organizations that arose within a disciplinary framework. This is changing as increasingly universities are creating organizational units such as mega-faculties and colleges which cross disciplinary boundaries and require more adventurous thinking about knowledge structures.

Educational issues

The immediate challenge for all institutions adopting work-based learning is to select staff who can cope with working with students operating outside their disciplinary comfort zone. This confronts the increasingly important educational challenge of the era: how can we teach what we don't know (Boud 1996; Boud and Miller 1996)? Work-based learning courses require teaching staff to change their role from being experts on the content of what is being learned to becoming animators and assessors of learning. This might often be in areas of learning and knowledge in which students and their workplace colleagues may be more expert. They may also have to engage in knowledge generated through work that does not map on to the knowledge structures with which they are most familiar.

Their immediate role is to assist students in interpreting the framework of levels and standards in the light of the knowledge they are pursuing. However, this is not easy, as they cannot draw simply on their own disciplinary experience of what is legitimate knowledge. Over time they will learn to create new conceptual maps to guide them in the uncharted territory of transdisciplinary knowledge, but in the short term they are faced with substantial learning needs of their own. This requires a degree of flexibility and responsiveness to changing circumstances that not all academics can meet. Professional development needs are greater than might be immediately apparent, as it is not a matter of induction into new procedures but a conceptual shift that is needed. Development programmes for staff must therefore persuade them of the need for such a shift, as well as providing the conditions under which such a shift can occur. This is the work-based learning challenge for the educational institution. In order to meet the needs of the partner, the university has to engage in work-based learning for its own academics.

The future of work-based learning and the future of the university

There is little doubt that the current models of work-based learning and practices are evolving and will change considerably over the next decade. But at the same time it is also highly likely that many of the issues, and the accompanying challenges work-based learning faces, will remain. In this section we consider the areas that we imagine will continue to construct our higher education practices and identities in the early part of this century. We have organized this section into two parts – research challenges and the demands of a new pedagogy – arguing that a full engagement with these necessitates, as well as contributes to, a reconfiguring of the structures and practices of a new higher education.

Research challenges

At present there is a large gap between work-based learning and collaborative research. The reason for this is a structural one. Work-based learning is, for the most part, located within the area of teaching and learning, while research is located in the area of research and consultancy. This division also often exists at the university and faculty levels. While it is one that may simplify programme delivery, it has longer-term consequences for both the development of research partnerships and the researching of work-based learning practices.

In terms of developing research partners, the establishment of new and enduring partnerships with external organizations is likely to continue as a strong feature of research in higher education institutions. The conditions for this lie with the increasing shift in the locus of knowledge production from universities to other sites (see Chapter 3), as reflected in and supported by government research funding arrangements that reward 'partnership' with industry and business. Organizational and government interest in research and new knowledge is not in the pursuit of knowledge for knowledge's sake, but in how knowledge will enhance the performance of employees and organizations, and will increase the production of intellectual capital (Edwards and Usher 2000).

There are a number of reasons why work-based learning partnerships offer new research opportunities. First, in order to forge a work-based learning partnership it is necessary to undertake considerable negotiation and to establish links between university and organization staff at many levels. It is much easier to extend rather than begin relationships with a given organization. Second, direct contact between academics and professionals within an organization occurs on an ongoing basis. Academics visiting a work site discover what is going on there and develop an understanding of what is important for the organization. They can spot opportunities for research at a much earlier stage than academics having only minimal contact with an organization. Third, the investment involved in establishing a work-based learning partnership and maintaining an elaborate infrastructure to support it may not be cost-effective if it only generates extra students. Liaison between universities and the relevant organization needs to be frequent and ongoing if work-based learning is to be effectively sustained. A large part of the infrastructure would need to be duplicated in a research partnership undertaken independently of work-based learning. Thus there is some advantage in using work-based learning as a seed venture to generate opportunities for research, and vice versa.

Unfortunately, the prospects for associating research with work-based learning partnerships are more problematic than they might at first appear. The great potential for research is unlikely to be realized if we persist in seeing work-based learning only within a framework of course delivery and as an adjunct to 'conventional' university work.

However, work-based learning programmes are not only sites of interest in terms of their potential for establishing collaborative research partnerships with organizations. They also provide a site that is conducive for researching the new kinds of teaching and learning practices associated with the concept of 'work as the curriculum'. While the work-based learning models explored in this book are a novel construct, these models are symptomatic of new pedagogical practices that can be found in contemporary educational developments. This is particularly the case in those models where knowledge is co-produced in partnership arrangements and where the curriculum is framed by work rather than by more conventional bodies of knowledge.

Empirical research conducted with work-based learning practitioners could provide useful understandings about these new forms of knowledge and learning. These could conceivably contribute not only to the future of work-based learning in a narrow sense, but also to broader changes related to the increasingly complex relationship between knowledge production and the university. What follows is a listing of some potential areas of research that focus on the new teaching and learning practices that are being constructed as the university opens its internal and external organizational and curriculum structures. They have been organized in categories that focus on each of the partners involved in the development and delivery of work-based learning programmes: the learner, the academic, the participant organization and the university.

Areas of research that focus on the learner include:

- the characteristics of learners/employees for whom work-based learning is the most effective kind of postgraduate study;
- the way learners/employees understand and manage the blurred distinction between being a learner and a worker and between learning and work practices;
- the extent to which participation in a work-based learning programme changes learners'/employees' relationship with their supervisors and/or the organization itself, professional trajectory and approach to learning and working;
- the effectiveness of the different kinds of educational resources (including material and academic support) that are needed for meeting the learning goals of the diversity of work-based learners and the participating organizations;
- the new kinds of textual practices in work-based learning that reflect and contribute to the conflation of employee and learner identities and practices;
- the way learners/employees transfer knowledge that is produced within a specific context of application to other contexts.

Research that focuses on the academic includes:

- the way academics manage cross- and/or transdisciplinary learning;
- the way academics manage the shift from being a teacher of a specific body of knowledge to being a facilitator of learning;
- the way academics assess learning that lies outside their disciplinary areas;
- the extent to which academic participation in work-based learning programmes changes teaching and learning practices in more conventional programmes, the identity of academics and understandings about what is worthwhile and legitimate knowledge;
- the way academics understand and manage the effects of working in two sites (the workplace and the university) in terms of double surveillance and accountabilities, and the struggles between oppositional views of what is worthwhile knowledge/learning;
- the new textual practices of co-production of knowledge (Scheeres and Solomon 2000) arising from the negotiations around the intersection of academic, professional and workplace discourses and their various accountabilities.

Research areas that focus on organizations in partnership with the university include:

- the motivations of organizations for establishing partnerships with universities;
- organizational understandings about the relationship between productivity levels and workplace learning;
- various views in the organization on what is worthwhile knowledge and the extent to which this changes during a work-based learning partnership;
- the relationship of organizational and university capability frameworks;
- the way various levels of employees in the organization understand and manage tensions that arise that are manifestations of differing views on learning processes, organizational priorities and what is considered to be relevant learning.

Research areas that focus on the university include:

- the extent to which work-based learning initiatives influence other programmes in the university, in terms of further or decreased involvement with organizations outside the university in determining new educational initiatives, and debates around disciplinary versus cross-disciplinary versus transdisciplinary organizational and curriculum structures;
- the individualizing of learning programmes;
- the development of cross-faculty structures and course developments.

These are but some of the research challenges that exist in our own areas of research. They can be multiplied many times across other academic and professional areas. Another important consideration in the fostering of work-based research that is linked to work-based learning is: who are the representatives of the university that interact with partners and partner organizations? As mentioned above, there is a danger in structuring work-based learning so as to ensure that the most skilled research academics have the least likelihood of interacting with partners. While there are significant exceptions to this, frequently staff negotiating partnerships, coordinating programmes, acting as advisers and undertaking assessments of work-based learning are neither research trained nor, with one or two exceptions, especially active researchers.

This provides a major challenge to universities, as the academics who are involved do have skills that are needed in work-based learning which insufficient numbers of their colleagues possess. More seriously, though, much existing research training and subsequent career development as academics deskills researchers for the kinds of transdisciplinary, applied and exploratory research that new forms of work-based research demand. Nor does it fit the normal patterns of inquiry associated with academic conferences and journals. It does not lead (so rapidly) to the kinds of outputs which academic peers recognize. It demands a responsiveness and flexibility which the present diverse mix of academic workloads, and pressures for 'equity' in workloads, does not permit. Someone with a typical load of coursework teaching, supervision of research students, administration and contributions to the university/profession cannot readily find time for the more intensive, drop-everything kinds of engagement that work-based research often demands.

Demands of a new pedagogy

Work-based learning as a pedagogical site challenges most of our conventional assumptions about teaching, learning, knowledge and curriculum. It is a disturbing practice – one that disturbs our understandings about our academic identity and its location. Indeed, work-based learning in higher education institutions disturbs most of the conventional binaries that have framed our academic work, including: organizational learning and university learning; performance outcomes and learning outcomes; organizational discourses and academic discourses; theory and practice; and disciplinary knowledge and workplace knowledge.

While these binaries have been useful in maintaining territorial distinctions between the pedagogical work of the university and that of organizations outside the university, their sustainability as opposing categories is problematic. Knowledge and learning can no longer be divided as contrasting facets of academic and workplace practice. Nor can it be argued any longer that there is a case for privileging one element in the binary over another. Perhaps more realistically (and more confronting) is that we understand the new pedagogical practices, which are exemplified in work-based learning, as located at the intersection of each element of the binary (McIntyre and Solomon 2000).

An engagement with the overlapping of each element means that we no longer regard them as necessarily oppositional. It suggests that the pedagogical work is located within a different frame and this different framing can account for, in part at least, the repetition of the word 'new' throughout this book's engagement with work-based learning. There is talk of *new* identities, *new* pedagogies, *new* frameworks of standard and levels, *new* forms of learning and working and *new* modes of knowledge production. Each of these 'news' reflects as well as contributes to the construction of *new* forms of pedagogy and a *new* kind of language that we use to talk about and inscribe our pedagogical work.

It could be argued that the significance of the *new* is only relevant to work-based learning because of its radical nature. It could be said that work-based learning is a marginal or even a transient pedagogic activity and therefore not really exemplary of mainstream teaching and learning practices. However, taking this position ignores the many other challenges that the university and academics are facing in their (arguably) more mainstream work. It ignores the way that these challenges are to a greater or lesser extent reshaping not just teaching and learning practices but also the structures of the university. The development of new conceptual and material resources that are shaping the transdisciplinary tools for work-based learning practices are in contrast to the old frameworks – but those pedagogical frameworks have become problematic across all kinds of pedagogical sites in the university.

Reconfiguring

In earlier chapters, we spoke of the serious challenges to the university's dominant understandings of what counts as legitimate knowledge and what is a legitimate site of learning and knowledge production. But these challenges are not confined to work-based learning activities. Certainly the key features of work-based learning – such as the pedagogical significance of the particular and the present, the situatedness of learning and the learner, the co-production of knowledge, the individualization of learning – are features (indeed, contested ones) of many of the educational practices within contemporary universities. In different sites the consequences of these are manifested in very different kinds of changes in terms of university structures and processes and in pedagogical practices. Yet what is common to most higher education institutions is that they are reconfiguring themselves – not simply by adding extensions to existing practices but by a reconfiguration of the existing spaces. The changing spaces of knowledge require more open, less rigidly bounded and more permeable structures.

The 'house of knowledge', in fact, is a useful metaphor for encapsulating the features of contemporary higher education (Solomon and Usher 1999). At present the 'house of knowledge' is undergoing reconstruction and renovation. This has considerable consequence for the current residents who are used to 'roomier' houses in which the walls between each part of the house cannot easily be removed. The new context for the university, which is expressed in microcosm in work-based learning, involves more than just making some extra rooms available for the new types of educational guests or building extensions in the grounds to house the poor relations. Instead it requires the 'house of knowledge' to be reconstructed on a more 'open plan' basis. Its rooms need to undergo complete reconfiguration, its entrances and exits need to be widened, its rooms need to be furbished with the latest technology and video surveillance needs to be installed in the grounds. This is so that the radically new kinds of learners and the new kinds of learning that are beckoning on the horizons of higher education can be accommodated. Among these, the work-based learner and work-based learning are the most challenging. The challenge is to make the architecture of higher education work for work-based learning, not against it. It is with that objective in mind that this book has been written.

References

Boud, D. (1996) The end of teaching as we know it. How can we assist people to learn what we don't know? *Australian Journal of Experiential Learning*, 35: 66–74.

Boud, D. and Miller, N. (1996) Synthesising traditions and identifying themes in learning from experience, in D. Boud and N. Miller (eds) *Working With Experience: Animating Learning*. London: Routledge.

Edwards, R. and Usher, R. (2000) *Globalisation and Pedagogy: Space, Place and Identity*. London: Routledge.

McIntyre, J. and Solomon, N. (2000) The policy environment of work-based learning: globalization, institutions and workplaces, in C. Symes and J. McIntyre (eds) *Working Knowledge: The New Vocationalism and Higher Education*. Buckingham: SRHE/Open University Press.

Scheeres, H. and Solomon, N. (2000) Whose text? Methodological delimmas in collaborative research practice, in A. Lee and C. Poynton (eds) *Culture and Text*. St Leonards, NSW: Allen & Unwin.

Solomon, N. and Usher, R. (1999) Open plan? Re-organizing the space of knowledge, Conference paper presented at *Re-organizing Knowledge: Trans-forming Institutions – Knowing, Knowledge and the University in the XXI Century*, 17–19 September, University of Massachusetts, Amherst.

Index

Aaker, A., 143
access, 8, 62, 75, 168, 210
accountability, 27, 209
accreditation, 106, 110, 130, 138
  claims, 108
  of prior experiential learning
    (APEL), 8, 19, 50, 62, 63, 65,
    66, 69, 71, 72, 105, 110, 168
  procedures of industry programmes,
    105
achievement, levels of, 167–82
advanced performance improvement
    activities, 131
advisers, role of, 53
Alderton, J., 92
Anderson, G., 52, 56, 67, 94
Anglia Polytechnic University, 158
Araujo, L., 115
Argyris, C., 120
assessment, 56, 64, 68, 69, 94, 96, 108,
    115, 118, 123, 136, 138, 155–63,
    173, 190
  criteria, 162, 164, 176
  norm-referenced, 160
  of prior and experiential learning
    (APEL), see accreditation, of
    prior experiential learning
ASSET Programme, 158
Atkins, M., 93

Bailey, C. H., 42
Ball, S., 23
Barnett, R., 78, 104, 136, 155, 212

Beckett, D., 91, 208
Beddowes, P., 88
Bement, J. M., 170
benchmarking, 177
benefits, economic, 81
Black, H., 158
Bloom, H., 88
Botkin, J. W., 115
Boud, D., 30, 56, 57, 93, 114, 187, 193,
    210, 220
Bovis Construction, 103, 104, 106, 108,
    110
Bowden, J., 39–42
Bowles, S., 204
Boyatzis, R., 97
Brennan, J., 75
British Defence Evaluation and
    Research Agency (DERA), 178
Brookfield, S. D., 56
Bryan, C., 174
Burgess, T., 87

Cambridge Programme for Industry
    (CPI), 113, 115
capabilities, 8, 78
  corporate, 18
  current, 135
  see also capability
capability, 87, 93
  corporate, 88
  demonstration stage, 95
  development, 147
  envelope, 94–8

exploration stage, 95
    individual, 6, 86–9
    organizational, 6, 89
    progress review stage, 95
Capability in Higher Education, 46
capable organization, 88
capstone units, 7
Chappell, C., 88
Coady, T., 207
Comerford, A., 109
competence, competency or
        competencies, 87, 93, 126, 136,
        157, 158, 162
    concept, 88
competencies
    core, 105
    current, 50
    generic, 8, 88, 220
    industry, 105
    recognition of current, 6
competency
    development, 107
    frameworks, 105
    holistic approaches to, 46
    models, 178
    movement, 208
competency-based
    frameworks, 46
    programmes, 92
compliance driver, 148
contestation, of programmes, 45–6
cooperative education programmes, *see*
        sandwich courses/placements
Cope, B., 25
costs, 136–7
Council for National Academic Awards
        (CNAA), 62–7
courses
    disaggregating, 38
    validation of company, 69
credit
    academic, 66, 68, 69, 123, 173,
        184–96
    accumulation and transfer (CAT),
        62, 64, 65, 67, 68, 69, 71, 72
    definitions, 177
    levels, 174–5, 177
    standardized, 173
    system, 75
    worth, 168, 169

critical
    action, 104
    distance, 42
    perspectives, 212
    reflection, 57, 136
Critten, P., 82
curriculum, work as the, 5, 6
customer expectations, 155–6, 161

Dale, R., 23
De Wit, P., 155, 156
Dearden, G., 68
Dearing, 185
Dewey, John, 9, 208
disciplinary community, 20, 51
    surveillance of, 30
discretion and discretionary practices,
        20–1
doctorate, professional, 178
Donaldson, M., 42

Edwards, R., 23, 222
Elster, J., 209
email, 13, 189
employer
    involvement, 108
    role of, 189
employers'
    experience, 70–1
    feedback from, 195
Eraut, M., 77, 91, 96, 114, 115
ethical concerns, 57
evaluation, 190–1
Evans, J., 93
Evans, N., 50, 63, 67, 73
experiential learning, 2, 77, 91

Featherstone, M., 23
fitness for purpose, 88, 103, 155, 160,
        163, 209
Foster, E., 93, 98, 100, 184
Foucault, M., 204
Fowler, G., 7
Fulwiler, T., 54
Further Education Unit (FEU), 63,
        155, 156

Garnett, J., 105, 110, 111
Garrick, J., 22, 25, 136
Gee, J., 24

generic attributes, *see* competencies, generic
Gherardi, S., 114
Gibbons, M., 31, 37, 206
globalization, 23, 205
Gonczi, A., 46
Gore, J. M., 40
grades and grading, 159, 160, 176

Hager, P., 46, 91
Harris, R., 88
Harvey, D., 24, 186
Hase, S., 87, 88
Heron, J., 21
Higher Education Quality Council (HEQC), 84, 98
higher education
  reconfiguring, 215–26
  repositioning in society, 205
Holly, M. L., 54
honours degree programme, 159
Howells, J., 168
Hughes, C., 53, 188, 189
human capital vision of higher education, 205

identity, 31
  as an active learner, 49
  ambiguity, 36
Illich, I., 208
independent studies, 8
industrial relations, 149
industry partnerships, 141–54
information and communication technologies (ICT), 24, 99
intellectual capital, 104, 110, 222

Jaguar Cars, 66, 72
JBS Computer Services, 66
Jessup, G., 156
journal or learning portfolio, 47, 54

Kanter, R. M., 88
Kaplan, S., 150
Karpin Report, 141
knowledge, 35, 114
  academic, 114
  co-production of, 21–2
  disciplinary, 22, 40, 126

framework, integrating disciplinary and professional, 39, 40
house of, 226
legitimate, 31, 226
Mode 1, 37, 38, 40, 45, 46, 51
Mode 2, 24, 25, 38, 40, 42, 45, 46
representation, 46
tacit, 91, 96
transciplinary, 22, 28, 216, 221
work-based, 40
and the work-based learning curriculum, 36–8
knowledge production, 24, 37, 206, 222
  sites of, 24, 27, 36
  workplaces differentially generative of, 36
Knowles, M. R., 52, 77
Kolb, D. A., 91, 107, 135

Latour, B., 211
Laycock, M., 94, 97
learner, situatedness, 45
learner-centred, approach to the curriculum, 47
learning agreement, 65–6, 69, 106, 107
  see also learning, contract
learning
  action, 54
  added, 47
  approaches to, 42
  assessable, 68
  autonomous, 89, 93, 196
  competitive advantage through, 143–4
  conceptions of, 36–42
  context, 56, 75, 117
  contextual, 23
  contract, 5, 9, 52, 65, 94, 97, 168, 170–1, 176, 179
  documenting, 56–7
  by doing, 75
  environment, 162, 219
  equivalence, 47
  identified, 47
  inducements, 145–6
  informal, 54, 91, 93, 114
  managing one's own, 90
  negotiation of, 53, 56–7

organization, 25, 207
and organizational performance
    144–5
outcomes, 7, 13, 28, 35, 46, 47, 50,
    80, 90, 95, 109, 156, 169, 186,
    187, 188, 192, 211
    different to work outcomes, 57
plans, *see* learning, contract
recognized, 47, 131, 146
resources, 53
self-managed, 92, 94
sets, 189
sources of, 169
supporting, 52–4
transfer of, 41
trapped within work setting, 40–1
for unknown situations, 39–42
variation in, 41
what is being learned, 36–42
while earning, 68, 71, 72
and working similarities and
    differences, 34–6
workplace sites of, 162
Learning from Experience Trust, 61,
    64
Learning Power Scheme, 97, 98, 99
Leeds Metropolitan University, 97
Leeds Training and Enterprise
    Council (TEC), 97
Lester, S., 115
level
    criteria, 98
    descriptors, 80
    indicators, 93, 96, 98
levels and standards of achievement,
    framework of, 6, 7, 27, 46,
    50–1, 56, 57, 219
Levin, B., 23
Levy, M., 138
Locke, John, 9, 208
Lyons, F. S., 169, 170, 174, 176

McClelland, D. C., 94
McGill, I., 54, 191
McIntyre, J., 24, 225
McKenzie, P., 146
Makarenko, A. S., 208
management development, 105, 107
Mandel, A., 50
Marceau, 205

Marginson, S., 23
market place, university's positioning
    in, 18
marketing, 84
Marshall, I., 185
Martin, E., 190, 196
Marton, F., 39
Mayo, A., 89
mentoring relationships, 29
micro-culture, 92
Middlesex University, 74, 75, 76, 78,
    79, 80, 81, 84, 105
Miller, N., 135
modular degrees, 184
modularization, 63

Napier University, 185
National Centre for Work-Based
    Learning Partnerships
    (NCWBLP), 79, 81, 103, 106,
    110
National Council for Vocational
    Qualifications (NCVQ), 61,
    158
negotiated
    external award, 96
    learning, 5, 8, 51–2, 170
    learning goals, 93, 131
    see also learning, contract
negotiated curriculum, 8
negotiation, 52, 95

Oates, T., 158
OECD (Organisation for Economic
    Cooperation and
    Development), 23, 24, 205
online
    learning, 11
    service, 99
Onyx, J., 127
organizational
    adoption, models of, 146–50
    culture, 25
    learning, 89, 142
    performance, 147
Osborne, C., 93, 98

partnership
    approaches, 142
    model and discourse, 21–2

partnerships, 4, 5, 25, 103–11, 218
   questions to be asked of, 219
Pedler, M., 88
peer learning, 13, 54
peers, role of, 54
performance
   improvement/management, 11, 145,
      146
   management driver, 147
Polanyi, M., 91
policy, 205, 208
Policy Studies Institute (PSI), 62
portfolio/s
   development and assessment, 50, 52
   prior learning, 170
   or records of learning achievements,
      9
   see journal or learning portfolio
Portwood, D., 67, 75, 78, 104, 129
post-structuralist theory, 40
power, 209
   relations, contested, 22
   relationships, new, 22
power/knowledge dynamics of work
      settings, 40
practice
   disturbing, 225
   epistemology of, 208
   knowledge of, 37
practices, disciplinary, 19
Pring, R., 155, 156
prior learning, 210
   documentation of, 7
   see also portfolio/s
problem
   of application, 41–2
   formulation, 98
problem-based learning, 128, 187
problem-centred approach, 127
problems, deciding what the problem
      is, 39
professional bodies, influences on the
      curriculum, 21
professional development, 12, 29, 83,
      113, 114, 145
proposal and portfolio, 131

quality assurance, 155–63, 209
quality audits, 84
quality matters, 156, 161

recognition of prior learning (RPL), 6,
      9, 19, 50, 210, 131
   see also accreditation, of prior
      experiential learning
      (APEL)
reflection, 54, 91, 97, 107, 212
   critical, 136
reflective
   assessment, 176
   practice, 193
reflective approach to learning, *see*
      reflection
regulation, sites of, 30
Reich, R., 205
research
   challenges, 221–5
   opportunities, 222
   partnerships, 218, 222
Research on Adult and Vocational
      Learning (RAVL), 3
resources, decreasing, 185
response times, 133
Ritzer, G., 153
Robertson, D., 74
Rose, N., 40
Rousseau, Jean-Jacques, 9, 208
Royal Society for the Encouragement
      of Arts, Manufactures and
      Commerce (RSA), 87

Sadler, P., 88
Sainsbury's Supermarkets Limited, 92
Sampson, J., 54
sandwich courses/placements, 7, 8, 68,
      184, 185
Saunders, M., 9, 205
savings of time and effort, 35, 49
Scheeres, H., 223
Schön, D. A., 91, 120
self-assessment, 94
   schedule, 57
self-confidence, 96
self-efficacy, 96
Senge, P. M., 88, 89, 115, 207
Sennett, R., 24
Shaw, M., 93, 98
Shether, G., 128
skills development, 97
Slaughter, S., 207
Slotnik, H. B., 91

small and medium-sized enterprises
(SMEs), 97
Smedslund, J., 41
Smith, E., 87–8
Solomon, N., 20, 25, 226
South East England Consortium for
Credit Accumulation and
Transfer (SEEC), 177
staff development, 83, 221
Stahl, T., 88
stakeholders, 167
standards, 28, 118, 167–82
academic, 27, 211
accreditation or legislated, 148
control of, 88
see also levels and standards of
achievement, framework of
Stephenson, J., 46, 87, 94, 97, 98, 196
Sternberg, R. J., 114
Stewart, T., 104, 110
strategic plan driver, 147
student
as customer, 161
perceptions, 194
succession planning, 148
supervisor, role as, 138
supervisory inputs, 189
Symes, C., 23, 168, 207

Taylor, S., 23
total quality management (TQM),
161
Toulmin, S., 24
transfer, see learning, transfer of
transferable
outcomes, 188
skills, 159, 191–2
Turpin, T., 20

university as a workplace, 25, 26, 75
University of Leeds, 97, 98
University of Portsmouth, 167
University of Technology, Sydney
(UTS), 126, 127, 141
university, future of the, 221–6
Usher, R., 30

validation
of company courses, 67
institutional, 79

variation, 39, 41
discerning, 39, 41, 42, 56

Waters, M., 23
Weatherhead School of Management,
97
Weaver, T., 88
Webb Associates, 103–10
Wicks, S., 155
Williams, R., 88, 92
Willis, P., 204
Wilmott, H., 25
Wimpey International, 66
Winter, R., 16, 157, 158, 159, 163
Woolwich Building Society, 64
work and learning, history of, 203–14
work as the curriculum, educational
implications, 45–8
work experience, 68, 184, 185
work, part-time, 184–96
work-based curriculum, 44–58
curriculum, elements of, 48–57
work-based learning
academic credibility of, 77–8
academic resistance to, 76
administrative system, 83
antecedents, 7–9
basic assumptions, 36
benefits of, 109–10
beyond the present and the
particular, 36–42
centralization in university, 82
challenges of, 26–30, 216–25
economic issues, 216–17
equivalence, 27, 28
institutional issues, 217–18
prudential issues, 218–19
quality issues, 219–20
challenges to
identity, 30
practices, 28, 29
characteristics of, 4–7
client, who is the, 123
credit tariff, 174
definition, 4
demands of a new pedagogy, 225–6
devolution of, 83
evaluation of, 122–4
features of, 77
as a field of study, 76–9

financial issues, business plan, 81
future directions for, 215–26
history, 7–9, 61–73
holistic approach to, 100
implementing, 126–39
industry perspectives, 141–54
infrastructure, 219
inscription environment, 211
institutional locations, 82–3
key features, 226
key learning themes, 47
and knowledge, 36–8
lessons from, 72–3
level of, 158
micro-culture of, 210–12
not identical to work, 49
origins of, 22
outcomes of capability-focused,
    90
pedagogy, 212
processes, 92
propositions, 78–9
purposes and outcomes, 156
role of the academic, 138–9
seductive qualities of, 18, 31
staffing, 218
standards for, 51
as a viable pedagogy, 210

work-based learning partners, contested
    control between, 132–3
work-based learning partnerships
    approaches to, 150–3
    cost-effectiveness approach, 151
    cross-sectoral approach, 152
    cultural change, 151
    desirables and undesirables, 150–3
    just-in-time approach, 152
    mass production versus
        customization, 153
    organizational requirements, 9–10
    stakeholder ownership, 151
    value-adding approach, 150
work-based learning programmes,
    recruitment of staff, 29
work-based learning studies, 78
work-based projects, 107, 110
work-based research and development,
    107
working knowledge, 28, 206
workplace behaviour, espoused theory
    of, 120
workplace supervisors, 52, 53

York Consulting, 98, 99
Yorke, M., 93
Young, M., 204

The Society for Research into Higher Education

The Society for Research into Higher Education (SRHE) exists to stimulate and coordinate research into all aspects of higher education. It aims to improve the quality of higher education through the encouragement of debate and publication on issues of policy, on the organization and management of higher education institutions, and on the curriculum, teaching and learning methods.

The Society is entirely independent and receives no subsidies, although individual events often receive sponsorship from business or industry. The society is financed through corporate and individual subscriptions and has members from many parts of the world.

Under the imprint *SRHE & Open University Press*, the Society is a specialist publisher of research, having over 80 titles in print. In addition to *SRHE News*, the society's newsletter, the society publishes three journals: *Studies in Higher Education* (three issues a year), *Higher Education Quarterly* and *Research into Higher Education Abstracts* (three issues a year).

The society runs frequent conferences, consultations, seminars and other events. The annual conference in December is organized at and with a higher education institution. There are a growing number of networks which focus on particular areas of interest, including:

Access	Learning Environment
Assessment	Legal Education
Consultants	Managing Innovation
Curriculum Development	New Technology for Learning
Eastern European	Postgraduate Issues
Educational Development Research	Quantitative Studies
FE/HE	Student Development
Funding	Vocational Qualifications
Graduate Employment	

Benefits to members

Individual

- The opportunity to participate in the Society's networks

- Reduced rates for the annual conferences
- Free copies of *Research into Higher Education Abstracts*
- Reduced rates for *Studies in Higher Education*
- Reduced rates for *Higher Education Quarterly*
- Free copy of *Register of Members' Research Interests* – includes valuable reference material on research being pursued by the Society's members
- Free copy of occasional in-house publications, e.g. *The Thirtieth Anniversary Seminars Presented by the Vice-Presidents*
- Free copies of *SRHE News* which informs members of the Society's activities and provides a calendar of events, with additional material provided in regular mailings
- A 35 per cent discount on all SRHE/Open University Press books
- Access to HESA statistics for student members
- The opportunity for you to apply for the annual research grants
- Inclusion of your research in the *Register of Members' Research Interests*

Corporate

- Reduced rates for the annual conferences
- The opportunity for members of the Institution to attend SRHE's network events at reduced rates
- Free copies of *Research into Higher Education Abstracts*
- Free copies of *Studies in Higher Education*
- Free copies of *Register of Members' Research Interests* – includes valuable reference material on research being pursued by the Society's members
- Free copy of occasional in-house publications
- Free copies of *SRHE News*
- A 35 per cent discount on all SRHE/Open University Press books
- Access to HESA statistics for research for students of the Institution
- The opportunity for members of the Institution to submit applications for the Society's research grants
- The opportunity to work with the Society and co-host conferences
- The opportunity to include in the *Register of Members' Research Interests* your Institution's research into aspects of higher education

Membership details: SRHE, 3 Devonshire Street, London
W1N 2BA, UK. Tel: 020 7637 2766. Fax: 020 7637 2781.
email: srhe@mailbox.ulcc.ac.uk
word wide web: http://www.srhe.ac.uk./srhe/
Catalogue: SRHE & Open University Press, Celtic Court,
22 Ballmoor, Buckingham MK18 1XW. Tel: 01280 823388.
Fax: 01280 823233. email: enquiries@openup.co.uk

WORKING KNOWLEDGE
THE NEW VOCATIONALISM AND HIGHER EDUCATION

Colin Symes and John McIntyre (eds)

Universities are undergoing a series of profound changes. One of the more pronounced of these involves the partnerships that are now being formed between business enterprises and higher education. The emergence of these partnerships has much to do with the changing economy, which is increasingly based around knowledge and information – the traditional stock-in-trade of the university. Knowledge capitalism has given a renewed impetus to higher education. One expression of this is work-based learning, which challenges the scope and site of the university curriculum. This book analyses this development from a number of perspectives: critical, historical, philosophical, sociological and pedagogical. Its various contributors argue that work-based approaches contain much that is challenging to the university, and also much that could help to create new frameworks of learning and new roles for academics. *Working Knowledge* offers a comprehensive examination of the new vocationalism in higher education.

Contents

Working knowledge: an introduction to the new business of learning – Learning for real: work-based education in universities – 'Real world' education: the vocationalization of the university – Knowledge that works: judgement and the university curriculum – Eros and the virtual: enframing working knowledge through technology – The policy environment of work-based learning: globalization, institutions and workplaces – Imposing structure, enabling play: new knowledge production and the 'real world' university – Deschooling vocational knowledge: work-based learning and the politics of curriculum – Learning to work, working to learn: theories of situational education – The organization of identity: four cases – Organizational gothic: transfusing vitality and transforming the corporate body through work-based learning – Index – The society for research into higher education.

208pp   0 335 20571 2 (Hardback)

USING EXPERIENCE FOR LEARNING

David Boud, Ruth Cohen and David Walker (eds)

This book is about the struggle to make sense of learning from experience. What are the key ideas that underpin learning from experience? How do we learn from experience? How does context and purpose influence learning? How does experience impact on individual and group learning? How can we help others to learn from their experience?

Using Experience for Learning reflects current interest in the importance of experience in informal and formal learning, whether it be applied for course credit, new forms of learning in the workplace, or acknowledging autonomous learning outside educational institutions. It also emphasizes the role of personal experience in learning: ideas are not separate from experience; relationships and personal interests impact on learning; and emotions have a vital part to play in intellectual learning. All the contributors write themselves into their chapters, giving an autobiographical account of how their experiences have influenced their learning and what has led them to their current views and practice.

Using Experience for Learning brings together a wide range of perspectives and conceptual frameworks with contributors from four continents, and is a valuable addition to the field of experiential learning.

Contents

Introduction: understanding learning from experience – Part 1: Introduction – Through the lens of learning: how the visceral experience of learning reframes teaching – Putting the heart back into learning – Activating internal processes in experiential learning – On becoming a maker of teachers: journey down a long hall of mirrors – Part 2: Introduction – Barriers to reflection on experience – Unlearning through experience – Experiential learning at a distance – Learning from experience in mathematics – Part 3: Introduction – How the T-Group changed my life: a sociological perspective on experiential group work – Living the learning: internalizing our model of group learning – Experiential learning and social transformation for a post-apartheid learning future – Experiential learning or learning from experience: does it make a difference? – Index.

Contributors

Lee Andresen, David Boud, Angela Brew, Stephen Brookfield, Ruth Cohen, Costas Criticos, Kathleen Dechant, Elizabeth Kasl, Victoria Marsick, John Mason, Nod Miller, John Mulligan, Denis Postle, Mary Thorpe, Robin Usher, David Walker.

208pp   0 335 19095 2 (Paperback)

SKILLS DEVELOPMENT IN HIGHER EDUCATION AND EMPLOYMENT

Neville Bennett, Elisabeth Dunne and Clive Carre

The last decade has seen radical changes in higher education. Long held assumptions about university and academic autonomy have been shattered as public and political interest in quality, standards and accountability have intensified efforts for reform. The increased influence of the state and employers in the curriculum of higher education is exemplified by the increasing emphasis on so-called core or transferable skills; an emphasis supported by the Dearing Report which identified what it called 'key' skills as necessary outcomes of all higher education programmes. However, there is little research evidence to support such assertions, or to underpin the identification of good practice in skill development in higher education or employment settings. Further, prescription has outrun the conceptualization of such skills; little attention has been paid to their theoretical underpinnings and definitions, or to assumptions concerning their transfer.

Thus the study reported in this book sets out to gain enhanced understandings of skill acquisition in higher education and employment settings with the aim of informing and improving provision. The findings and analyses provide a clear conceptualization of core and generic skills, and models of good practice in their delivery, derived from initiatives by employers and staff in higher education. Student and graduate employee perspectives on skill delivery and acquisition are presented, together with a clearer understanding of the influence of contexts in skill definition and use in workplace settings. Finally, important questions are raised about institutional influences and constraints on effective innovation, and the role that generic or key skills play in traditional academic study, and in workplace effectiveness.

Contents

Generic skills in the learning society – A conceptualization of skills and course provision – Beliefs and conceptions of teachers in higher education – The practices of university teachers – Student perceptions of skill development – Employer initiatives in higher education – Employers' perspectives on skills and their development – The graduate experience of work – The challenges of implementing generic skills – Appendices – References – Indexes.

224pp   0 335 20335 3 (Paperback)   0 335 20336 1 (Hardback)

NEW DIRECTIONS IN PROFESSIONAL HIGHER EDUCATION

Tom Bourner, Tim Katz and David Watson (eds)

This book exemplifies the growing involvement of universities in professional education at its highest level. It also demonstrates the increasing importance of education for the professions in the work of universities.

It contains a wealth of practical examples and ideas about how universities can respond to the changing needs of students' initial professional training, continuing professional development and lifelong learning.

At the heart of the book is a series of analytical case studies of developing practices that respond to the challenges to higher education at the start of the new millennium. These chapters address important themes in developing professional higher education: partnership, independent learning, reflective practice, new technologies, intranets, world wide web, distance learning, the international dimension, work readiness, assessment and standards. Many of the case studies test out ideas in action.

The result is a valuable handbook for practitioners of professional education in higher education and an important resource for staff and educational developers and higher education managers.

Contents
Part 1: Setting the scene – Lifelong learning and professional higher education – Issues of professionalism in higher education – University education for developing professional practice – Part 2: Case studies – Partnership in higher education – Independent learning and reflective practice – Using new learning technologies – Using the internet and the world wide web – Distance learning and the international dimension – Preparation for professional practice – Assessment and standards – Part 3: New directions – A framework for personal and professional development – Professional doctorates: the development of researching professionals – Practitioner-centred research – References – Index.

272pp   0 335 20615 8 (Hardback)   0 335 20614 X (Paperback)

STOCKTON - BILLINGHAM

LEARNING CENTRE

COLLEGE OF F.E.

STOCKTON - BILLINGHAM

LEARNING CENTRE

COLLEGE OF F.E.

openup
ideas and understanding
in social science

www.**openup**.co.uk

 Browse, search and order online

 Download detailed title information and sample chapters*

*for selected titles

www.**openup**.co.uk